THE COVID TRAIL

THE COVID TRAIL
Psychodynamic Explorations

Edited by
Halina Brunning and Olya Khaleelee

First published in 2023 by
Phoenix Publishing House Ltd
62 Bucknell Road
Bicester
Oxfordshire OX26 2DS

Copyright © 2023 to Halina Brunning and Olya Khaleelee for the edited collection, and to the individual authors for their contributions.

The rights of the contributors to be identified as the authors of this work have been asserted in accordance with §§ 77 and 78 of the Copyright Design and Patents Act 1988.

All rights reserved. No part of this publication may be reproduced, stored in a retrieval system, or transmitted, in any form or by any means, electronic, mechanical, photocopying, recording, or otherwise, without the prior written permission of the publisher.

British Library Cataloguing in Publication Data

A C.I.P. for this book is available from the British Library

ISBN-13: 978-1-80013-136-1

Typeset by Medlar Publishing Solutions Pvt Ltd, India

www.firingthemind.com

We dedicate this book to all who perished due to Covid-19

Contents

Acknowledgements — xi
About the editors and contributors — xiii
Introduction — xix
by Halina Brunning and Olya Khaleelee

Part I: The shock of the new

1. Stepping into the unknown — 3
   by Halina Brunning

2. Disorientation, loss, and mourning — 9
   by Birgitte Bonnerup

3. What is social dreaming telling us about the new terrain? — 29
   by Halina Brunning

4. Guide to the new terrain — 37
   by Mario Perini

Part II: Reparation, resilience, recovery

5. Despair and endurance: the experience of NHS staff during the Covid crisis — 61
   by Barbara-Anne Wren

6. Multi-system failure of the body and the body politic — 79
   by Richard Morgan-Jones

7. Power, fragility, and recovery — 97
   by Winnie Fei and Zhang Jian Li

8. Vulnerability and resilience in a time of Covid — 105
   by Tim Dartington

Part III: The fourth humiliation of humankind

9. The virus as symbol for the fourth narcissistic blow to humankind — 121
   by Claudia Nagel

10. Covid—an intrusion of the Real — 139
    by Simon Western

11. Questions of denial—Covid as a catastrophe — 157
    by Andrzej Leder

12. What the International Listening Posts are telling us about Covid — 171
    by Rob Stuart and Olya Khaleelee

Part IV: Our new Covidian world

13. The Long Covid at an individual and societal level — 193
    by Anthony Berendt

14. The future of organisations and leadership 213
    by Leslie B. Brissett

15. Dark beam of light: what Covid is telling us about
    race relations 233
    by Leslie B. Brissett

16. The traumata of Covid: learning from the pandemic 251
    by M. Gerard Fromm

Follow the Covid Trail 269
by Halina Brunning and Olya Khaleelee

Conclusions 275
by Halina Brunning and Olya Khaleelee

Index 281

Acknowledgements

We wish to thank all invited contributors who made this book possible by describing a specific aspect of the Covid phenomenon, sharing their own understanding and experience. The unusual agreement was reached between the two authors and the fifteen contributors that each chapter will be written under a very specific title, so as to create a coherent Covid Trail. For this flexibility and willingness to experiment we thank them all.

Images used in the book are accredited to:

Cover illustration by Edvard Munch, *The Sick Child*, 1907
Part I original photograph by Thor Simony, 2020
Part II image by Edvard Munch, *Separation*, 1896
Part III original photograph by Halina Brunning, 2018
Part IV image by Edvard Munch, *Norwegian Landscape*, 1900

Permissions

Chapter 2 "Disorientation, loss, and mourning" by Birgitte Bonnerup includes quotations from three poems, reprinted with permission from

Naja Marie Aidt and Laurence Laluyaux, RCW Literary Agency, Søren Ulrik Thomsen and Susanne Nied (translator), and Lone Hørslev and Gyldendal group agency.

Chapter 4 "Guide to the new terrain" by Mario Perini is based on an expanded and updated version of "Panic and pandemics: from fear of contagion to the contagion of fear" by Mario Perini in *Psychoanalytic Reflections on a Changing World*, edited by Halina Brunning (2012) and published by Karnac, London. Copyright © 2018 by Routledge. Reproduced by permission of Taylor & Francis Group.

Chapter 6 "Multi-system failure of the body and the body politic" by Richard Morgan-Jones features a cartoon originally published in *The Management of Risk of Recycling Trauma in the Context of Conflicting Primary Tasks: An Analysis of the Use of the Group Dynamic of Incohesion Basic Assumption Activity* by Richard Morgan-Jones in *Organisational and Social Dynamics* 6(1): 22–41. Reproduced with the kind permission of Phoenix Publishing House.

Chapter 13 "The Long Covid at an individual and societal level" by Anthony Berendt includes an extract taken from "November" by Ted Hughes, which first appeared in *Lupercal* by Ted Hughes, published by Faber & Faber. Reproduced with permission of Faber and Faber Ltd, licence no. P211021/180.

Chapter 16 "The traumata of Covid" by M. Gerard Fromm. Parts of that chapter are based on chapter 11 and the epilogue of Gerard Fromm's book, *Traveling through Time: How Trauma Plays Itself out in Families, Organizations and Society* (2022), reprinted here with the kind permission of Phoenix Publishing House.

About the editors and contributors

Editors

Halina Brunning is a chartered clinical psychologist, freelance organisational consultant, and executive coach. Halina has published extensively on clinical and organisational issues, and has edited seven books for Karnac including *Executive Coaching: Systems-Psychodynamic Perspective* (2006). She conceived the idea of a trilogy of books which examined the contemporary world through a psychoanalytic lens. This approach continued in her latest book co-written with Olya Khaleelee: *Danse Macabre and Other Stories: A Psychoanalytic Perspective on Global Dynamics* published by Phoenix Publishing House, 2021.

Olya Khaleelee is a corporate psychologist and organisational consultant with a particular interest in leadership and organisational transition and transformation. She was director of OPUS: an Organisation for Promoting Understanding of Society from 1980–1995, is a professional partner of the Tavistock Institute, and was the first female director of the Leicester Conference on the theme of Authority Leadership and Organisation. She has published extensively in the areas of leadership and system psychodynamics in organisations, and beyond, into society.

Contributors

Anthony Berendt qualified in medicine in 1983, specialised in infectious diseases, and for twelve years was medical director of specialist and acute teaching hospitals. He gained a master's in leading and consulting in organisations from the Tavistock and Portman NHS Trust and the University of Essex in 2019, and works in leadership development, coaching, and consulting, particularly within health care. He is a member of the International Society for the Psychoanalytic Study of Organizations (ISPSO) and OPUS, is former commissioning editor of the online leadership journal *BMJ Leader*, and is a senior associate tutor, Department for Continuing Education, University of Oxford.

Birgitte Bonnerup holds an MA in psychology, University of Copenhagen, is an authorised psychologist, and a qualified specialist and supervisor in organisational psychology and psychoanalytic psychotherapy. In her practice, Bonnerup & Hasselager Registered Psychologists, her work is as a therapist and organisational consultant. She holds a position as external lecturer on the Master's Programme in Organisational Psychology, University of Roskilde, Denmark. She is a staff member at the Institute of Group Analysis in Copenhagen. Birgitte has organised and directed several group relations conferences. She is a member of ISPSO and OPUS. In 2019 Routledge published *Love and Loneliness at Work*, her book co-written with Annemette Hasselager.

Leslie B. Brissett is director of the Group Relations Programme, company secretary and principal consultant/researcher at the Tavistock Institute of Human Relations. He co-directs the Dynamics at Board Level Programme and co-edited *Dynamics at Boardroom Level: A Tavistock Primer*. He has directed six Leicester Conferences, including the first outside the UK, in Bavaria in 2020. He launched a programme of work, Tavistock Awakening Organisations (TAO) that seeks to explore both the nature of spirit within a secular context and to develop the capacity for organising within a spiritual context.

Tim Dartington, PhD, is a social scientist and consultant to groups and organisations. He has written extensively on the dynamics of systems of health and social care in relation to vulnerable groups in society. He is a professional partner of the Tavistock Institute, where he was employed as a researcher, and has staffed and directed Tavistock group relations conferences, including the Leicester Conference. He is also a long-standing member of OPUS: an Organisation for Promoting Understanding of Society.

Winnie Fei, PhD, CEO and academic principal of the Tavistock Institute of Human Relations in China, was responsible for bringing the advanced methods and technologies of the Tavistock Institute into China in 2017, conducting certificated training in partnership with the Tavistock Institute accredited to an international standard. She gained her PhD in psychology of religion from Peking University. She is a Tavistock consultant with a Practitioner Certificate in Consulting and Change, and a certified group supervisor and group therapist, the Irvin Yalom Institute, USA. She is committed to applying Tavistock methods and technologies to Chinese enterprises, organisations, health education, and welfare services.

M. Gerard Fromm, PhD, is a distinguished faculty member and the former director of the Erikson Institute of the Austen Riggs Center, and a fellow of the American Board and Academy of Psychoanalysis. He is president of the International Dialogue Initiative, an interdisciplinary group that studies the psychodynamics of societal conflict, and a past president of the International Society for the Psychoanalytic Study of Organizations. His most recent book is *Traveling through Time: How Trauma Plays Itself out in Families, Organizations and Society* published by Phoenix Publishing House in 2022.

Zhang Jian Li holds several posts: director, Beijing Qingyuan Si Meng Sinology Center; vice president, US–China Education Trust; cultural director, Beijing Handicraft Association; and chief consultant on Chinese culture, the Tavistock Institute of Human Relations in China. He specialises in analysing problems from the perspective of philosophy and Jungian psychology, combined with national psychology and religious psychology, so that people can get a glimpse of the far-reaching background of individual and group phenomena.

Andrzej Leder, PhD, is a professor at the Institute of Philosophy and Sociology of the Polish Academy of Sciences. Andrzej works on political philosophy and the philosophy of culture, applying phenomenological and psychoanalytical tools, especially Lacanian psychoanalysis. He has published books in Polish, English—*The Changing Guise of Myths* (2013), and in German—*Polen im Wachtraum: Die Revolution 1939–1956 und ihre Folgen* (2019). His main work in political philosophy, *Sleepwalking the Revolution. Exercise in Historical Logics* (2014), was widely discussed in Poland and nominated for literary and scientific awards. He is also a practising psychoanalytical psychotherapist.

Richard Morgan-Jones works internationally as an organisational and group relations consultant. He is a supervising psychoanalytic psychotherapist at the British Psychotherapy Foundation, and a member, British Psychoanalytic Council and OPUS. He is a mentor, A. K. Rice Institute; visiting faculty member at the Indian Institute of Management, Ahmedabad, India, and the Higher School of Economics, Moscow; associate consultant of Work Lab, New York; and director of Work Force Health: Consulting and Research. He is the author of *The Body of the Organisation and Its Health* (Karnac, 2010).

Claudia Nagel, PhD, is a professor at the VU, Vrije Universiteit Amsterdam, holding a chair on change and identity in organisation sciences. She works as consultant, coach, author, and senior advisor to international organisations and their board members. As an economist (MBA), organisational psychologist (PhD), and chartered psychoanalyst (ISAP), Claudia is an expert on strategic management, leadership, and change processes. She runs Nagel & Company, is president of ISPSO, and visiting professor at Hull University Business School, UK. She publishes extensively on behavioural strategy and other psychodynamic subjects. Her most recent book *Psychodynamic Coaching* was published by Routledge, 2020.

Mario Perini, MD, co-founder of IL NODO Group, is a psychiatrist, a psychoanalyst, and an organisational consultant. He is a member of the Italian Psychoanalytic Society, IPA, and ISPSO. He has been working as a consultant in the public, private, healthcare, and voluntary sectors, and also as a trainer for professional and management education, a Balint group leader, and a group supervisor. While working in private practice as a psychotherapist and an executive coach, he teaches group and organisational dynamics at the Turin University Department of Psychology.

Rob Stuart is a psychodynamic counsellor registered with the British Psychoanalytic Council. He trained at Birkbeck College, University of London and spent five years as an honorary psychotherapist at Central and North West London NHS Foundation Trust. He is the current director of the Listening Post at OPUS: An Organisation for Promoting Understanding of Society, and an active member of Extinction Rebellion and other climate related protest groups.

Simon Western, PhD, is founder of the Eco-Leadership Institute and is CEO of Analytic-Network Coaching, a leading advanced coach training company. He is an internationally acclaimed author on leadership and coaching. His book *Leadership: A Critical Text* (Sage, 2019) is now in its third edition and is taught at business schools in Australia, the USA, and the UK. Previously a family psychotherapist, he is past president of ISPSO, adjunct professor at University College Dublin, and honorary professor at Moscow Higher School of Economics.

Barbara-Anne Wren is a psychologist and organisational consultant. She has a keen interest in using narrative to develop individual, role, and system resilience as described in her book *True Tales of Organisational Life* (Karnac, 2016).

She is a founder member and previous chair of the UK National Network of Practitioner Occupational Health Psychologists, director of Wren Psychology Associates, consultant psychologist at the Royal Free London NHS Foundation Trust, and an honorary fellow of the Royal College of Physicians in Ireland.

Introduction

The Covid Trail was created at a time of real urgency and despair.

This project, like a number of previous ideas, having quietly organised itself and matured out of sight, perhaps even unconsciously, announced itself ready and fully formed when its time had arrived.

It was inspired by one of the authors walking along the Wandle Trail in South London, not far from her home, when like most Londoners during the lockdowns, instead of indoor activities, she was reliant upon walks to connect with friends and family. In so doing, she discovered the beauty of the Wandle river.

She thus allowed nature, as opposed to the city centre of London, to envelop and transport her deeper into this ancient unknown terrain. She is mindful that the river itself has for years been cemented over and has only recently been released, excavated in its full beauty, together with the natural habitat that supports it, appropriately now jointly called the Wandle Trail.

This book is an exploration of the new unknown terrain that Covid has presented to us. This is a dangerous, dark terrain, full of foreboding, that we are all exploring in our own ways, using such resources as lie at our disposal. To explore it is to follow its trail and to note each of its sharp yet subtle twists.

For us, a pair of experienced psychologists and writers, to edit this book together we needed to find a way of thinking about and understanding the world, supported by a common language. That language is psychoanalysis and system psychodynamic thinking.

Motivated by a desire to express what is hidden, dangerous, and difficult to express, this book takes us on a trail that starts with disquiet, disorientation, and loss. Through attempts to make sense of a narrative that we would rather not recognise, the book slowly shakes off the sense of disorientation in the initial fragmented narrative, and looks for a guide to lead us through the pandemic. This guidance cannot offer a guarantee of survival, but it acts as a psychic container for the necessary understanding that we all seek.

The first disorienting part of this book thus ends with a containing coherent guide to the trail. There is not so much light at the end of this trail, for we cannot guarantee the future, but there is a clear path to follow, despite its meandering and dangerous nature.

The second part of the book is devoted to pairing despair with resilience through balancing power with vulnerability. We take an international perspective while tracing how this pattern of resilience paired with vulnerability plays out in all four chapters.

In the third part of the book we delve into the realm of psychoanalysis, to seek solace, or at least a deeper understanding of the phenomenon of Covid and the pandemic, as we examine the role that we as human beings have played in sowing our own environmental destruction in this unfolding catastrophe.

The fourth and last part of the book offers a glimpse into the post-Covidian world which forces us to fully recognise the longer and deeper impact of Covid upon our bodies, relationships, constructs, and civilisation.

To create this book, we were fortunate to have been able to bring together a team of amazing colleagues from around the globe who speak our language. Of course, this language is not necessarily English per se, but that of psychoanalysis.

This is a book that simultaneously deals with lived-in reality and with the hidden aspects of existence. One way of uncovering the hidden aspects of reality is through symbolism and visual representations. Let us then explain the choices we made in selecting the five images.

INTRODUCTION xxi

The cover image, *The Sick Child*, by Edvard Munch is an evocative and poignant scene of an ominous loss: a scene of a family bracing itself for the death of a child. At the time of Covid when family membranes were sharply pierced by unexpected and brutal loss and the inability to attend to the process of dying, this image stands for all losses.

The image associated with Part I of the book, The Shock of the New, is a photograph by Thor Simony taken at Moen, a small island in the south east of Denmark. The image represents the disquiet of an empty snow-covered platform which simultaneously represents the presence of absence and the absence of presence, leaving the viewer uncertain as to the swimmer's fate and safety. The lifebuoy indicates the omnipresence of danger, the horizon is unclear, the water icy cold … If only we had had our own personal lifebuoys when Covid struck …

Part II, Reparation, Resilience, Recovery, is about surviving the greatest inflicted injury and how we dealt with it as individuals, systems, and cultures. The best image to illustrate this is again by Edvard Munch: *Separation*. Here the wounded heart of a lover is on fire as well as much of his body, while he tries to support his own falling frame, having nearly died because of his lover's ethereal disappearance … loss not yet mourned appears to threaten his own life.

The image associated with Part III, The Fourth Humiliation of Humankind, is a photograph taken by one of the authors (HB) at the front of the National Theatre in London two years before the pandemic struck. A group of friends have come together in a joyous welcoming reunion, but hovering ominously above their heads and invisible to them, is a punishing Finger of Destiny. It seems to say: *You do not even know that you have been selected …* We cannot be sure how this selection will play out but certainly, humiliation and punishment are already visible, at least to the viewer, if not yet to the group of friends. If only they knew … And now it is already too late, for we have all been selected for suffering and humiliation.

For the last part of the book, Our New Covidian World, we selected the lustrous image of *Norwegian Landscape*, again by Edvard Munch. What is striking here is the intense luminosity which is playing on the landscape making it simultaneously familiar and unfamiliar, multicoloured and irradiated, real, and surreal. Is this uncannily familiar yet strange landscape the essence of the Covidian world?

The volume ends on a physical trail built of each chapter's essence, arranged in the same way as the book: from shock, disorientation, and fear through mobilisation of resilience, a realisation of the enormity of the changes humanity faces, and an attempt to comprehend these processes as a guide to this permanent "new normal".

We wish to thank all our contributors for working within the prearranged structure and for trusting the process. In this Introduction we decided not to describe the actual content of the book nor to introduce the contributors as their chapters will speak volumes.

Let the images guide you along this Covid path.

We leave you free to explore the trail …

Halina Brunning and Olya Khaleelee
Autumn 2021

Part I

The shock of the new

Photo courtesy of Thor Simony, 2020

CHAPTER 1

Stepping into the unknown

by Halina Brunning

Step 1

A poem for a new era

> What is the highest value to hold onto
> in the time of cholera
> asked the author of a famous
> Bolivian volume
> when everything you know
> everything you rely upon
> everything that makes you who you are
> is different now, either lost, dangerous
> or no longer accessible?
>
> How can you love when you cannot touch
> how can you live when utterly alone
> how can you nourish the family
> when not allowed to shop for food?
> what do you do when darkness descends
> when neither your past achievements

your future ambitions
nor the soothing tones of a piano
recital help to lift your spirits
when flowers have lost their scent
when long road ahead no longer for walking
when playful behaviour
of your kid your cat your dog
no longer lifts you from
the phenomenal heaviness
when the car once your pride and joy
has not been cleaned for weeks
for you cannot spark the energy any more
when the radio in full volume emits only
forebodings warnings and new prohibitions

When the earth shakes in its foundations
when the lightness has been replaced by darkness
and forms its pole opposite the "new normal"
so you no longer know where you are located
when the human race has run out
of power to control its destiny
how can you spark the last vestige
of faith when all hope is gone?

March 2020

Step 2

The Covid story

Who could have predicted what would be happening early in the promising new year of 2020? The year arrived just like a magical 20/20 vision proposing nothing less than a full-sighted perspective before Covid struck.

Now the world is locked in the grip of a disease so brutal that the mightiest countries and their heads of state are falling ill: and anyone, prime ministers, presidents, royalty, and celebrities, must submit to its deadly embrace, rendering riches, fortunes, fame, and power null and void at the kiss of the virus.

Unpredictable graphs ascending then descending, then ascending again show the steep rise of victims per country, per continent, adding a ghastly record to the totality of global mortality statistics. Alarming and urgent action in search of a vaccine was so far away, therefore we needed to rely on a test, to check on the health of the population. Cross infection within all groupings with which we are familiar and which are most intimate to us: our families, our lovers, our friends, colleagues, and neighbours, are also designated as the most dangerous to us, just as we have become to them.

We are all in the hands of hospital staff, themselves exhausted, infected, worried, besieged by Covid-19, and traumatised by what they have seen and what they need to attend to! What motivates hospital staff to keep on working and sacrificing their own health for the health of the nation is a delicate, painful, and complex question.

Who thinks about the non-medical staff, about the porters who cart the ill into intensive care and the dead to their final destinations? Hollowed out by fatigue, lack of appreciation, poor pay, long hours, and again and again by their self-sacrifice. Just like firemen, they run towards danger when all others run the other way. The dark shadows under their eyes, do we even notice these people? For sure we do not: they are the invisible but essential institutional substructure!

Can I invite the reader to imagine being a hospital porter for half a day?

How does it feel gently to push a trolley with a dying patient from the ICU to a corner ward? Or to put a flimsy cotton cover over a dead body before wheeling a recently diseased person to the mortuary? How can you bear doing this all day, every day, day in and day out? You may feel that you have no choice or love for this work, but work you must, not forgetting the night shifts. You cannot be finicky or choosy: your boss allocated you to a shift and so you comply.

But if you, the busy reader, who is used to clapping for the doctors and the nurses, more recently also for the care staff, were to stop for a moment to also think about the hospital porters: can you see a calm and strange beauty in this monotonous movement between illness and the critical state, between life and death, between agony and reaching the temporary resting place when all is lost? Only they, the hospital porters, will accompany you on that journey …

For these are the ancient boatmen, they are the Charons crossing the river Styx with the dead, carefully delivering their bodies to rest in Hades.

Clap for the hospital porters before they die themselves!

Who will then take their bodies to Hades?

April 2020

Step 3

Bang bang you're dead

She had a bad feeling all weekend, fear gripped her chest, her breathing was noisy and shallow, and, not recalling a similar experience of being unwell, she reached for her phone and dialled the emergency services. A disembodied voice instructed her to call 111. After an exhausting wait, the length of which morphed from minutes to hours, she was connected to the main office. Information about her was conveyed to the Nightingale Hospital, miraculously erected in under ten days to catch the new cohort of Covid-19 victims.

An ambulance was dispatched to take her on a new journey that might well be her last, who knows? *Trust me love*, said a fully gowned and masked ambulance driver, *we'll get you there in no time* or get you there in time. Which is it? she wondered. Banter is just banter, she recalled this familiar phrase from her recent past … Was it recent past or distant past? She did not know or care. The past is past but is there any future? This was her question, yet there was nobody around she could ask. The ambulance arrived in Docklands, an area she once associated with the recovery of London, but now when her own recovery was in doubt, she no longer cared where she was located.

Masked men put her on a trolley and wheeled her towards a vault as enormous as the connected hangars for several jumbo jets; the ceiling was high, the noise in the hangar a weird mix of humming and crying, all other-worldly, half human, half machine.

Spacious cubicles arranged on both sides of the hangar, each bed attached to a ventilator. All hope and joy had evaporated from her body, exhausted as it was already by the journey between home and this wired and weird place.

Would it be my last resting place? (for recovery was rather unlikely) she asked of herself. The crackling noises from her lungs were alarming. On her left and right two spacemen were trying to attach something to her body … Will I fly? she asked herself.

She coughed again: this time it was painful. *Take your time please*, said one of the spacemen kindly and patiently. She tried to smile but all life was now departing from her.

A bang bang gong of metal upon metal woke her from her reverie. She saw they were trying to attach a respirator to her or perhaps her to the respirator. *That is enough*, she said quietly, more to herself than to anybody else …

CHAPTER 2

Disorientation, loss, and mourning

by Birgitte Bonnerup

> *The novel coronavirus spreads in the same way as, for example, the common cold and the flu, as virus is transmitted from the respiratory passages of an infected person to another person's respiratory passages or mucous membranes in one of the following ways: droplets or contact.*
> —Danish Health Authority, July 1, 2021

Simply-stated facts. And from these facts sprang a pandemic we did not (have the courage to) see coming. With all the disorientation, loss, and mourning that it brings with it.

In my attempt to understand what we are living through, I have turned to poets for help. Poets who have written about the human condition, about mourning, disorientation, and how to go on living.

What is happening? First: disorientation

In 2020, the novel coronavirus spread from country to country, transforming the public space and the possibility of transport between countries and regions, not to mention day-to-day practices in organisations, working tasks, leisure activities, and social interactions.

Deserted cities, empty offices, and closed schools throughout most of the world. In our relational spaces, hygiene, physical distancing, and the absence of presence became the norm. Hugs, handshakes, and kisses disappeared from our close and more distant relationships.

Time passed, vanished—and some things will never be the same. Some things have been lost, others maybe gained, perhaps new insights. In this chapter, my focus is on the disorientation, the temporarily lost, the forever lost, the mourning, and how we still manage to heal and move on.

Coronavirus is an invisible threat: a threat without body, intention, volition; a threat that simply exists. A threat that we have to fight with the measures we are least inclined to take: distance; isolation; absence. Closeness became a threat. We can bring a deadly disease to those we love most, or they can bring it to us. We have become each other's threats.

The losses we have suffered over the past months of living with the coronavirus are at once simple, difficult to identify and to understand. Some losses are temporary—hopefully. Others are permanent. Perhaps, closeness will return, travel will again be possible, but the dead do not come back to us. Lost time does not come back.

An important side story

In 2009, we lost our twenty-seven-year-old daughter. Within twenty-four hours, she died from meningitis, leaving behind her husband, twin boys aged two, sisters, parents, friends, and family in chaos and mourning. Our world was turned upside down, we were, and are, marked for life, young children without their mother, a young man without his wife and with the sole responsibility for his sons, sisters without their older sister, and as parents, we had to bury our child. As many others have experienced, we received support and understanding from some; other relations were a disappointment, and some relationships could never be properly repaired.

We knew what we had lost—a daughter, mother, sister, wife, friend—although we did not grasp the full extent of the loss. I knew that I must, could, and would carry her with me as the internal object she would have to be from then on. I knew what I had to do, I was able to, and understood the obvious necessity of looking after grandchildren, daughters, son-in-law, marriage. It was not always pretty, but I and we managed as well as we could.

We had places to go: friends and colleagues who were not directly affected by our loss. Some did not know her but were able to feel with us in our grief, which we will always carry with us in our family. We have places where our grief resides, connected by pictures, rituals, and the cemetery, as Søren Ulrik Thomsen (2011) (translated by Susanna Nied) writes in this poem:

> Every year on the date
> that arbitrarily became your birthday
> we take the train to Århus
> to visit your grave
> which happens to be the place here in the world where you are not.
> On our way through the city we buy flowers and talk as on any other day
> until we're standing in front of the stone.
> And on the way back it always rains.
> Since none of this has meaning
> and it takes place anyway
> it must be of the greatest significance.

For a time, our loss pulled the rug out from under our feet. Like balls in a pinball machine, we tumbled through the first years, supported in our grief, but also in our efforts to take on our life and work to the best of our abilities. Relationships provided a guard rail to hold us, and other people helped clear some of the obstacles from our path. I leaned heavily on the patience and support of friends, not just during those initial dreadful months but during the years that followed.

Why this personal story? Because it is a story of the inevitable experiences of disorientation, loss, and mourning that are part of any life. But also, a basis for an attempt to understand both the unique and familiar aspects of the disorientation, loss, and mourning of this particular time. A time of pandemic with no idea how long it is going to last, just as we have no idea how it is going to unfold around the world.

Pandemic

Many of us were slow to grasp the seriousness of the novel coronavirus. It spread from China, and at first, the Chinese authorities' brutal way of dealing with the risk of infection and the spread of disease was the scariest aspect. That gradually changed, however. From being an abstract and remote threat, the risk of spreading or catching infection became a concrete threat in most of the world. Schools, universities, shops, libraries closed, surgical procedures were postponed, and everyone who could had to work from home. While wearing a mask in the public space used to be strictly forbidden, face masks now became mandatory: on public transport, in the—still open—supermarkets and grocery stores, at the doctor's surgery. The handshake (the hug, the peck on the cheek), traditionally a marker of friendship and courtesy towards friends, acquaintances, colleagues, patients, clients, and customers now became a potential source of infection, and we stopped touching each other as a gesture of friendship. Our usual courtesy routines had to change.

Did we believe it? Yes and no

I see Covid as a threat that cannot be overstated, but it is a matter of debate how that should be translated into practice. We have seen large-scale denial of the threat of coronavirus and of the severity and scope of the pandemic from some of our political leaders. We have seen attempts at a balanced approach to managing the pandemic, as politicians and health experts, to the best of their varying abilities, have handled the complicated task of shutting a society down and the even more complicated task of gradually opening it again—and the down again and up again … and down again. The criticism has at times been shrill and at other times disturbingly absent: the fact that the task is difficult does not mean government administrations and experts should not have to answer for their decisions and statements.

Covid and anxiety

Freud operated with three forms of anxiety: realistic, neurotic, and moral (Freud, 1933a). The fear of Covid is based in reality. The Covid pandemic was and is a threat to us and our everyday life, implies the risk of death, and may pose a threat to the world as we know it. It is the fear of losing, and the fear of the risk of losing, closeness, relationships, health, economy, the social fabric of our communities. We are far from properly understanding the full scope and extent; some aspects of our lives will probably be fairly quick to return to the normal we knew; others will change in minor ways, and yet others will be forever changed. The pandemic is a real threat, and not to fear the spread of the virus can only be seen as denial. The pandemic, the invisibility and dangerousness of the virus, the distancing, the hygiene procedures, and the knowledge that we may be a (potentially deadly) threat to someone else also activates neurotic anxiety: what might I suddenly feel the urge to do? Kiss a stranger (and thus kill him)? Our attempts at controlling the pandemic and the risk of catching the infection from someone close to us underscore how pervasive our loss of control is.

And constant nagging doubts: was I thorough enough when I washed my hands? Am I doing enough to protect and care for clients who, with great anxiety, show up for face-to-face therapy sessions? How do I provide a sense of security and containment online? Are there things I miss? Don't understand? What is my understanding of the other, of the group work in the here and now when I have so little practice sensing the other here and now in an online context? Am I good enough? What *is* good enough?

Clear and permanent losses

The pandemic has been associated with obvious and easily recognisable painful losses. Bereavement, illness, bankruptcies, economic losses. Unemployment and the loss of a life's work. Many have suffered concrete losses due to the pandemic; irredeemable losses that must be addressed with respect.

Loss of time

> Little children too dream of their past
> which is huge and dusky
> full of scents and unrecognizable figures

> reflected in polished floors.
> Even the very old feel bereft
> when they sit staring in dayrooms
> and suddenly remember
> that they have lost their parents.
>
> (Thomsen, 2011)

On my analogue watch, time moves round in a circle. The seasons change, and summer returns when the winter is over. But time, too, is disappearing. Few of us know how much time we have left, but time that has passed does not come back. Young people have lost years of their youth. Their youth years turned out very different from what they had imagined. Learning and working online was not what most of them had dreamt of. Partying was dangerous, and casual kissing, kissing some frogs to look for a prince, became a high-risk activity. Not just unprotected sex but simply kissing became unsafe. For many, parties, concerts, festivals, and other contexts where young people could meet and explore their bodies in relation to other bodies, were replaced with (chaste) walks in nature.

Old people too lost precious time with others; a lost year is even more significant to someone who is painfully aware that they have only a limited number of years left.

Grief over lost time, events that did not turn out as expected, weddings, exams. Funerals cannot be postponed, but they also cannot be repeated. Winter evenings alone, summer evenings alone. Children grow up and mature as time passes, even if we do not get to see them. The hidden Covid babies that could not meet the rest of the family and were suddenly one year old. The isolated teenagers who came out of their rooms—the boys now young men with beards. Whether the years left to us are few or many, no one knows. Lost time does not come back.

Potentially temporary losses

Loss of the taken-for-granted

Taken-for-granted experiences of being in the world have been limited for a long time, for many people.

In his book *Resonance*, Hartmut Rosa (2016) writes about skin and breathing as fundamental elements of being a human being in resonance with others. The skin, he writes, "forms a doubly sensitive, literally *breathing* and *responsive* organ of resonance that mediates and gives expression to the relationship both between body and world and between person and body" (p. 51). Later, he writes about breathing (and the ingestion of nourishment): "Every corporeal subject must ceaselessly process 'world' through his or her own body, incorporating and then releasing it in a continuous process of exchange. These are the acts of *breathing* and *ingesting and excreting nourishment*" (p. 52). He adds that "Breathing as the most basic act of life and the most fundamental process of metabolic exchange between subject and world, plays an essential role in how human beings relate to the world, how we are situated in the world" (p. 62).

Necessary distancing and the shift to online contact has led to a significant reduction in these basic experiences of being alive, as we have been (largely) unable to touch others, much of our breathing has been through a face mask, and we have lived with the knowledge that every breath might potentially lead to infection. Perhaps we have lost a natural ease in the way we socialise.

Loss of data

We lack data when we are not together. We lack data when we only meet online.

> Everything is data, this poem is data, the days are data and the day.
> This day today, which is full of seconds, and
> dreams, you and the pigeons on Toftegårds Plads.
> The lovely sky here
> stretching over Valby and the smell from the bakery are data.
> Mortality,
> the human condition, is data and
> the dystopias, the pigeons and Dropbox.
> The telephone that I carry with me everywhere, which
> delivers my data, is data.
> The fragile thread
> that *nearly* snapped
> when we *nearly* lost each other

> is data, the fear of losing is data. Losing data.
> DNA, cells
> and breathing are data, the way
> the air pulls and tugs
> at the web of branches in our lungs
> my rattling snore are data. The scar under my eye, your lemon scent and
> your iris
> are data, that special *recognition*
> we know as being in love are data.
>
> (Hørslev, 2018)

An apt description. Distance and absence mean a loss of data.

Loss of micro moments and passages

Micro moments are the tiny situations in which relationships are established, cooperation is affirmed, the severity of a conflict is toned down. A nod in the hallway after an exchange of opinions that became a little too heated, a smile of recognition when we see each other in the morning, a quick cup of coffee in-between seeing patients and providing care, a few words about events in domestic life over the weekend or even a little venting over top management and their lack of understanding for everyday conditions on the floor—all of these exchanges help maintain relationships and affirm our existence in the organisation. A colleague who notices that you could use an arm around your shoulder. Mirroring of existence and the possible development of relationships. Widely unnoticed, micro moments help maintain relationships, shape our ways of meeting and crossing boundaries and swords, and contribute to balance and connectedness. Not quite like the mortar in-between the bricks in a building. But not too far from it, either.

Every system is defined by a boundary. Some boundaries have been too closed, with a lack of oxygen (or other elements) as a result. Some families do better when everyone is not together all the time, and the constant presence of schoolchildren sent home for online learning, the lack of distance in the family, and the lack of contact with others have increased the risk of parents dropping out of their parental role and failing in their roles and tasks as adults. Organisations where many people did come in for work—in person—had to split up into smaller, closed units. Formal meetings were held online or cancelled. Natural and taken-for-granted meeting places across the organisation's subsystems became rare. Canteens closed, meetings going online, less teamwork, all with the purpose of reducing the infection risk in the workplace. The online setting was convenient in many ways, and it found its own form, as both the technical systems and the users evolved. It became possible to have relevant dialogues and meetings, even though it meant missing out on the quick glances, the sensation of the other participants' scent, information from our peripheral vision, the benefit of knowing who is looking at whom and how people are positioned in the room. We cannot even be sure that the others have the same visual image of the group as we do.

Passages through boundaries became brief. Many workplaces had developed a bad habit of going straight from one meeting to the next, without breaks in-between. Previously, a few moments were necessary to move a body, maybe a cup and a notepad. Now, meetings are separated only by a split-second click. For people who worked from home, the passages between work-related and family systems were much shorter than the normal travel time. Meeting over. Screen off. And in an instant, the head of department switched to being a mother with an infant. The loss of passages with some extension in time and space to go from one system to another. From one role and task to another. Sometimes resulting in a confusion about roles.

Loss of routines and presence

People who worked from home partially lost contact with their organisation. Primarily virtual, the workplace team turned into rows of postage-stamp size pictures. Without bodies, scents, legs, shoes. Many have preserved their sense of connection to the actual task, but online meetings notwithstanding, organisations and colleagues increasingly turned into "organizations- and colleagues-in-the-mind" (Armstrong, 2005). Micro moments and data were lacking, and in some cases the relationships suffered.

Other organisations have been busier than ever; called and able to adjust to a new reality. The motivation for some of the changes were obvious. Space and staff were needed to deal with a different patient population. In the hospitals, some wards were temporarily closed and replaced by Covid wards, staff had to take on tasks they did not want, were afraid to take on, or—in some cases—came to see as interesting new tasks, with attention and recognition from management and the general public. Over time, some of the front-line workers became fatigued, and staff from other departments had to step in. Some hospital departments saw their patients stay away because patients were afraid to come in, or because they did not want to add to the workload when there were so many Covid patients in hospital. Some types of illness dropped in number due to the reduced rate of contact and the many hygiene measures. The number of people hospitalised with influenza dropped dramatically in Europe (SSI, Statens Serum Institut). Other diseases became rampant because some people, paradoxically, did not wash their hands often enough, thinking that hand-sanitiser was sufficient. Both organisations and the patterns of disease changed.

Others, too, were busy. Preschool teachers had to come up with new procedures for parents to drop off and pick up their children, schools had to be partitioned in new ways, home schooling had to be developed, shops faced a huge task with added cleaning, signage and so forth, and employees felt exhausted.

Overlooked losses

There were and are many losses associated with the pandemic, which is still far from over, and with its ramifications. There is also the loss of attention to other losses. The losses that there was no room for. The ones that were not about the pandemic or working from home. People who died from cancer, went bankrupt, got divorced. People who were bullied or who failed their exams. Including less traumatic experiences, such as burglaries, lost pieces of jewellery, or broken bones. How do you deal with feeling slightly under the weather when others are suffering? Many losses have nothing to do with Covid. Other illnesses and difficulties were overshadowed by Covid, and, as a result, those affected did not get the physical or psychological support they would otherwise have received and benefited from.

Other forms of disorientation—in the wake of a loss

Easily comprehended losses are by no means easy to overcome. But they are visible. They can affect any one of us, and they strike us in different ways. They give rise to individual and collective experiences of loss and related emotions. However, coronavirus remains a ubiquitous and diffuse threat. The pandemic and the steps we need to take to deal with it led to disorientation and loss. And the losses lead to a different form of disorientation, at a societal and relational level.

Spring 2020 came and went. The idealisation of hospital staff in particular began to fade, and society began to show new forms of division: who was most deserving of sympathy?

In Denmark, in 2020, many people worked from home. After the idealisation of doctors and nurses and, to a lesser degree, retail workers, transportation workers (who secured a steady supply of highly coveted toilet paper, which, according to news stories, was being hoarded in large parts of Europe), and school and preschool teachers, that was widespread in spring 2020, the focus shifted to the strain of working from home. When working from home peaked in Denmark in autumn 2020, it included 26% of the labour force, or 40% if we include everyone who worked partially from home (*Danmarks Statistik 21*, 2021). Big shares, but still surpassed by the number of people who continued to show up in person. Nevertheless, the press was full of articles about working from home, and at some point, I got the impression that almost everyone did so—apart from a nurse, a doctor, and a bus driver. There was also some degree of division between professions as to who is most at risk. In Denmark, teachers described themselves as cannon fodder when schools were due to reopen—something that irked preschool teachers, who had kept nurseries and kindergartens open almost since the start of the pandemic.

Who is better at preventing the spread? Some municipalities had far higher infection rates than others. And one wondered—how could they not get it under control? The picture became more nuanced once the affluent municipalities also had trouble keeping the rates of infection down; that seemed to be what was needed to add more nuance to the debate.

Unsure authorities

If we are fortunate enough to have grown up with good-enough care from relevant persons of authority, we are able to have realistic expectations of authority figures and governmental agencies, and their necessary use of power with the intention of fighting the pandemic. We have seen major differences between different countries in terms of the authorities' willingness and ability to grasp the threat, manage it, and address it in accordance with human rights and democratic principles. However, the authorities too have been, and are, in doubt. What is the right strategy? Who should be vaccinated first? The young, since they are the ones who are most likely to spread the infection (or so we think)? Or the old and the vulnerable, because they are more likely to succumb to the virus and to put a strain on the hospital system when they are infected? Which vaccines should be rejected as inadequate, can we get sufficient supplies, and is the population going to be willing to take the vaccines? What should reopen first—fitness centres or universities? Easy to make a decision that might later prove wrong and lead to criticism. Difficult to find what W. R. Bion called "the selected fact" (Abel-Hirsch, 2019, p. 234) that enables decision-making in complex situations—and impossible to wait for science to provide firm evidence to guide every single decision.

Not just governments have to find a way and make decisions based on incomplete facts. Where I live, many directors and managers had to find solutions on their own, virtually overnight. What to do when the children in a residential institution cannot simply be sent home to their family if they are infected? How to handle the risk of infection in a kindergarten that has to stay open? What to do in a shop if the customers insist on NOT respecting the rules about distancing and using hand-sanitiser? The individual managers had a sense of authority and autonomy—for once—but also felt isolated, abandoned, burdened with too much responsibility. In some settings, it was suddenly very easy to delegate responsibilities and task management to the local managers who were close to the staff and the users.

Loss of relationships—for now or forever?

Conditions have changed for relationships—with family, friends, colleagues, and more or less random strangers who might prove to become new, significant people in our lives. Physical distancing, fewer occasions and opportunities to socialise. Sure, online relationships are better than none. But it is not the same as being together, breathing in the same air, seeing each other from different angles, shifting one's feet and noticing that the others notice.

Then there are the people we do not see. Distances and boundaries that cannot be overcome. Families who are unable to meet, and when they do, the next reunion is uncertain and difficult. Perhaps because the physical meeting has become so idealised that it is almost unattainable? Because our family/group "in the mind" has fallen out of step with reality during periods of lockdown, working from home or pressures at work? Or because the difficulties that always exist between people in groups become more prominent and also more difficult to handle due to the lack of habits, rituals, and micro moments? Or because we are bound to feel anger and frustration and need to project it somewhere? Sometimes, extensive repairs are needed, a process that requires time, tolerance, and energy.

Loneliness

The pandemic has led to many different kinds of loneliness. Leaders with big responsibilities, limited data, and little experience to lean on; employees who have to remain isolated from their family because they are potential carriers of infection; families that close in on themselves; people working from home facing the combination of being part of an organisation and still spending many hours on their own. Those who have to live in physical isolation, dependent on online contact, facing anxiety, uncertainty, and loss.

Loss and mourning make us lonely. It is inherently difficult to be with someone who is mourning. And even harder if we have limited energy and vitality. Fear of each other makes us lonely. The isolation during lockdown, shuttered city streets and empty metro trains, online contact bereft of touch and the sharing of air; all these factors left many people lonely. Tired of looking at themselves on a screen, alone in their own company once they switched off. For some, solitude turned to loneliness, with all the pressures and difficulties that involves (Bonnerup & Hasselager, 2019). Winnicott (1958) has written about "the capacity to be alone" and how it develops in early infant–parent interactions. This capacity is put to the test when someone is cut off from physical everyday interactions with others for an extended time. Being on one's own, partially cut off from contact with the outside world, gives the "brutal superego" greater latitude: "The super-ego's contradictory and impossible demands are unlikely to be modified by reality and the meeting with others" (Bonnerup & Hasselager, 2019, pp. 90–91) when one spends too much time alone, and the brutal superego is unchecked. The individual has to rely, to a high degree, on good internal objects or, as Buechler puts it, "How aloneness feels depends on who you are with when you are alone" (Buechler, 2011, p. 16).

Who has done this before?

"It takes a village to raise a child." An African proverb, that stresses the importance of more than "just" a parent to provide the child with a safe environment (widely quoted, Wikipedia, August 4, 2021). However, the pandemic has isolated some families, and parents have not been able to lean on their parents' experiences—what did you do when I was a Covid baby? Outside families, too, in our leisure life and workplaces, there was no one to ask—what did you do during the last pandemic? What procedures, routines, and rituals did you use to handle the organisational and relational pressures?

Now, the expectation that there will be SOMEONE to ask, that SOMEONE will have the right experience, is challenged. We share this experience of lacking certain knowledge, lacking reliable authorities, having to rely on our own ability to assess situations and make decisions in a world with many questions, uncertain answers, and potentially disastrous consequences.

Nowhere to turn

The loss of my daughter is without a doubt the biggest tragedy of my life. But I understood my grief; knew, to some extent, what I had lost. And I had people to turn to. Other people who understood what I was going through as well as people who knew nothing about my loss and who had the same expectations of me as always. That supported me and gave me a break from the grief that was ripping me apart and, thus, also help to pick up my life again. However, coronavirus is everywhere: in families, groups of friends, organisations. Every system is affected by the coronavirus pandemic. No one has an unaffected place from where they can contain the others' fear, anxiety, anger, and despair and the dilemmas that are suddenly part of everyday life. Everyone's everyday life was and is infected with coronavirus, all at the same time.

Loss and meaning

Let me quote the closing lines of S. U. Thomsen's poem (2011) again:

> Since none of this has meaning
> and it takes place anyway
> it must be of the greatest significance.

Coronavirus has caused very concrete and brutal losses as well as temporary losses whose long-term consequences we are not yet sure of. Loss of time, loss of closeness in relationships, loss of countless micro moments, loneliness, loss of data from social interactions.

Loss raises the question of meaning. What is the meaning of my losses? Of everything? What is the meaning of Covid? Nature's punishment for humanity's stupidity and greed? Evil individuals' attempt at claiming world domination and controlling us all, both mentally and in concrete terms? Bad luck and an inability to think clearly and bear the consequences? We need to mobilise our thinking to understand our world, as children, as adults, in this new reality.

> The infant needs a lot of help in developing its own meaning, the appearance of things that have meaning … The baby needs something of an auxiliary ego to enable the baby to make sense, to make a meaningful sense, of what comes through the eyes and ears … This is the way upon which Bion focuses on containing. That the baby's experience, which is very difficult for the baby to make sense of, gets transferred into the containing object … So

> the containing object can give it a sense of meaning, the baby acquires the conception from the object of how to see the thing that's in front of it, whether it is sight, or hearing or whatever, the perception is given a form through the interchange between the baby and its containing object/mother/whoever ... who can make sense of it.
>
> (Hinshelwood & Abram, 2021, mins. 20.00–25.00)

We have work to do to find meaning in the pandemic and in its causes and effects, and no one is in a position of having tried this before, a safe position that would allow them to guide others in their search for meaning. We need to find shared meaning, not uniform meaning, by *thinking* in the broadest sense of the word and having the courage to think for ourselves as well as together.

"Loss is a brutal gift"

A loss can bring something positive with it, even if that does not mean the loss was "worth it". In their book *Life after Loss*, Volkan and Zintl quote Rabbi Harold Kushner: "'I am a more sensitive person, a more effective pastor, a more sympathetic counselor because of Aron's life and death, than I would ever have been without it. And I would give up all of those gains in a second if I could have my son back'" (Volkan & Zintl, 2015, p. 38).

But a loss can be a gift, albeit it a "brutal gift", as Volkan and Zintl call it (p. 7). It can bring increased insight. Greater sensitivity. A deeper appreciation of others' presence and perhaps—hopefully—a better understanding of other worlds and the planet we need to protect.

According to Volkan and Zintl (p. 5), loss and our development through mourning depends on 1) the survivor's emotional make-up: "Those who had inadequate support for childhood needs or who have sustained a series of losses may have difficulty grieving", 2) the nature of the loss: "A relationship that was overtly dependent or laden with unfinished business is harder to let go", 3) the circumstances of the loss (for example, in the present case, the fact that it is a global pandemic, with incomprehensible and overwhelming losses), and 4) that we are "a culture of death deniers".

Our personal history, relational experiences, and the stability of the substance of internal objects affect the course of our mourning. In "Mourning and Its Relation to the Manic Depressive State", Melanie Klein writes:

> The poignancy of the actual loss of a loved person is, in my view, greatly increased by the mourner's unconscious phantasies of having lost his *internal* 'good' objects as well. He then feels that his internal 'bad' objects predominate and his inner world is in danger of disruption. We know that the loss of a loved person leads to an impulse in the mourner to reinstate the lost loved object in the ego (Freud and Abraham). (Klein, 1994, pp. 103 ff.)

Mourning takes time and energy

Freud writes about grief in "Mourning and Melancholia": "Mourning is regularly the reaction to the loss of a loved person, or to the loss of some abstraction that has taken the place of one, such as one's country, liberty, an ideal, and so on" (1917e, p. 243). In a later passage, he adds,

> Reality-testing has shown that the loved object no longer exists, and it proceeds to demand that all libido shall be withdrawn from its attachments to that object. This demand arouses understandable opposition … [but] normally, respect for reality gains the day. Nevertheless its orders cannot be obeyed at once. They are carried out bit by bit, at great expense of time and cathectic energy, and in the meantime the existence of the lost object is psychically prolonged. Each single one of the memories and expectations in which the libido is bound to the object is brought up and hypercathected, and detachment of the libido is accomplished. (pp. 244–245)

After noting that the process is a painful one, Freud concludes, "The fact is, however, that when the work of mourning is completed the ego becomes free and uninhibited again" (p. 245).

But what does that mean in a potentially endless series of losses, when it is difficult to say when the actual pandemic is over and what we might return to? Mourning will probably form a parallel track in society; some will have suffered concrete losses, others more diffuse ones; and society will have lost something significant that we probably barely recognise, just as we do not know what will come, what we should put in its place.

Angry with the virus?

Anger is part of the grieving process, and anger can facilitate the process in which the libido gradually detaches and can be invested anew. The object is not forgotten, it is stored and exists in our imagination. However, how does that work when we are speaking of a virus and a pandemic? What and who can we then direct our anger at? Everyone and no one. Some specific morons have exacerbated the situation. I shall mention no names. And with the benefit of hindsight, it seems clear that many decisions could have been better. The virus is not an evil subject at which we can direct our anger. But the anger is there as part of the grief; one of the many and fairly complicated emotions the loss gives rise to. It is not sufficient to be angry with some distant authority figure, even if the anger may be quite relevant. Anger has to find its way, and many people are angry, for many different reasons; and this anger may be expressed and manifested in many different ways: irritation, touchiness, pettiness, greed, miserliness, attacks and violence—anger has many expressions. We need to be prepared for big and small outbursts of anger and ready to understand the bigger outbursts as expressions, also, of a collective unconscious anger and a collective unconscious desire for simple explanations and quick fixes.

Summer 2021

What is the question we need to answer?

Vamık D. Volkan has written about grief and transgenerational traumas (2017). What do we pass on to future generations? If nothing else, that consideration compels us to address our loss and grief, to avoid leaving an overwhelming legacy of issues for coming generations to deal with.

How do we make room to mourn our concrete and less concrete losses, our definitive and more temporary losses? Mourning is important. It is important to know our loss and its full scope and impact. It is important to approach each other with curiosity, with a desire to understand each other, also when the thing we hope to understand is so provokingly different. This is not in order to cling to loss and mourning, but in order to be able to let go and move on, enriched by this new and deeply incomprehensible experience.

It is also important to be able to alternate between mourning and the continued process of living; not as two separate worlds but as two sides of our existence that go together, where the two aspects, so to speak, take turns being the focus of our attention, as neither aspect is sufficient to stand on its own (see, e.g. Stroebe & Schut, 1999).

To be able and willing to make repairs in relationships, groups, organisations, communities. To linger in the depressive position. To understand the other's otherness, because our individual experiences and life strategies are different; to maintain our ability to think under pressure; to allow disorientation to serve as an occasion to think and to give mourning and loss room to exist. So that new insights, relationships, priorities may emerge, as the libido continually and once again finds its way.

It is a learning process, but not everything we learn is good new learning, and there are unnoticed learning processes that we only become aware of down the road. We may hope that they, too, can lead to something good.

I close with a quote from Naja Maria Aidt's book *When Death Takes Something from You Give It Back* (2017):

> When death takes something from you
> give it back
> give back what you got
> from the dead one
> when he was alive

References

Abel-Hirsch, N. (2019). *Bion. 365 Quotes.* Abingdon, UK: Routledge.
Aidt, N. M. (2019). *When Death Takes Something from You Give It Back.* D. J. Newman (Trans.). Minneapolis, MN: Coffee House Press, 2019.

Armstrong, D. (2005). Emotions in organizations: Disturbance or intelligence? In: D. Armstrong, R. French, & A. Obholzer, *Organization in the Mind. Psychoanalysis, Group Relations and Organizational Consultancy.* London: Karnac.

Bonnerup, B., & Hasselager, A. (2019). *Love and Loneliness at Work: An Inspirational Guide for Consultants, Leaders and Other Professionals.* Abingdon, UK: Routledge.

Buechler, S. (2011). Someone to watch over me. In: B. Willock, L. C. Bohm & R. C. Curtis (Eds.), *Loneliness and Longing: Conscious and Unconscious Aspects.* Hove, UK: Routledge.

Danmarks Statistik 21 (2021, February). Newsletter from Statistics Denmark. www.dst.dk (last accessed July 16, 2021).

Freud, S. (1917e). Mourning and melancholia. *S. E., 14*: pp. 237–258. London: Hogarth.

Freud, S. (1933a). *New Introductory Lectures on Psycho-Analysis and Other Works. S. E., 22.* London: Hogarth.

Hinshelwood, R. D., & Abram, J. (2021). Holding and containing, part 2. IPA webinar, June 7.

Hørslev, L. (2018). *Dagene er data* (The days are data). Copenhagen: Rosinante.

Klein, M. (1994). Mourning and its relation to the manic depressive state. In: R. V. Frankiel, *Essential Papers on Object Loss.* New York: New York University Press.

Rosa, H. (2016). *Resonance: A Sociology of Our Relationship to the World.* J. C. Wagner (Trans.). Cambridge: Polity.

SSI. Statens Serum Institut (2020, August 20). The 2019/20 influenza season was very unusual. www.ssi.dk (last accessed March 29, 2022).

Stroebe, M., & Schut, H. (1999). The dual process model of coping with bereavement: rationale and description. *Death Studies, 23*(3): 197–224.

Thomsen, S. U. (2011). *Shaken Mirror: Poems.* S, Nied (Trans.). Copenhagen: Gyldendal.

Volkan, V. (2017). *Immigrants and Refugees: Trauma, Perennial Mourning, Prejudice, and Border Psychology.* Abingdon, UK: Routledge, 2018.

Volkan, V., & Zintl, E. (2015): *Life after Loss.* London: Karnac.

Winnicott, D. W. (1958). The capacity to be alone. *International Journal of Psychoanalysis, 39*(5): 416–420.

CHAPTER 3

What is social dreaming telling us about the new terrain?

by Halina Brunning

What is social dreaming?

"Social dreaming" was developed by Gordon Lawrence at the Tavistock Institute in 1982 (Lawrence, 1998, 2000). Social dreaming focuses on thinking and new knowledge that is embedded in dreams on the assumption that dreams do not belong to the individual dreamer but belong to "the matrix". The matrix can be a physical or a virtual space in which dreams are shared. The matrix thus becomes the containing environment in which the process of social dreaming takes place, mirroring the matrix of the "undifferentiated unconscious" that operates while we are asleep and dreaming. In this space the exploration of the unknown takes place as dreams are being shared. No hierarchy of dreams is assumed, rather a democratic dialogue between dreams can take place via free associations to the shared material. Dreams can thus be linked to find connections between them and, furthermore, may be turned into a hypothesis addressing the underlying meaning contained in the interlinked dreams. The emerging pattern can tell us something new about our personal and societal preoccupations. New and often surprising thinking can emerge from this process.

Sensing new danger

During the Social Dreaming Matrix held in Poland in December 2019, a number of dreams were being offered containing references to a catastrophe.

These dreams referred to a past catastrophe, such as the Second World War, which even now represents a deep and traumatic subject in Poland. Towards the end of the matrix, however, there was a shift as dreams and associations which were referring to an *impending new catastrophe*, unknown, as yet not experienced.

Dreamers referred to both categories of danger: the old and the new, either by sharing a sense of being out of control, feeling lost, confused, unable to save one's own children; feeling powerless to prevent danger that engulfed one's life, or by expressing fear that no structure of support, be it human, natural, or man-made can stop us from falling into a void. This void was unknown and unnamed at that time—December 2019.

Yet this new danger in the matrix was clearly related to the *function of breathing*. Dreams described attempts to stop breathing and trying to do something paradoxically different to stave off death, like questioning whether breathing was actually at all necessary for staying alive.

Dreamers reported living at a time where all had changed and become unrecognisable:

> *The town was my own town, yet it was different, there were no people around, nobody I could trust to take care of my children. Life cannot go on without breathing. What kind of future will our children have without towns and without breathing?*

Dreams offered in a pre-pandemic Poland at the end of 2019 spoke presciently of a new danger to life and to our civilisation, it being an example of the as yet undeclared *unthought known* as proposed by Bollas (1987).

Apocalypse now

Early in 2020, the year the coronavirus pandemic erupted and took a global hold on humanity, three International Social Dreaming Matrices were held online, the first virtual session being in May 2020.

The extracted essence from these matrices could be seen to refer to the new un/reality and its surrealistic elements, like a coffin resting on the bed.

The matrix denuded us of all illusions by showing that nothing is what it seems; the image of a locked up cage was offered ambiguously in as much as we are all locked up, but would prefer to lock up the enemy (the virus) instead.

The virus, our chief enemy, was seen to be of male gender. Bare knuckle fighting was described in different guises with examples of symbolic breakdown of the social order and a growing lack of trust in authorities, noting that children demanded answers from ignorant adults.

Many seemingly unrelated dreams offered in panic looked for safe containing structures. Dreamers were longing for and describing our idols, seeking protection and salvation. Symbols of mother, gods, Mother Earth, our collective idols were being evoked and summoned to help us. Yet regardless of that, we were still rudderless, on a sea swollen by tsunami, and the remaining symbol was only a coffin with a dead mother resting on a bed …

The second Social Dreaming Matrix in 2020 had a very different flavour in that it approached "the tragic position".

We were no longer searching for societal containers to locate and channel our anxiety. Why would we do that, if the main containers available were all coffin-shaped?

During the first matrix we were in touch with *the real.*

In the second matrix, instead, we were in touch with *the surreal.*

Apparently, we are observing ourselves going on with our lives, but nothing is what it seems anymore: we are changed, our life is changed, our future has changed. We have lost our innocence, our capacity to enjoy simple pleasures, to understand and predict the future, for we no longer have the navigational instruments to help us find our way from among many confused pathways.

The only thing we are seeing is the possibility of a second wave and with it a dawn of a frightening new civilisation … civilisation both unknown and unknowable where new rules might apply and where a hybrid of new beings—human/animal/viral—might appear. Are we waiting for a new messiah?

The third Social Dreaming International Matrix in June 2020 started with a number of references to symbols and elements usually associated to the Second World War. The images were frightening: the forests, selection for survival, hidden cemeteries, being naked in a public space, long black tunnels, baths that were not real baths but ovens, the importance of blond versus dark hair and blue versus brown eyes. Undoubtedly, these are the signifiers of the Holocaust.

These elements featured as though unconnected, yet all were equally foreboding.

Pictures representing the fragility of life, decay, and death featured prominently in the first half hour; many dreams rushed out, and even more associations were offered.

This was bridged to *"and time will tell"* as we entered a more contemplative period during the matrix. We recognised the uncanny events that unfolded, feeling half dead, half alive, filled with fear and hope mixed with uncertainty. This led to a question: *Where will hope come from?*

> A mother and a daughter in two different cars set out on the road. The mother knew she took the wrong turning but failed to correct her route, unlike her daughter who took the right turning. Both women symbolised the generational differences associated with climate change attitudes: different paths of knowing and acting.

Fatherland versus mother tongue: this split and division of roles took us to the issue of leadership, asking whether, if women were to be allowed more of a leadership role, would the world look different? Evidence was quoted that the nine countries that did best during the pandemic were all run by women.

Recognising that the lockdown will end soon, the preoccupation then moved on to the question of what kind of world will we be returning to. Can we clean out our stuff/our shit before we emerge? Can we use the lockdown period as a kind of reset, or will the primitive elements in each one of us be dominant once more?

I caught up with the stream of the International Social Dreaming Matrices in December 2021, at the time when the newcomer Omicron first appeared on the scene. Noticeably, the number of participants had shrunk, as well as the expressed overt anxiety during the session.

In place of anxiety *transformation* was now centre stage in a number of dreams. This transformation was filled with inner toxicity; at its core, noticeable in a number of dreams was the process of innocent, pure, and beautiful objects filled with joy and promise unexpectedly turning sour, empty, or dangerous. Against this process of decay a question was asked: Whom can we trust, on what can we rely? Spirituality, religious beliefs, and churches were described in a variety of ways through the matrix. Searching for safe containers was again the underlying theme. We must rebuild churches so that we can be rebuilt, was the symbolic conclusion of the 2021 International Matrix.

We shall now take a brief look at other social dreaming matrices taking place around the world at the time of the pandemic.

One such social dreaming matrix accompanied this year's 37th Annual Symposium of ISPSO, the International Society for the Psychoanalytic Study of Organizations, which was held virtually in July 2021. Sessions took place twice daily for a week in the morning and evening to connect members across the global time span.

Let us extract the essence of this matrix where members from all continents shared dreams and nightmares from the ongoing global pandemic.

A sense of being lost in familiar places accompanied the ISPSO matrix without offering any safe resting place … Dreams talked about a state of vegetating rather than living, a sense of dreamers being locked in a maze as surreal as Maurits Cornelis Escher's drawings, from which there was no escape. The weirdness of the experiences was heightened by a sense that everything was reversed, back to front and nothing offered comfort or succour. The most upsetting feature was the terror of the known as opposed to the unknown, since we all represented a danger to each other, potentially becoming secret killers of our nearest and dearest. No place offered security, not even the familiarity of our own domesticity. No respite or rescue was available, no safe spaces, neither inside nor in any public sphere to contain our anxiety. Even cats were potentially spreading Covid on their silky fur! Everything we loved turned into ash. Envy was expressed towards cats for their legendary capacity to have nine lives when we, mere mortals, had only been given one life, which was now about to expire.

Dreamers collectively eschewed reliance on our own intelligence as a way out of danger. What surrounded us were walls with graffiti and warnings (*the writing on the wall*) listing our sins and encroachments against the earth, against nature, against each other.

Eros was no longer strong enough to offer us any salvation when Thanatos dominated the world. Humanity and the civilisation we have co-created are vulnerable, fragile, isolated from resources and impervious to rescue, suspended between the sin of abundance and the fate of abandonment.

From here to eternity?

What can we discern from the social dreaming matrices about the new terrain?

The Social Dreaming Matrix held in Poland in December 2019 represented a prescient realisation that humanity as well as our current civilisation is on the precipice, facing new mortal danger that might lead to a new world *dis/order.*

The four online International Social Dreaming Matrices at the start of the pandemic and later in 2021 represented a desperate search for new safety in the shape of *any* holding psychosocial containers. Dreamers came to a shocking realisation that no safe containers were available due to death of the mother figure. As the mother figure was no longer available to contain and soothe her needy and frightened children, we had all become orphaned …

While the second matrix was also contemplating the end of our civilisation as we know it, the third matrix was a tentative look at the emerging new reality and the possibility of finding a deeper understanding of the age in which we live.

The new terrain sketched in the four matrices linked to the anticipated attack on parenting, blaming parents for their inability to protect their offspring against the impending new danger to the world and to humanity. This was visible in the Polish and in the International Social Dreaming Matrix, the death of the mother in the first session leading to the articulation of demands for a more maternal environment, standing for a more containing political leadership. This is where the hope briefly resided.

The presence of the evil within society and the evil resident within each one of us was expressed, but was not elaborated; dreamers escaped quickly from this theme, making no links to other observations. We are all implicated in the co-creation of this dangerous and perhaps irreversible worldly mess.

The ISPSO Symposium Matrix held a year later, in July 2021, referred obliquely to a sense of loss of hope, and the destruction of humanity and civilisation, even though by then, unlike the time of the earlier social dreaming matrices of 2020, there was a widely available vaccination programme against Covid. This could have offered hope, yet hope was still elusive. Why?

The essence of this deep sorrowful mood was probably linked to a shared sense of guilt, shame, and remorse about the extent to which this dangerous state of affairs in the world was the result of our own greed, selfishness, narcissism, and exploitation of each other and of earthly resources, and was thus created by all of us. We only had ourselves to blame …

Within this context it now makes sense to see why the fourth International Social Dreaming Matrix of late 2021 was preoccupied with spirituality as opposed to the voracious consumption and greed referred to in earlier events.

Noting with a degree of resignation that all good objects have thus been poisoned and have now been lost, a desire to rebuild goodness was expressed. If we rebuild churches, we will also be rebuilt and will have a new container for our salvation, the matrix seems to say.

At least hypothetically, this is how all the matrices read now.

It would appear that, independently of conclusions drawn from the International Social Dreaming Matrices, the International Listening Posts arrived at identical conclusions (see Chapter 12). Three further chapters in this book address this assumption from a more theoretical position, finding resonance with the unconscious conclusions reached by the dreamers.

References

Bollas, C. (1987). *The Shadow of the Object: Psychoanalysis of the Unthought Known*. Abingdon, UK: Routledge.
Lawrence, W. G. (1998). *Social Dreaming @ Work*. London: Karnac.
Lawrence, W. G. (2000). *Tongued with Fire: Groups in Experience*. London: Karnac.

CHAPTER 4

Guide to the new terrain

Panic and pandemics: from fear of contagion to contagion of fear*

by Mario Perini

From time immemorial epidemics threatened man's survival, mental peace, and the social order that man has come to create. As Walter Pasini (2010) writes in his presentation of a recent symposium on "old and new epidemics":

> Plague, smallpox, syphilis, cholera, tuberculosis, influenza have changed mankind's history for their impact on men's life and health, and their demographic, financial and social effects. The great epidemics created panic and anxiety as they decimated entire populations. If one single person's illness or death represents a tragedy for his/her family, the collective death adds on feelings of impotence and fear concerning men's fate.

Besides being a haunting ghost, a terrible memory of the past, epidemics have recently also become a present nightmare, a source of

---

* This chapter is an expanded and updated version of "Panic and pandemics: from fear of contagion to contagion of fear" by Mario Perini, in H. Brunning (Ed.), *Psychoanalytic Reflections on a Changing World* (pp. 213–232), published 2012 by Karnac. Reproduced by permission of Taylor & Francis Group.

individual and collective fears, so much harder to bear in that they symbolically represent all the unseen or disavowed insecurity, complexity, and vulnerability belonging to our current life, as well as the archaic anxieties and "nameless terrors" belonging to every human being's early childhood experience.

During the last decades on the stage of an increasingly globalised world—where everything, even risks, tend to happen on a worldwide scale—more than thirty new infectious, epidemic or pandemic illnesses appeared, the so-called "emergent infections": AIDS, SARS, Ebola virus, "bird flu", "prions illness" ("mad cow disease"), "swine flu", and the new entry, Covid-19, are only the best known among these new threats, while the traditional ones (malaria, typhus, cholera, tuberculosis, etc.), although no longer feared in Western countries, are still going on and killing thousands of people in the poorest countries.

During 2020 the Covid pandemic shook the world. While causing fewer casualties than expected, it demonstrated the extent to which "the king is naked", namely, how vulnerable our social systems are and how inadequate our managerial, scientific, technical, and communicational abilities have been shown to be. Above all, it highlighted how deeply unprepared governments, technical bodies, and mass media were when faced with the need to manage not just the virus and the illness, but also the spread of fear among the populations.

In order to deal with present and future challenges—as Pasini outlines—we need to start by keeping in mind the lessons from the past, and the understanding of the history of epidemics. To this relevant warning I would also add one more: in order to deal with challenges involving anxiety, fear, and panic for thousands or even millions of people, we also need to understand better these human emotions, the way they develop, what may enhance or mitigate them, what their psychological and social dynamics are, and how they impact on individual and group behaviour, as well as on organisational functioning.

The centuries of fear (Treccani Encyclopedia, 2009)

Words like "epidemic", "infectious", "contagion" are still able to trigger fear by their mere sound, although modern medicine has by now eradicated, at least from industrial societies, most of the infectious diseases which have been plaguing mankind for centuries.

The first evidence of an epidemic may be traced back to the Egyptian and the Babylonian epochs, and terrible pandemic plagues devastated ancient China as well as the Mediterranean lands during the Trojan War. Ancient and modern history describe cyclical periods of major plagues over the centuries throughout the known world. In 430 BC Athens was overwhelmed by a plague, as Thucydides narrates in detail; the Western Roman Empire, just prior its destruction by the barbaric invasions, had already been weakened by plague and smallpox epidemics; the Byzantine Empire during the reign of Justinian was lashed by bubonic plague. In the Middle Ages first leprosy, and then tuberculosis added to the plague. The greatest epidemic of the pre-modern era, the so-called Black Death, developed in central Europe by 1345, probably carried from Asia through the caravan routes. Within a few years it had spread all over the continent, striking Constantinople in 1347, Florence, Marseilles and Paris in 1348, and many other countries in the following years, until it petered out in Russia in 1351.

With the great discoveries, sailors brought to Europe syphilis that they had contracted in the Americas, while the natives were decimated by the illnesses imported by the conquerors: smallpox, measles, and even the ordinary cold. During the seventeenth century, due also to the Thirty Years War, the plague struck again in Europe, spreading death alongside other then endemic illnesses, such as malaria and smallpox, and new killers like spotted fever.

In the following century the plague paid another visit to Europe: to Austria in 1711 and to the Balkans from 1770 and 1772, reappearing sporadically by the second half of the nineteenth century, simultaneously with a big Eastern pandemic which led to more than 12 million dead in China and India.

During the first half of the same century cholera had struck Italy, while in England the new working class was paying the price of the Industrial Revolution with a heavy toll of thousands of victims of tuberculosis, which then went on to infect France, Germany, and Japan. Furthermore, tuberculosis appeared to be a fatal gift of colonial expansion, spreading mainly in Africa and in the southern seas; smallpox, measles, diphtheria, and influenza also gradually crossed countries and continents and was exported almost everywhere.

Influenza and viral illnesses were the absolute protagonists in the epidemics and pandemics of the twentieth and early twenty-first centuries.

The discovery of the bacterial origins of many infectious diseases, an increased concern for public health, the practice of vaccination, and the new drugs, antibiotics, allowed the eradication of nearly all the sources of traditional plagues and epidemics, or at least enabled the containment of their diffusion. The last enemies however, viruses, appeared harder to fight against than bacteria, and from their ranks arose what may be considered the two most dreadful "plagues" of the contemporary age: AIDS and the flu pandemics.

The first HIV epidemics—which presented the world with a new disease, AIDS—date back to the 1980s. Oddly enough, although this illness is still far from being defeated and goes on bringing pain and death among the emergent and the poorest nations, people's fears and the attention of the mass media have almost completely moved away to focus on the flu.

During the twentieth century, influenza viruses, always the origin of large epidemic events, have provoked three pandemics: the Spanish flu (1918–20), which claimed approximately twenty million victims; the Asian flu (1957), which killed two million people; and the 1968 Hong-Kong influenza, which resulted in one million dead. In this first decade of the twenty-first century influenza viruses spread panic within the globalised world on three occasions: SARS in 2003, bird flu in 2005–06, and the last one, the type A influenza so-called "swine flu", in 2009. And now, starting by the end of 2019, we have the Covid-19 pandemic.

Well, after all, it is evident that epidemics are not just a health problem, as they also imply social, cultural, political, financial, and also psychological processes which require complex, multidimensional approaches. Besides being a terrible memory of past plagues, they have recently also become a present nightmare, a source of individual and collective fears, so much harder to bear in that they symbolically represent all the unseen—or disavowed—insecurity, complexity, and vulnerability belonging to our current life in a fast globalised world, as well as the archaic anxieties and "nameless terrors" belonging to every human being's early childhood experience. In short, an *"epidemic of fear"* (Perini, 2010; Strong, 1990).

In what follows, I want to offer a contribution to this necessary process of understanding.

On fear and its vicissitudes

The first shield against all fears is the mother, but with growth this protection appears increasingly defective, partial, and full of ambivalence, which enhances the role of individual and social psychic defences. Faced with unbearable fears, the mind may try to repress, displace, or deny them or the dangers, to project them onto others, to find reassurance in some rational explanation, or to split the reality into a bad, dangerous outside world to be warded off, and a good, safe, and idealised place—including legal and illegal drugs—to withdraw to in search of salvation.

Social defences (Krantz, 2010; Menzies, 1961) may also serve the purpose of avoiding fear: the social system itself, its institutions and politics may be involved in a defensive set of beliefs, actions, and organisational routines aimed at protecting their members from an experience of fear, provided the latter accept to live within a social bond essentially based on dependence, fidelity, obedience, and conformism, or on the splitting and projection of all responsibility for the danger into the demonised Other—the scapegoat, the enemy, which therefore has to be feared, excluded, blamed, or even destroyed. As a result, all theories and catchphrases which sound reassuring and optimistic exert a strong seduction for public opinion, even when apparently false or manipulated; another consequence is how rapidly and superficially these defensive systems identify dangers, enemies, faults, unhealthy foods, the causes of cancer, terrorists, etc. Nothing would please us more than having a quick fix to heal most fears, to find a name for them, and to point a finger at a culprit: splash the monster across the front pages, and allow people to resume peaceful sleep at night.

Another problem is the fact that these social defences are not just unconscious processes managed by individuals, groups, or communities searching for safety. As Freud pointed out in *Group Psychology and Analysis of the Ego* (1921c), their capacity to convince people, blinding their critical functions, is well known to leaders and to anybody who wants to achieve or exert power over others. That is why occasionally the "politics of fear" arises and develops, by riding or feeding on collective anxieties and conflicts.

Epidemics as psychosocial processes: spaces and symbols of fear

The relation between epidemics and contagion has been taken for granted, but for a considerable time the science, the culture, and partly also people's opinions attributed them to other causes. Quite paradoxically, however, the concept of contagion—a transmission of illnesses from one person to another person (or from animal to person)—is really a very old one. For centuries the official medicine has been supportive of different explanations, adding to those coming from popular fantasies and superstitions, and from religious doctrines.

From its very origins, during the Middle Ages and, to some extent, even now, the Catholic Church had been declaring that epidemics represented nothing but God's punishment for men's sins, drawing on the accounts of biblical plagues and furnishing people's terrors with a reassuring cultural container based on the dynamics of guilt, punishment, and penance. The modern institutions responsible for dealing with contemporary epidemics—the government, the healthcare and the financial systems, and to a great extent the media—are, besides their "rational" tasks such as to anticipate the outburst of an epidemic, to identify its etiological agent, to interpret its trend and dangerousness, and to make decisions on what resources should be organised to face it and how they should be deployed, also expected to manage individuals' fears, group phantasies, and mass panic among the population: in short, to work as a social defence against an epidemic of fear.

Over such a terrain, where emotional, unconscious, and irrational aspects reign supreme, even among those charged with the task of governing the process, the logic of science, rationality, and critical reasoning will not have a sufficiently strong hold. Hence the great importance of a sophisticated social communication in situations of alert and panic; if not inspired by a deep understanding of personal and social aspects of human fear (and particularly the fear of contagion), such communication may boil down to a series of procedures and informational routines, and risks being perceived by people as a superficial, bureaucratic, and self-absolving reassurance, inevitably turning into a source of mistrust and of further insecurity.

These considerations bring us directly to the core of the problem, namely that an epidemic such as Covid-19 is not just a health problem, but a complex, multidimensional psychosocial process, focused on the individual/society interface and on the overlap between these two-way relational dynamics: one part of this is the way the social order impacts upon individuals' behaviour and responses; the other refers to how people's mental functioning interacts with and gets to shape or change social systems, sometimes to a great extent.

In his article on "Epidemic psychology" Philip Strong (1990) points out how an epidemic may become "*a medical version of the Hobbesian nightmare—the war of all against all*", and how the spreading of the biological disease may be followed by psychological epidemics of fear, suspicion, panic and stigma, fierce moral and ideological controversies, all kind of interpretations or fantasies, and veritable wars of religion around causes, responsibilities, and solutions to be adopted.

The fear of contagion has some very specific characteristics. One is the *fear of the invisible*, something that is among us but cannot be seen, because it is too little (like bacteria and viruses), too big (like pollution, radioactivity, the stock market, or a pandemic process), or too familiar but somewhat uncanny (Freud, 1919h) like air, water, food, the next-door neighbour, or worse, our friends and our beloved. The core unconscious fantasy in the fear of epidemics is that "the enemy is among us or even one of us"; its hallmark is a set of paranoid defences, involving splitting (between the guilty and the innocent, the pure and the contaminated) and projection of guilt and blame on individuals and groups supposedly responsible for the contagion. The paranoid attitude tends therefore to transform the epidemic of fear and even more of confusion into an epidemic of mass suspicion towards the Other as a plague-spreader, a role that in our times of global connectedness has been extended from one single person to entire groups or even systems, for example the Chinese secret laboratories or the Big Pharma conspiracy or the "medical dictatorship".

From a psychoanalytic perspective we could see how such paranoid transformation of mourning may well serve to fight the depressive view of human frailty and a related *fear of abandonment*, while conspiracy theories, involving the idea of malignant all-powerful organisations, are somewhat reassuring if confronted with the discouraging evidence that, faced with this little virus, even the highest powers and giant organisations appear substantially disarmed and helpless. In short, thinking of some diabolical Big Brother acting in the shadow might be more comfortable than discovering that there is nobody at the helm.

Another relevant consideration, though it might appear quite obvious, is that these epidemics of fear, interpretation, and action seem to be much more severe when the disease is new or strikes in a new way, as with Covid-19 and the related *fear of the unknown*, the unpredictable. Two aspects are relevant here: one relates to the way in which social systems are equipped with norms, routines, narratives, roles, beliefs, etc., in order to deal with novel and unknown issues; the other raises a difficult psychological question: whether fear is more triggered by what is completely unknown or by what is somehow deeply known but still unbearable and therefore impossible to think about and articulate (Bollas, 1987).

In order to try to manage social processes involving anxiety, fear, and panic for thousands or even millions of people, like the Covid-19 pandemic, we need to understand these human emotions better, namely:

- The way they arise and develop
- What may enhance or mitigate them?
- What are their psychological and social dynamics?
- Which defence mechanisms they mobilise
- How do they impact on individual and group behaviour, as well as on organisational functioning?

Some useful distinctions would be:

- *Between "normal" and pathological fear*, where the former, however useful for survival and adaptation, might prove unbearable, and the latter, as a disguised expression of internal dangers based on unconscious fantasies, anxieties, and related defences, is generally inaccessible to evidence, reasoning, or reality testing
- *Between psychological defences*, like repression, projection, or denial, working on an individual basis to keep fears out of the mind, and *"social defenses"*, like authoritarianism, scapegoating, or inter-group

fight–flight dynamics, that try to remove them from collective consciousness
- *Between defence and protection*, where the latter acts as a container for primitive anxieties, also at an institutional level, to protect individuals and the environment from their potential damages, such as stress, mass panic, and social paranoia.

Social defences are concretely embodied in institutions, like the government, the Church, the army, the World Health Organization, and their primary task is containing collective anxieties such as the fear of contagion, and managing the group or mass dynamics influenced by basic assumptions such as dependence or fight–flight. Another example is the police, whose task is to protect us from other people's antisocial behaviour, but sometimes also from our own potential destructiveness, like when it acts to forbid people from joining gatherings which might enhance the risk of contagion.

Nowadays in this role of an idealised "manager" of primitive fears of illness, contagion, and death, the Church has been widely replaced by medical science, which is called on in this pandemic to act as an *institutional container* against such anxieties. From this perspective, we could say that both the Church and the healthcare system have now established themselves as parallel institutions (or sometimes parallel religions) acting as social defences against Covid anxieties and relying upon these psychosocial functions to increase their cultural and political influence and authority.

But, as we know—and as even Pope Francis said, coming to quote Freud—behind all idealisations lies some devaluation. So during the Covid-19 epidemic we passed through a phase, filled with war language and metaphors, presenting doctors and nurses as our brave warriors against the virus—the enemy, inviting us to tell them thank you and to clap our hands from our balconies, etc.; provided they first save our lives and then eventually die in glory, as *heroes* or even martyrs. But, should they survive, when the pandemic is over and there will be the last body count, they risk being considered incapable, or worse still, cowards, deserters, or betrayers, and therefore they deserve to be pursued by lawyers, assaulted in emergency departments, or be subject to media lynching.

Like emotions, defences may also be relatively "normal" and adequate, as well as excessive and pathological or counterproductive. Denying one's own fear of a contagion may expose an individual to becoming infected or to infect other people, and for a disease to become more severe if left untreated. At a systemic level, defensive social devices like police control, home confinement, or the "tracking apps" might come to perform a socially destructive role when used by a totalitarian government.

As mentioned above, the first "bodyguard" against fear is the mother, later on the family or its social and organisational equivalents—the government, the healthcare system, mass media—as long as they can remain able to listen and to show concern, that is, to act as a good-enough mothering system. Well, a bitter and frightening discovery from the current Covid-19 pandemic is that we all are orphans, namely we are both "motherless" and "fatherless", because all social institutions—which René Kaës (2012) called "*metasocial* guarantors"—turned out to be unable to offer maternal protection against a threatening world as well as paternal guidance oriented by a shared reliable knowledge. This pandemic actually demonstrated how vulnerable our social systems are, and how inadequate and deeply unprepared governments, technical bodies, and mass media may be when faced with the need to manage not just the virus and the illness, but also the spreading of fear among the population.

Another point could be the *space* dimension of this epidemic of fear, and its symbolic elements. For example, social distancing, a sensible strategy for reducing the risk of contagion, ended up establishing in the collective mind a configuration "outside vs. inside", while these two spaces are experienced as competitors, and therefore cannot be easily integrated: as a result, outdoor life, squares and beaches, theatres and pubs, nightlife and restaurants, travels abroad, all these symbols of freedom seem unable to negotiate with lockdown, homeland rhetoric, taking refuge in domestic spaces or the inner world, which tend to represent safety. When primitive fears are overwhelming and splitting becomes dominant, the "outside" may turn into a bad place because there we have the viruses, the strangers, the enemies at the door, while people isolated in a good "inside" space may feel protected by their family or tribe, by daily routines, personal beliefs and biases. But if safety only lies in isolation, this may become an antisocial drive, leading first to withdrawal and mistrust, then to exclusion, ostracism, or even persecution of the scapegoated other.

One could argue that there are also "transitional spaces", bridging the gap between inside and outside, from international relationships to house windows and balconies, and also the digital space with smart working, e-commerce, new media, and within individual and group minds a space for reflection on internal object relationships and social relatedness.

But we cannot escape from conflict and ambivalence, and the evidence that closeness and intimacy may become a risk. Squares filled with crowds may host a rebellion against authority or simply a mindless denial of dangers. And what about the poetics of "Home sweet home"? Rooms where partners or families have been forced to stay together all the time, often in narrow spaces, may turn into places inhabited by growing stress, intolerance, and even violence outbursts. The same balconies where people were singing together or applauding healthcare workers showed other people shouting insults against an infected neighbour who was being taken to hospital by stretcher bearers.

A pandemic like Covid-19 may deeply test and even undermine the conventional social order, bringing about a breakdown of its structure together with a *collapse of its culture of omnipotence and invulnerability*, as well as highlighting its hidden distortions, failures, and unresolved businesses, such as a narcissistic decay, a loosening of social bonds, or a general crisis of leadership and authority. Faced with such primitive individual and collective fears how could a human society try to manage?

What psychoanalysis teaches and might help us to achieve (and to maintain) would be essentially *awareness*, which combines the courage to face a frightening truth with the capacity for thinking. So, we could say that when challenged by an epidemic of fear *thinkability* would be a good enough vaccination. This means that a collective mental space to work through those fears should be offered at a proper time and provided with enough authority to inspire reasonable decision-making processes. Otherwise the place for thought is bound to be filled by action, a generally impulsive and mindless kind of action, driven by fear or its denial, or by the projection of vulnerability, impotence, and guilt.

Two interrelated concepts, both coming from Bion's thinking, could be helpful to build a "reflective space" for dealing with the pandemic fears: *patience* and *negative capability*. Patience means a tolerance for waiting and an ability to give oneself time for thinking; negative capability implies being able to bear uncertainty for a while instead of rushing into action or explaining away what should be first tolerated and understood (Bion, 1970). One contribution of psychoanalysis to the management of fear might therefore be to enlighten the general picture in terms of developing "weak thinking" and a deeper understanding of the problem, rather than a strong set of "how-to" prescriptions.

As a more general attitude what we need to learn from the experience of the pandemic is how to reimagine human relations beyond this manifest collapse of our myths of omnipotence and invulnerability, by taking time to pause, make sense, and connect, and then act better together.

As Strong (1990) points out, "The epidemic of fear is also an epidemic of suspicion. There is the fear that I might catch the disease and the suspicion that *you* may already have it and might pass it on to me." The central character of the drama is the "untore", a term used in seventeenth-century Italy to denote a plague-spreader, as vividly described in Manzoni's 1827 novel *I Promessi Sposi* ("*The Betrothed*").

In our times of global connectedness the role of plague-spreader has been extended from one single person to entire groups or even systems. During contemporary pandemics one continues to be afraid of individuals, but the suspicion extends rapidly to embrace groups such as: strange people, foreign communities (like Chinatown), enemies (like Islamic terrorism), or large organisations, hidden powers, and obscure interests. This is the case with recent pandemics, when heavy doubts have been raised about the financial interests of some corporations (food industry as well as pharmaceutical companies) or against the governments themselves, accused of playing with people's lives for political reasons or even of spreading new plagues through their secret laboratories for the purposes of biological warfare.

Although in these suspicions there is probably more truth than one could imagine or wish for—as was the case of the "anthrax envelopes" sent around by Al-Qaeda in 2001—undoubtedly they are right in the range of delusional persecution and magic omnipotent fantasy.

Looking at this with a psychoanalytic lens we could see how such paranoid transformation of mourning may well serve to fight the depressive view of human frailty, and how conspiracy theories, involving the idea of malignant all-powerful organisations, are somewhat reassuring if confronted with the discouraging evidence that, faced with pandemics, even the highest powers appear substantially disarmed and helpless.

The use of epidemics as a social defence, displacing internal insecurities on an external bad object, allows individuals and societies to maintain a fantasy of locking out dangers and fears, and making themselves immune against them. In this sense, epidemics appear not very different from wars (Eisold, 1991). The combination of a splitting of reality and a special mobilisation of energies (including the crucial role of mass media) may help for a while to divert attention both from individuals' everyday problems and from governments' failures.

What makes the difference is the very nature of danger, which in epidemics is invisible and difficult to spot, and this makes them more similar to terrorism than to war. Where the enemy might be "any one of us", including the family, no team spirit or social solidarity, that is likely to work in wartime, can develop or survive. As Strong (1990) reminds us, this may turn into a war of all against all:

> A ... characteristic of novel, fatal epidemic disease seems to be a widespread fear that the disease may be transmitted through any number of different routes, through sneezing and breathing, through dirt and through doorknobs, through touching anything and anyone. The whole environment, human, animal and inanimate may be rendered potentially infectious. If we do not know what is happening, who knows where the disease might not spring from? (p. 253)

As the core risk is contagion, namely contacts, relationships, empathy, and social interactions, the sole safety lies in isolation, not so much in a medical sense, as a means of preventing the transmission of infectious agents, but rather as an antisocial drive, leading first to withdrawal and mistrust, then to exclusion, ostracism, or even persecution of the scapegoated other.

These defensive dynamics are similar to those of social phobias: primitive anxieties from the individual's inner world, matching with everyday "endemic" worries and the global insecurity of present-day life, are fully displaced onto an external object. This object is firstly perceived as bad, dirty, strange, and ill—the epidemic and the virus—and secondly as some kind of plague-spreader. In this sense the "fear of contagion" rather than dirt, phobia, or pathophobia appears closer to xenophobia, the fear of strangers.

The idea of epidemic as an exotic production and of strangers as typical "untori", vehicles of contagion, wards off the troubling evidence that the danger is with us, inside our family or in human nature. Immigrants, especially when illegal, are the best candidates for the role of plague-spreader: they are poor, not very clean, coloured, badly spoken, they steal (our jobs and our things), rape, peddle drugs, kill—surely they are the ones who brought this damn virus here! They look like us, but actually they are different: in fantasy "they are not what they appear", that is to say they are kind of alien, unreliable objects, precisely dangerous as they seem familiar, just like air, water, daily bread, and the next-door neighbours during an epidemic.

Again, in such gross biases there may be some truth, and after all, most infectious agents really do come from across the border; but this idea of illegal immigrants as potential plague-spreaders essentially reassures us against further puzzling evidence:

- That we ourselves could be a vehicle of epidemics as tourists or business travellers or peace-keeping soldiers
- That to some extent the main "plague-spreader" is globalisation, the human, financial, and social costs of which are still far from being understood, mastered, and contained.

Another link which could be explored is the one between infectious and mental diseases. This connection is somehow obvious if one thinks of how easily an epidemic might drive people crazy or bring to mind what Foucault (1961) describes in his *history of madness*, namely how old *lazarettos* isolating infected people were being gradually transformed into asylums for "lunatics". But subtler links may be also found in certain persistent attempts to discover some infectious agent as a source of psychic disorders (jokingly called a "schizococcus theory"); and at least partly in the strong emphasis that some theories, even within the psychoanalytic field, place on traumatic events as the origin of mental diseases. It is as if there was a shared wish to ascribe madness to some external agent instead of having to acknowledge what Marion Milner (1987) called "the suppressed madness of sane men".

What we need to be aware of is, as Bion suggested, the defensive meaning and use of theories, which basically protect us from facing a world so often uncanny, unknown, inexplicable, and unpredictable. In the case of epidemics, what is being avoided is the evidence that all the time we live among viruses and bacteria, which since time immemorial have been our constant "travel companions". Some of them may actually be useful, like intestinal bacteria, or the germs involved in the production of antibiotics or biological agriculture, but more often than not they are dangerous, reminding us of what our technological hubris would sometimes try to make us forget: our human limits and own vulnerability.

The last point I wish to discuss is how the fear itself may spread and act as a kind of epidemic. Let us consider an epidemic of fear following or concomitant with an epidemic illness as a social pathology overlapping the biological disease, the two being relatively independent from one another. A wave of fear and panic indeed may explode among a population even when very few individuals have actually been infected. On the other hand, a society may come to adapt itself to periodic epidemic cycles, at least when the illness is known, so that epidemics may become "normalised and institutionalised", just as AIDS has now become during the last thirty years or so.

When an epidemic of fear is underway one can see panic and irrationality going well beyond ordinary citizens, to strike even those who should be either best-informed about the disease, like doctors, or well-equipped to find the best solutions, like government bodies and officials. As mentioned above, this epidemic causes serious damage to the social order as a whole and particularly to social cohesion, solidarity, and the collective ability to deal with the problems. The main symptoms of such social pathology seem to be confusion and stigmatisation.

Confusion appears from the very beginning of epidemics as a collective process of an "exceptionally volatile intellectual state" (Strong, 1990), an inability to decide whether the situation is serious or not, and a flood of explanations on how it could have originated (sometimes hiding moral or ideological judgements), as well as of suggested strategies to solve the problem. This leads to a general disorientation that is usually amplified by mass media. People experience this as evidence of a profound disorganisation of the public authorities, which as a result become more and more denigrated, their warnings and instructions increasingly ignored and unheeded.

Stigmatisation is not a product of epidemics, as it is a permanent potential process in all societies, along with beliefs, stereotypes, biases, and myths. An epidemic may help underlying stigmata to surface, and be applied to the specific situation (as was the case of AIDS and homosexuals), resulting in what Strong calls an "epidemic of stigmatisation":

> the stigmatisation both of those with the disease, and of those who belong to what are feared to be the main carrier groups. This can begin with avoidance, segregation and abuse and end—at least potentially—in pogroms. Personal fear may be translated into collective witch-hunts. Moreover, so we should note, such avoidance, segregation and persecution can be quite separate—analytically at least—from actions aimed at containing the epidemic. Such behaviour can occur with all types of stigma, not just with that of epidemic disease. We are dealing here with magic and taboo, not just with quarantine. (1990, pp. 253–254)

Unveiling hidden social issues

It has been said that in extremely dangerous conditions such as epidemics or wars, human beings reveal their true nature, particularly the dark instinctual side hidden behind a well-mannered, civilised façade. This is certainly true, but more than that, an epidemic may represent a powerful test for the social system itself. Experience shows that large-scale epidemic diseases (or pandemics) may deeply undermine the conventional social order, bringing about a collapse of its structure or a corruption of its culture, as well as highlighting its hidden distortions, failures, and unresolved questions. Strong gives a vivid description of the former process:

> All kinds of disparate but corrosive effects may occur: friends, family and neighbours may be feared—and strangers above all; the sick may be left uncared for; those felt to be carriers may be shunned or persecuted; those without the disease may nonetheless fear they have got it; fierce moral controversies may sweep across a society; converts may turn aside from their old daily routines to preach a new gospel of salvation; governments may panic. For a moment at least, the world may be turned upside down. (1990, p. 255)

The emergence of the shadow side of a social system seems extremely hard to recognise mainly because it's so easy to hold an epidemic responsible for anything that is going wrong; however, claiming that the plague has revealed such and such bad facets of our society also risks unveiling just that sort of crusading spirit and moralising frenzy which is an integral part of the epidemic's social pathology.

It is certainly possible that inhuman behaviour of individuals or organisations portrays the narcissistic decay and lack of solidarity of postmodern communities, that isolation and difficulty of working in groups is an expression of a growing liquidity (Bauman, 2000, 2005) and a loosening of social bonds, so that transgressions and crimes may indicate a general crisis of leadership and authority. However, all these hypotheses would remain as vain intellectual exercises unless a collective mental space to work through them was offered at a proper time and provided with enough authority to promote an uncomfortable awareness, and to inspire reasonable decision-making processes.

Otherwise, the place for thought is bound to be filled by action, namely the storm of control measures (not always so mindful) taken to contain the epidemic: a generally impulsive and mindless kind of action, driven by fear or its denial, or by the projection of vulnerability, impotence, and guilt.

If we agree that great epidemics and pandemics, when additionally studied by historians and social scientists, may enlighten not only the evolution of science and health care, but in particular, the demographic, economic, structural, and cultural changes occurring in human societies, then we could assume that such exploration should result in increased understanding and awareness.

But here we close the circle by connecting back to the issue of fear, because it is well known—above all from the perspective of psychoanalytic psychology—that fears and anxieties are major obstacles preventing us both from being aware of and understanding our external and internal realities.

How could we heal or at least contain collective fears or mass panic? You cannot just tell people: "Hey, listen, you must not be afraid!", or spread clouds of valium throughout the planet. Neither the politics nor the official medicine today seems able to create enough safety and trust to reduce such fear.

From this point of view admittedly even the knowledge we have from individual and social psychology is not likely to provide effective solutions for such unpredictable and uncontrollable phenomena. One can just reiterate the following common-sense points:

- That facing fears should be better than denying them or turning a blind eye to them
- That putting them into words and creating reflective spaces for their exploration is already a good enough way to reduce them
- That experience shows us how the simplest solutions may be highly attractive but actually are often mostly deceptive.

Can psychoanalysis be of help?

Psychoanalysis also puts forward awareness as a good enough antidote to fears, saying that if adult people want to face their own anxieties as well as to consider real dangers, they should be able to match a mature vigilance of actual reality with the capacity to get in touch with their own "inner child" and early ways of experiencing fear, while at the same time giving up any pre-packaged, conformist, and mechanistic responses offered by the current culture.

As Gaburri and Ambrosiano (2003) point out:

> Strong emotions—and fear among them—require a response which is to be specific, namely the result of a work made by the adult in order to hold and to some extent share the child's point of view, finding a way to get through. Resorting to group

prefab responses ... only shows that adults cannot stand to let themselves to be *infected* by the child. (p. 113)

The contribution of psychoanalysis might therefore be to enlighten the general picture in terms of developing or encouraging a "weak thinking" aiming to achieve a deeper understanding of a problem, rather than a strong set of "how-to" prescriptions. This is similar to what Bion intended when he spoke of a "negative capability" (1970) to bear uncertainty for a while instead of rushing into action or explaining away what should be first tolerated and understood. Some authors (French, 2000; French et al., 2002, 2009) emphasised the use of such capability as a specific quality of leadership, particularly in turbulent conditions or environments, when mind, thought, and linking are under attack from the pressure of primitive anxieties.

The first pathway to try to face epidemic panic would therefore imply setting up a rather steady political as well as clinical governance of the phenomenon. Here a psychodynamic approach may help the development of an appropriate "situational" leadership and support its capacity for keeping on thinking when things become tough.

Trying to work directly upon mass opinions and behaviour would be a sign of unforgivable omnipotence, if not arrogance and manipulation. What people need when facing real danger is the feeling that they are in the mind of their leaders and wisely and realistically led by them. They also need leaders who make them feel safe and prevent them from experiencing pain, often in a magical way, and this is what triggers omnipotence among those in charge of making crucial decisions.

But a good enough leadership should be aware that when emotionally driven, a population must be respected and treated as *reasonable adults*, but also they need to be understood as *frightened children*. That is why, in order to lead them towards real safety and security, an authentic parental attitude and state of mind is generally required; also, in terms of neither pursuing popularity nor reassuring people by false and seductive solutions. Such qualities are to some extent intrinsic in some individuals' personalities, but they may even be inspired and fostered with suitable means, such as psychoanalytically oriented in-depth coaching or role consultancy, organisational diagnosis, and group relations training, to enhance both awareness and the exercise of personal and delegated authority.

As you also need to deal with day-by-day problems and emergencies while keeping in mind the overall frame, a systems psychodynamic consultation to the numerous bodies involved in emergency processes and related decision-making might help them to maintain the necessary "binocular vision": upon the here and now as well as the future; on both individuals and large groups and systems; considering rational, mature, and task-oriented functioning, but also taking into account the primitive, emotional basic assumptions dynamics.

One last point where psychoanalysis may offer a contribution is after the storm, that is, by helping to learn from the experience, in order to be prepared to deal with future crises without repeating the same errors. Repetition compulsion is a general tendency of the human mind, both in individuals and in populations, and in some cases might even prove useful as a way of sparing energies and maintaining homeostasis. But it also represents a by-product of traumatic experiences badly worked-through, and the resulting stress disorder may thus obstruct the capacity for thinking and learning. The last "swine flu" pandemics expired unexpectedly, while people were prepared to see millions dead on the streets and while the local authorities were holding emergency meetings to decide where to locate the necessary mass graves! A sigh of relief has been breathed worldwide, but two clouds are still hanging on the horizon: new pandemic waves are maybe expected by 2022 (*the future is still uncertain*) and it seems that few lessons have been learnt from these past events as yet (*the past is still to be deciphered*).

On such a large and complex scale, learning from experience is nearly a "mission impossible", but just by looking at what happened, some elements are actually available for insight and reflection. The extraordinary level of panic which affected all layers of our societies, individuals as well as organisations, powerful statesmen as well as ordinary citizens, scientists as well as uninformed people, shows the power of the global, overwhelming uncertainty under which we continuously live. It warns us all of the urgent need to reduce the weight and the duration of widespread insecurities; of the need to rebuild trust and a safer basis for coexistence and co-operation; to restore more mindful authority and leadership structures, which may act as learning organisations; and to create reflective spaces and institutional containers capable of holding and transforming societal anxieties—as well their own worries—as a potential drive for action.

This obviously will not prevent epidemics from occurring, nor people from feeling scared by the last plague, as in the case of Covid-19; but it may help to use a crisis that we have overcome (not just passed over) as a tool to cope with the next one.

Finally, as Guerrera (2010) noted, with reference to the Lehman Brothers' bankruptcy and the market meltdown: "A crisis is a terrible thing to waste."

REFERENCES

Bauman, Z. (2000). *Liquid Modernity*. Cambridge: Polity.
Bauman, Z. (2005). *Liquid Life*. Cambridge: Polity.
Bion, W. R. (1970). *Attention and Interpretation*. London: Tavistock.
Bollas, C. (1987). *The Shadow of the Object: Psychoanalysis of the Unthought Known*. New York: Columbia University Press, 2017.
Eisold, K. (1991). On war: a group relations perspective. *Psychologist-Psychoanalyst, XI (Supplement)*: 32–35.
Foucault, M. (1961). *Madness and Civilization: A History of Insanity in the Age of Reason*. London: Tavistock, 1965. (Originally, *Histoire de la Folie à l'âge classique*. Paris: Librarie Plon.)
French, R. (2000). "Negative capability", "dispersal" and the containment of emotion. Paper presented at the Symposium of the ISPSO, London. *Bristol Business School Teaching and Research Review*, 3, Summer 2000.
French, R., Simpson, P., & Harvey, C. (2002). Leadership and negative capability. *Human Relations*, 55(10): 1209–1226.
French, R., Simpson, P., & Harvey, C. (2009). "Negative capability": A contribution to the understanding of creative leadership. In: B. Sievers, H. Brunning, J. de Gooijer, L. J. Gould, & R. R. Mersky (Eds.), *Psychoanalytic Studies of Organizations*. London: Karnac.
Freud, S. (1919h). The "uncanny". *S. E.*, *17*: 217–256. London: Hogarth.
Freud, S. (1921c). *Group Psychology and the Analysis of the Ego. S. E.*, *18*: 67–143. London: Hogarth.
Gaburri, E., & Ambrosiano, L. (2003). *Ululare con i lupi: Conformismo e rêverie* ["Howling with Wolves: Conformism and Reverie"]. Turin, Italy: Bollati Boringhieri.

Guerrera, F. (2010, September 16). Interview in *La Stampa*.

Kaës, R. (2012). *Le Malêtre*. Paris: Dunod.

Krantz, J. (2010). Social Defences and 21st century organizations: A tribute to the contribution of Isabel Menzies Lyth. *British Journal of Psychotherapy*, 26(2): 192–201.

Menzies, I. E. P. (1961). The functioning of social systems as a defence against anxiety: A report on a study of the nursing service of a general hospital. In: *Containing Anxiety in Institutions: Selected Essays*. London, Free Association, 1988; and in: E. Trist & H. Murray (Eds.), *The Social Engagement of Social Science: A Tavistock Approach. Vol. 1: The Socio-Psychological Perspective*. London, Free Association, 1990.

Milner, M. (1987). *The Suppressed Madness of Sane Men: Forty-four Years of Exploring Psychoanalysis*. London: Tavistock.

Pasini, W. (2010, April 24). Presentazione a "Vecchie e nuove epidemie". Convegno di studio, Bologna ["Old and new epidemics": introduction to a Symposium, Bologna]. http://scienzaonline.com/index.php?option=com_content&view=article&id=393:vecchie-e-nuove-epidemie-convegno-di-studio-sabato-24-aprile-2010-archiginnasio-di-bologna-ore-10-12-&catid=55:eventi&Itemid=70 (last accessed May 2010).

Perini, M. (2010). Si vis pacem para bellum: Psychoanalysis, peace education and conflict literacy. In: H. Brunning & M. Perini (Eds.), *Psychoanalytic Perspectives on a Turbulent World*. London: Karnac.

Strong, P. (1990). Epidemic psychology: A model. *Sociology of Health & Illness*, 12(3): 249–259.

Treccani Encyclopedia online (2009). Epidemie e contagio: i secoli della paura [Epidemics and contagion: The centuries of fear]. www.treccani.it/Portale/sito/altre_aree/scienze_della_vita/percorsi/epidemie.html (last accessed March 2010).

Part II

Reparation, resilience, recovery

Separation by Edvard Munch, 1896

CHAPTER 5

Despair and endurance: the experience of NHS[1] staff during the Covid crisis

by Barbara-Anne Wren

In the beginning there were no words.
There was a rumble in the distance. And the splitting. Right from the beginning the splitting was there. The dichotomy that kept the impending reality at bay. "It's happening, it can't be really happening." "It's a plague, it's the flu." The television delivered stories and images but that was "on TV" covering a faraway land. Wuhan, and bats and doctors in white coats, and "foreign" scientists and people flown back to quarantine in the UK. A city on the other side of the world in lockdown. What?

A new lexicon exploded into our lives: quarantine, lockdown, Zoom, exponential, r ratio, flatten the curve, unprecedented … on and on it went, the emergence of the vocabulary we would need to begin to navigate this reality. Not new words of course but an alien language to most, with a futuristic feel, but also echoes of the past. Paradox and contradiction were all core to this experience as time would continue to prove. Maybe these new words belonged to other (less evolved) people? Here in the UK,

---

[1] The NHS stands for the National Health Service. It refers to the UK Government-funded health care services and is the largest employer in the UK employing 1.4 million staff.

we were carrying on. We would dispatch this virus quickly. The racing would go ahead.[2]

In the beginning there were the images.

Shattered and weeping Italian doctors, body bags, closing borders (yes, these were images with deep reach and powerful, painful resonances), opera music ringing out across valleys where trapped, safe people showed solidarity from their balconies. A hospital built in a week (Are they mad? What's going on? What do they know? Also, what terrifying efficiency …). Twitter roared into a new life and has been roaring ever since, but in those early days allowed the Italian doctors to vent and rage and grieve but mostly try to help. "This is real, it is coming your way, don't think it isn't, we *didn't think it could happen to us, prepare … prepare … prepare …"*

Yes. Many of them did die.

The cost of work was now forever to be calculated using a different equation. This was the beginning of a slow, subtle recalibration ("I didn't sign up for this," "I can't do this again," "I don't think I will ever be the same again," "I thought I was strong …"*)[3] that is ongoing, still shaping us all, our relationships to ourselves and our work, our work organisations, and our various private and public worlds. Our emerging understanding of what we can bear to witness, to say and see, to let go of, and to hope for. Our understanding of what words are possible to speak today (though maybe not tomorrow depending on how that goes …) to tell us what is happening to us. To allow us to persevere. At the start we needed something to hold on to. For we were in freefall whether we could see it or not. But what could that thing be? The past? The future? Our country? Our work? Our professional identities? Our loves? Our family? Each other? What tribe would keep us safe? What language could they speak to us to help us locate ourselves during these times? Oh, and where had certainty gone? What is this new world in which we live now?*

In the beginning words failed us.

---

[2] This was Cheltenham Races which against scientific advice were not cancelled and became one of the first three UK virus super spreader events estimated to have between them caused 100 deaths, 500 hospitalisations, and 17,000 infections. (John Vidal in *The Guardian* 20/2/2021).

[3] Direct quotes from NHS staff with whom I worked during the pandemic.

They lost their meaning, became porous or negotiable, elusive, just out of reach, they belonged to a world that had just slipped away, without warning, it seemed to many. How could they be the anchors needed when the terrain they had been held fast in was now bubbling away like quicksand? Like abandoned animals, people clung to each other in different ways, forced to rely on the parts of themselves that were beyond words as they shuffled towards the unknown. Terror, shock, the will to survive, the fear of loss and annihilation all roared up and drove us towards figments of safety, and words needed to catch up. Meanwhile lockdown and its imperative to disconnect and be separate from each other cruelly thwarted this terrified longing, this craving for safety and attachment.

At the same time there was work to be done.

Eventually, when everyone was belatedly sent home and the UK lockdown did begin, in hospitals across the UK the crisis was met head on by the work of NHS staff. Hours and endless hours and days unfolded of sheer graft, impossible effort, exquisite tenderness, huge creativity, and innovation, also (whisper it) exhilaration and excitement and adrenalin ("This is what we trained for," "Suddenly the system revolving around putting patient first became possible," "The sense of belonging, of camaraderie and teamwork was exhilarating and rewarding," "I have never felt prouder of my staff").[4] *Many staff suppressed their own terrors (or were forced to) and ran towards the burning house that was the healthcare system, with little time to think about how long it might take to put out the fire, or whether there might be another larger building burning further out there, somewhere they couldn't see yet, or whether they should occasionally retreat from the heat to recover or attend to their other roles. For this burning house provided purpose and meaning and focus, a sense of belonging, a way to obliterate the terror and helplessness and wordlessness of those early days, and all the primitive fears they reawakened. Only later would there be time to count the cost … (not much time: the house is still burning, there is little space to recover, words are still struggling to catch up …).*

This chapter reflects on the experience of designing and delivering psychology interventions to respond to the needs of NHS staff and organisations in the context of this shock and crisis. It will use story to convey the emotional undertow of working in health care during the

---

[4] Direct quotes from NHS staff.

first seventeen months of the Covid-19 pandemic, to trace the various cyclical journeys from despair to endurance and back and round again made by healthcare staff, who found themselves tasked with meeting the needs of tens of thousands of patients who were suddenly stricken and gasping for air. In this context of peril and suffocation the work required of psychology became one of crafting spaces and finding words to hold healthcare staff who barely had time to breathe themselves. The chapter concludes by reflecting on the impact of trying to put this work into written words. The physical and emotional experience of reaching for language to give form to the work of containing unmanageable terror and loss (at a time when societal and political containers are splintering), led to a sudden unravelling expressed in illness and fatigue in the writer. Practitioners need solid ground too! But it continues to shift. It is hard to locate words and hold them for long enough on this shifting ground. And parallel processes (the need to suppress in order to persevere, in this case) will always demand attention. The chapter closes by reflecting on the imperative to attend to them when supporting staff and systems in uncontained times.

Coming up for air: What can psychology offer healthcare staff in a pandemic?

What can psychology offer to staff going through a collective trauma in a healthcare system reeling from shock while already depleted? What reimagining of psychology work is needed to craft an offering that is flexible and relevant and accessible, and what steadying frame will hold the work when the ground the psychologist is standing on is shifting also? The experience of working in health care through the pandemic has not been a linear one of helping individuals and staff groups move from despair to endurance, but a circular, cyclical one, of witnessing and holding the moving over and back between both states as the kaleidoscope of shock and chaos continued to turn, revealing and concealing horrors, creating impossibly powerful resonances, and demanding an ability in staff to simultaneously confront and deny realities in order to persevere with their work and their lives.

The work of psychology became that of allowing the safe emergence (over time, and at intervals) of what was needed to be denied in order that staff could achieve the task of the NHS healthcare system: to keep as many patients as possible alive at whatever cost and in the direst circumstances, in the face of an initially unknown illness. Healthcare staff were required to contain the uncontainable and unbearable while remaining in touch with their humanity. Both staff and the system were pushed beyond their limits in this task.

Crafting a response to healthcare staff's distress: the work of a psychologist during the pandemic

The work described here is drawn from developing and delivering psychology interventions for NHS organisations during the first seventeen months of the Covid-19 pandemic. The work took place at the following levels:

Individual
- Providing brief therapeutic interventions to distressed staff some of whom became unable to work.
- Providing role consultation for leaders and managers whose roles and responsibilities changed in unimaginable ways as the crisis progressed.

Group
- Providing group interventions for senior clinicians and leaders, to help them to plan for the impact of the pandemic on group dynamics, staff engagement, organisational commitment, and team and service effectiveness.
- Debriefing psychology, psychotherapy, and psychiatry groups redeployed and mobilised to provide in-house staff support for their NHS colleagues.
- Development of bespoke group interventions for groups reforming after redeployment.
- Development and facilitation of group debriefing for executive teams.

Organisational
- Design and development of organisation-wide storytelling spaces to allow staff to witness each other's pandemic experiences, in order to validate distress and disorientation, honour courage and

commitment, allow the unspeakable to be spoken; and begin to conceptualise an overwhelming and ongoing experience.

This work was iterative. Dominant issues recurring in individual sessions and small group work were used to craft the organisational storytelling events, so that themes could be amplified and attended to at a system level, and staff who might not need or want psychological support[5] could access sessions where they could witness experiences like their own. It took place at both micro and macro levels with ongoing reverberation between both levels. Similarities of experience across settings were striking, allowing this creative, dynamic process to inform the ongoing development of the work and tailor the offerings made to individual organisations over time.

For example, at regular intervals overarching themes derived from individual and group work would be offered to all staff in an organisation; inviting storytellers to join a monthly panel in the organisation-wide reflective space. This created curiosity and invited experience to be elicited and simultaneously considered from a new perspective. Once chosen, each individual panel member then spent time with the psychologist to prepare their stories, deepen and develop themes. The aim was to move the stories towards a state when they could be shaped into generous offerings for the group, rather than be told to meet the storyteller's own needs (see Wren (2016) for a fuller description of this process). In the organisational sessions the stories were shared and meaning making took place with reference to individual and system level experience. Session numbers varied but ranged between fifty and eighty staff for each session. Titles covered included:

- When patients must die alone: *staff bear the unbearable*
- Danger, safety, and impossible choices: *the impact of the pandemic on senior clinicians and managers*
- Fear, guilt, and collateral damage: *parenting in the pandemic*

---

[5] For various reasons: the feeling that other people's needs are greater, shame, some denial of vulnerability but also fear of unravelling if they stopped and attended to themselves.

- Missing home, missing family, missing rituals: *caring for other people's families when your own are out of reach*
- Loneliness and longing: *connection and disconnection in Covid times*
- Working without touch: *the impact on staff*
- Fear of contamination: *anxiety about bringing Covid "home".*

Location

Requests for group work accelerated in each surge phase and the task grew to incorporate the process of location:

- Where are we now in this crisis?
- How best can we conceptualise the psychological and emotional challenges (individual and group) right now in this surge?
- What are the steadying factors in the here and now that will allow each worker to persevere with the least harm?
- What can we hope for?
- What must we let go of for now?

This process of "locating" was carried out with reference to the virtual world, within which so much communicating and relating (and all of this work) was taking place. The resulting lack of opportunity to calibrate one's own experience with reference to the other, the group, or the organisation was named. As was the loneliness of carrying significant burdens in healthcare work at a time of heightened awareness of the limited emotional capacity of others (for the same reasons) leading to a self-silencing and suppression that was invisible, and only became conscious when there was an opportunity to tell a story from beginning to end in these sessions.

Time

The changing relationship to *time* as well as *location* over the course of the pandemic was also incorporated into this thinking and named in the work. That is the *cumulative* impact of working without touch and physical presence, the invisible costs of the ongoing loss (how long now since …?) of so many opportunities to diffuse tension, celebrate success, create connection, and alleviate solitude: a coffee, a hug, a drink after work, the chance to have a group experience, to move between intimates and acquaintances, a movement that deepens their felt value, along with the ability to engage deeply with both. The reality of the sense of time becoming distorted without rituals large and small, and without these markers of the day and week, and the boundary between work and home, was regularly named and explored.

Relentlessness

In the first phase shock produced adrenalin which produced action, but for most the underlying assumption (conscious or unconscious) that made this mobilisation possible was that there would be an end point. Since the end of 2020 the need to accommodate and survive an open-ended "ending"—in truth a paradigm shift—has been at times accepted and at others denied, with various forms of magical thinking at individual, group, organisational, societal, and political levels. All these levels reverberate against each other in different rhythms, and thus rupture the possibility of clear or consistent containment. The naming of this deprivation in group sessions, of the loss of the sense of an ending, and the associated pain and fear, aimed to make these absences present for them to be attended to, and thought about, by individuals and groups. This was a relief for healthcare staff whose ability to regress to magical thinking was severely compromised by their inability to avoid the onslaught of Covid cases that would result when magical thinking happened at a societal, political, and community level. Each new surge deepened their closeness to realities that could be avoided elsewhere and limited the opportunity for healthcare staff to recover. For a fall in Covid cases simply meant an immediate, overwhelming pressure to address the harm caused to the patients who had had to wait for treatment until the crisis subsided, while watching society relax, knowing this would lead to an increase in Covid cases. Staff found it helpful to name this impossibility of "recovering" from work strain while still bracing for the next onslaught.

Once named, staff were encouraged to manage this paradox (the impossibility of bracing for impact while releasing their grip on the acute phase of each surge), in various ways: narrowing the frame of the lens through which they were making sense of their experience, not looking too far ahead, instead considering where now was the solid ground for them—both at work and at home. What was the smallest opportunity for nourishment or distraction that could for a moment restore them to themselves?

To respond aptly to paradox and complexity, this psychological work needed to develop quickly, to generate possibilities for hope in a time of despair, to be agile and flexible, to consider deeply how best to hold staff when the terrain was so uncertain and the future so unclear, and to help them see where the lifeboats were at any one moment in time, ensuring they could float (even just for now). Put simply it aimed to create space for them to breathe.

Language

The uses of language felt increasingly important—words like "well-being" and "resilience" were avoided, "perseverance", "endurance", "survival", "good enough", and "restorative" were words offered to staff to consider and reconsider their experience and their relationship to work right now, and the challenges it brought, some of them completely unimaginable just six months previously. The lack of steady ground, the impact of lockdown with all its associated strain were regularly named, in an effort to help staff to attend to the many layers of context impacting on individual, family, and organisational experiences of this crisis, and make sense of their felt ability to cope (or not) in any given moment. For it was a crisis that continued to move quickly, and to make relentless demands for adaptation and for courage.

Metaphor was useful as were visual images (a unique feature of this trauma was the arrival of visual before actual experience), and amplifying single sentences that were spoken helped staff give their own precious words space, and give themselves permission to pause. The courage needed simply to listen was named to convey confidence that for the moment it was enough, and it was bearable, and would allow them to know where they were standing, who was around them, what they were doing and how they were feeling. So many rich heartfelt words were spoken when this pause was achieved, and the space was created:

"When will we know how much we have lost and how much we can recover?" ... one doctor said in one session, having described a serious overdose by his partner (who had had a very late miscarriage during the pandemic) while he was working in a redeployed capacity in ITU. This powerful, heartfelt, and poignant sentence captured the experience at so many levels, along with the unbearable reality of not knowing how much recovery will be possible, how and when it will come about, and the sense of sorrow needing to be borne indefinitely. The sessions allowed for the safe emergence of sentences such as this, and for these utterances to be used to prompt thinking in other sessions and craft stories for the large organisational space.

Over time it felt important to thread in other words, to use the position of the psychologist to speak the unspeakable—to name the horror, to articulate what seemed unbearable and in the second surge to actively use language to prepare organisations and their staff for the natural human fallout of exhaustion, depletion, and lack of recovery time. To introduce the idea of cruelty, for example, as stories were emerging of bad behaviour towards staff who had had to shield and stay away from work, of scapegoating, and of splitting within teams, and of lack of compassion for patients. Now in the autumn of 2021, there are anxieties about how to manage strong feelings of anger towards unvaccinated patients, and words like aggression and retribution become important to say out loud, their use creating new spaces and opportunities for understanding.

At each stage, the aim of the psychological work has been to involve staff actively and openly in attending to and considering the use of language as a form of containment, to explore directly how to capture the experience of new realities and to work at a macro level to share emerging conceptualisations that could helpfully humanise the variety of staff experience, and aid in the acceptance of unwanted feelings and organisational realities. For example, the following differentiation in terms of emotional challenges of each pandemic stage was shared:

First wave
Shock, mobilisation, and pride
While the start of the crisis created profound shock in the system it also produced a high adrenalin response at individual, group, and organisational level. This allowed a huge amount of work to be done and change

to be achieved, and created a sense of belonging, purpose, and pride. It also created optimism that the pace of system change and the intense focus on patient driven care would lead to real change in hospital systems once the crisis had subsided.

Second wave
Less clapping, more death (and all in the territory of collateral damage)
By the time of the second wave there was little adrenalin left, staff were tired, and there were new challenges. For many staff this phase was worse than the first wave due to these factors and the high death rates, now in younger patient groups. In addition, many of the hopes resulting from the first wave did not come to fruition and the disappointment of limited system change had to be managed alongside the pressure of maintaining service provision (in contrast to the first wave when many services were paused). The growing awareness of the collateral damage (growing waiting lists, delayed presentations, and resulting advanced illness and mental health problems) added to the burden of this stage of the crisis.

Third wave
"I don't think I can do this again"
Now as we move through the third wave with a long winter looming the tiredness has persisted and there is high anxiety about what is coming next and the ability of the system to meet the challenges of winter 2021. Resources are depleted, staff are less forgiving of each other and of their managers and leaders, irritability, anger, and disillusionment are higher, and many are concerned about their ability to persevere. There is high anxiety in staff about being redeployed again in the event of a spike of Covid cases. Leaders' and managers' fear of high sickness absence may be well founded as staff shift into survival mode after a relentless seventeen months having experienced winter levels of healthcare service demand during the summer of 2021 as Covid cases increase while other viruses present unusually early as population circulation accelerates. Many staff are actively considering their options if they are pushed beyond their limits again.

Some groups were developed specifically for those in senior roles, to enable them to process the emotional impact of trauma and turbulence while supporting others to remain effective in role. The urgency of the crisis, especially in the first wave, had made the filing away of emotional experience imperative for leaders, heightening the necessity to focus on task (rather than meaning), to ensure the responsive functioning of their organisation at a time of danger. The complexity of avoiding catastrophe in real time while anticipating imminent further service crises was a real ongoing challenge for those in leadership roles.

The aim throughout this work has been to help staff and organisations to continue to attend realistically to themselves, to develop a level of coherence and clarity that could enable them to persevere in the ways that could minimise harm to themselves or others. So maybe now it is time to let the themes and the stories speak for themselves.

Bare bottoms, the terror of being a patient, and the fear of exposure: *a state of disarray, nakedness writ large, vulnerability exposed*

A senior ITU nurse became overwhelmed with anxiety and had to go on sick leave. Once off work she was gripped by a terror of catching Covid. The fear was not of breathlessness, pain, or of dying, but of being admitted to her own unit and, in her words, "colleagues seeing my bare bottom". In intensive care units throughout the country patients were being proned,[6] requiring great physical effort to turn them regularly. Inevitably, dignity was compromised in this process given the extreme pressures on ITU units. (This was the tip of the iceberg; safety could be compromised too.) This nurse had a background history of significant trauma. Her role working in the care of trauma victims in ITU allowed her to manage this background history through caring for vulnerable others. The possibility of being a patient herself, the terror of feeling vulnerable and exposed, created an intolerable pressure on this defence of the patient as "other" and the clinician as a powerful rescuer. This defence had sustained her and allowed her to build a role and identity

---

[6] Proning is the process of turning a patient with precise, safe motions from their back onto their stomach, so the individual is lying face down. It allows for better expansion of the dorsal lung regions, improved body movement, and enhanced removal of secretions which may ultimately lead to improvements in breathing—crucial in recovery from Covid.

on which to rebuild her life. Now that it was broken, she was unable to work and needed therapy to process the reawakening of past trauma.

Dior bag: *where did frivolity go?*

The very first healthcare assistant I saw for individual work told me in our first meeting that if she didn't die in the pandemic, she would buy a Dior bag. She was a thirty-year-old married mother of three boys with everything to live for, but like clinicians up and down the country she was preparing for the possibility that she wouldn't survive. Her planned reward was both brilliantly frivolous and a stark reminder of what she was losing at more than one level. It was a matter-of-fact statement that she made about the Dior bag, and in our sessions, she veered from this pragmatic place to extreme distress. As the first wave deepened, she found it increasingly hard to care for her children, finding their need for her when she got home almost unbearable. She felt extremely guilty about this but felt powerless to change it. Quite quickly she found that she could no longer sleep with her partner and he moved out of their bedroom. As for many others, regular twelve hour shifts in PPE in bright lights and hot temperatures led to an unbearable state of over-stimulation and exhaustion for this woman. She found she did not want to be touched when she was at home. She survived the first wave and arrived at our last session smiling and holding up a Dior bag. She told me that she had resigned and found work in a private hospital. The work was simpler and more straightforward with no risk of having to treat Covid patients or be redeployed to ITU. She told me she could never put herself or her family through that again.

"If I die you are the reason my girl will grow up without a mother": *leadership in times of mortal danger, are we in the army now?*

In a debriefing space for senior managers and leaders many stories were told of inner conflict and guilt. Managers had to redeploy staff to unfamiliar areas, and in the early days of the pandemic PPE was inadequate and little was known about how to treat coronavirus. Strong directives were issued by the Department of Health and many managers had to override their own misgivings and follow national level guidance. Often this guidance was issued quickly with various U-turns and changes of direction. Aside from this, many managers had to move from facilitative styles they were comfortable with and with which they had created relationships of trust with their staff, to directive styles—that is, from negotiating and guiding to issuing orders. Staff resisted directions and attacked managers in many ways, unsurprisingly. In one group a manager told me about how one of their staff shouted at her in a large group that she would be responsible for her child being motherless if she died. She wept as she told this story and shared the sense of horror about the level of responsibility she had suddenly assumed (been assigned) for the lives of her staff. Versions of this story were repeated in many groups. The sense of being complicit in causing harm or exposing staff to harm has been a recurrent strain for managers.

Unclaimed property and lost lives: *the impossibility of connecting task and meaning in the leadership moment*

The chief executive of a large London teaching hospital asked for a debriefing session for his team fourteen months after the pandemic started. He had some guilt about not organising it before now but they "couldn't find the time". In negotiating the time of the session, they had to be persuaded to reserve more than an hour tagged on to the end of an operational meeting. Eventually, a two-hour space was agreed. A simple introductory exercise designed to elicit memories of a single meaningful and a single challenging experience took up most of the whole two hours. The aim of the session was explained simply—an opportunity to slow down, to shift from a task focus to a consideration of the human who had had to perform the tasks needed, to ensure the organisation survived the crisis. An opportunity to listen to each other but also to themselves. One of the team told a powerful story which for a moment took our breath away.

Her very senior role was complex and highly pressured and there had been some serious acute crises with potential catastrophic outcomes to manage. During this time what seemed like a lesser problem kept bubbling up and distracting her from her main work. One day she decided she needed to get this task off her "to do" list and to meet one of her colleagues in the storage room to understand the problem for herself. The issue was lack of space. She rushed down between meetings to join her colleague outside the room she had been advised to look at.

She described the sound of the door swinging closed behind them as they entered the room and then looking up and seeing shelves upon shelves of belongings: clothes, phones, glasses, hearing aids, sticks, handbags, housekeys, coats, all abandoned and filling up the space. For this was the issue that kept pulling her away from her work: where to store the mounting pile of personal items belonging to patients urgently admitted and still in the hospital or now dead from coronavirus and with families not allowed on site. The image stopped her in her tracks and evoked for her (a woman with Jewish ancestry) images of the belongings found in liberated concentration camps. Suddenly stricken by the memory and this connection she began to weep. The group were shocked by the depth of her distress, her association to this terrible historical trauma, and the memories that both were now evoking for her and for them. Until now she had been unable to make the connection between the enormity of her task and the losses bubbling up underneath the operational work she was doing so skilfully. She was distraught at this knowledge of the increasing piles of lost property continuing to eat into hospital spaces: a harrowing reminder of the people that had been lost and were continuing to be lost. The subsequent group discussion allowed for a consideration of the true emotional impact of this work and when and how best to attend to it in leadership roles.

What is the role of psychology in a pandemic?

In her book *Dying: A Memoir*, the writer Cory Taylor (2016) described the experience of living with a terminal illness as *"living in two lands at the same time: the land of vigilance and the land of denial"*. Perhaps the experience of living through a pandemic, a time of mortal danger, compares to this. The work of psychology then becomes one of creating safe passage between these two states, of facilitating a conscious process of location and relocation in order to persist. Maybe the aim of the work described here has been to allow healthcare staff safe movement between these two states of mind, over and back, again and again, without becoming trapped in or overwhelmed by either, and while retaining some ability to work and to love. And all the while avoiding the danger of magical thinking and its denial of risk (clinical and organisational), with the hope that this increases the capacity to bear the feelings of loss and grief, so that sadness and realism can guide action (individual and organisational), and splitting and scapegoating can be minimised. For in pandemics, it is not only viruses that are contagious, and maybe psychology can help individuals to consciously locate and relocate themselves, in order to relate to experience and feelings safely and wisely.

Becoming unwell during the writing process—experiences beyond words and limits

I say maybe because I am still making sense of it all too.

    I sat down to write properly on July 19, 2021 which was, in the UK, "Freedom Day": a highly contentious day when many lockdown restrictions were lifted despite the serious misgivings of many scientists. It was also the start of a ten-day heatwave in London and that morning it felt like writing in a furnace. Although I had sketched paragraphs, written notes, and decided on a structure, what emerged when I gave the writing some real space was the italicised two pages at the beginning of the chapter. The language took on a life of its own, and I was unsure whether this was in fact a professional piece of writing, fit for a book chapter. For suddenly I was right back at the beginning, reliving my own terror and shock, and at the same time, remembering in a rush so many of the stories I have heard in the past seventeen months. They seemed to rush up and out, jostling for space and overlapping with each other. Words like "shuffling" appeared on page 2 as if from nowhere, except I suddenly remembered a nurse who told the powerful story of her train journey to work in the first lockdown with only NHS staff on the train, all getting off at the same station and *shuffling* in the early morning light towards their hospital. This was in the early stages of limited PPE with everyone but NHS staff at home, frightened and in shock, in lockdown. She said that the shuffling conveyed a sense of a group of people singled out and silently accepting their fate, reminding her of a film she had seen set in a concentration camp. This was just one of so many stories that created physical shivers in everyone who heard them, ripples into our own lives and memories. Small and tentative words became twinned with large screens and huge images, also hidden, unspeakable sorrows. Later this resonance would appear in the story described above.

It was by sitting down to try to make sense of it all through writing that the stories were suddenly released in me; they rushed out in fact, and now, caught up in the London heat, my own feeling of being overwhelmed grew. In the afternoon I had two patients booked in—intensive care nurses who I have seen regularly throughout the pandemic and who had been doing well. But on this day, they both arrived on the screen weeping because of "Freedom Day" and what they thought it would mean for them: the fear of further redeployment, the suffering and death that they would have to witness. Afterwards I lay down in the shade and felt suddenly exhausted. *When would it ever end? Could I even bear to write about it? How could I ever finish?*

A strange time followed of fatigue and nausea. I wrote intermittently, I took a break and came back to write, and now I have reached my word limit. I have permission to end! Though I have had supervision and reflective space during this time I think that the impact of reaching for words to write down released something I had suppressed—the scale of the traumas I have witnessed, the need for permission to stop. A process I had been attending to in staff: the cost of containing others in times of limited containment was of course relevant to me and needed expression. My body spoke first. Reaching for language brought myself into view, for where do I draw the words up from but my body—and that connected me to a layer of invisible impacts. Another iterative process. Round we go again! We do of course continue to need what we are helping healthcare staff to work without. The paradox continues. And the parallel processes. So will the writing. The importance of continuing to attend to the significance of the loss of solid ground and physical presence in our pandemic lives, to plan for sustainable working in virtual times, seems all too real. Meanwhile the stories speak for themselves.

References

Taylor, C. (2016). *Dying: A Memoir*. Edinburgh, UK: Canongate.
Wren, B. A. (2016). *True Tales of Organisational Life*. London: Karnac.

CHAPTER 6

Multi-system failure of the body and the body politic

by Richard Morgan-Jones

> *The world is wrong. You can't put the past behind you. It's buried in you; it's turned your flesh into its own cupboard*
> —Claudia Rankine, *Citizen: An American Lyric* (2005)

Introduction

The thesis of this chapter is that the crisis of the Covid pandemic has revealed a significant meeting point in a much-neglected frontier that deserves to be named and explored. This frontier is between a) the experience and representation of the body and its need for health, and b) health provision for society through government of its body politic. If neglected, both are at risk of storing up trouble for the interdependence between economies and sustainable health policies. The metaphor of long Covid uses descriptions of the range of invasive effects across the organs of the body that debilitate individuals who seem not to be able to recover from the virus. This describes the traumatising "body blow" to the social, economic, and political order and its failures to meet the health and dependency needs of individuals.

This interdependency suggests a frontier between these two mutually invading phenomena. This need to belong to a larger societal body of thinking and health beliefs, that is revealed in attempts by societal groupings to make sense of the virus, by adhesion to sets of shared assumptions around what will keep them safe as members of a larger group. It is suggested that these subgroupings are at risk of antagonising each other and undermining a more common-sense view of health that can co-operate with and activate moves by a body politic towards a healthier and more robust social fabric. This task is undermined by policies that ignore the dependency needs of vulnerable individuals and the health services on which they depend.

Background

The world is being shaken by a new "world war". All wars come fear-laden and carry intimidations. This war is against the enemy of a global pandemic and accompanied by fear for the survival and health of individuals across each and every nation and continent in the world. In the early stages of the pandemic, the fear of death, infection, and lasting illness stalked the streets and emptied them. Because of the UK government's apprehension at demanding a lockdown while also entertaining wild thoughts about a policy of unrealistic herd immunity, it disastrously delayed implementation for two weeks, costing the lives of possibly 20,000 victims. In the event, it was people's fear of the unknown threats of this infectious disease that made them stay at home. This created a double intimidation, partly from the virus, partly from the oscillation in government policy between lax and stringent policies that earned them a reputation for unreliability. Such vacillation was born of anxiety in leadership when dependability was urgent. This double intimidation resulted in inner confusion for citizens. On the one hand, there were the unfathomable consequences of the virus that caused fear. On the other, there was the intrusive and urgent fear of the privations and intimidation of demanded cures, including lockdowns, social isolation, and body hygiene. These infectious fears include you the reader and I do not underestimate the struggle for courage in facing some of the details and the meanings of what is something of a horror story being described and analysed in this book.

What is infectious, invisible microbes or fear itself?

This chapter follows previous work in my writing, research, and consulting across a range of fields that has sought to make connections between individual experience of being a body vulnerable to ailments and the meaning of these ailments in psychological terms. This is not a search for psychosomatic symptoms of individuals, but rather exploration of the way aspects of the wider society have created, through ailments, an expression of complex dynamics, carried by individuals, of the wider context including the political. Through a book and a series of international workshops entitled *The Body of the Organisation and Its Health* (Morgan-Jones, 2007, 2010), I commissioned a cartoonist to draw some images with captions, to communicate that the exploration of ailments could be representative of organisational diseases. My aim had been to communicate the way physical ailments were treated by employers and governments, as the individual responsibility of the sufferer to take up the sick role, get treatment under a doctor, to recover and return to work. I suggested that this ignored the research that linked high team sickness rates to low morale and work stress risk for which organisations took little responsibility. This took an essentially epidemiological approach that included working with an epidemiologically trained occupational health physician, researching ailments among staff in hospital for stress related illness presentations (Morgan-Jones, 2010, pp. 110–112).

One conclusion I suggested was that the huge investment by the HR and managerial as well as governmental initiatives in reduction of work stress placed such responsibilities on the individual, ignoring collective and societal exploration of causes and cures, for which employing organisations carry an often neglected, legal and ethical responsibility. If I had waited for a pandemic such as this one, I could have produced ample argument that there were crucial unnoticed links between individual ailments and collective failures in health provision, which is now what the world has been suffering.

"It's the organisation's body you ought to be examining, not mine, Doc!" (Morgan-Jones with Barwick, 2007, 2010).

When I commissioned this cartoon I little thought that the image I had designed would become prescient for the way people in 2020–21 had been required to wear masks in public indoor spaces, for fear of infection by an illness whose treatment and prognosis were so deeply unknown. This virtual imaginative connection was realised in a vivid and dramatic way through the pandemic and alerted us to the crucial link between the individual, organisational health, and the health of the body politic.

Fear of death, illness, and the need for dependency

Being ill is scary. Having a family, community, or a society that is sick and infectious is doubly scary, as the very frameworks that contain illness are suddenly in jeopardy. There is a tendency in human nature to avoid facing reality through denial, and projecting blame or vulnerability upon others. It is possible to see this process as one of facing humiliations that need to be modified to reduce unrealistic grandeur, demeaning, and distancing of others, who deserve adequate care and thoughtfulness. However, necessary psychological and emotional reflection may also herald coming to terms with the realities of losses and past traumas in life; moving towards a humbling and realistic perception of one's self and one's real worth together with a need for others, in a way that is more open to the future with all its uncertainties.

Psychoanalytic thinking suggests that when traumas from the past have not been faced, reactive defences against them create a tendency to repetition, as if by unconsciously repeating the same mistakes there could be a different outcome. Such an individualised metaphor can also apply to social groups, nations, and even the global population itself. There is no doubt that the onslaught of the pandemic with its millions of lives lost, multiple bereavements, lack of hospital care, and the inevitable wait for available vaccine can rightly be described as a humbling experience that sobers humankind to its limitations.

Historian Walter Benjamin (1940) wrote that "When the angel of history cannot perform his or her duty the process of history produces unsolved conflicts and losses that are not yet mourned, which, as we know, is what ghosts are made of." Like the trauma of invasive and civil wars of the twentieth century, unresolved conflicts about the past are likely to create ghosts. The repetition of past trauma, and in the case of Covid, the provocation of many mental health problems, due not just to the invasive nature of the threatening disease, but to the lockdowns and intrusive confinements stretching family resources that may already have been vulnerable. This has left whole populations as well as individuals vulnerable to often invisible experiences, including loss of contact with family and friends, losses of loved ones through illness and death, loss of secure livelihoods, confined spaces, and reduced distractions of daily life, travel, entertainment, and recreation. The tragedy of loved ones dying without the physical comfort of being in the same room as close relatives, or family being unable to attend a funeral, provide haunting images that still throw shadows over our communal and family ties. The abiding fear is that such confinements will recur internally if not externally in reality, creating permanent anxieties and risk to mental health.

But how is loss associated with failure to resolve past trauma? Freud distinguished between mourning and melancholia (1917e). On the face of it they appear similar, with dejection, and the loss of libido, vitality, and an important attachment figure. What differentiates melancholia is that the person or people are tormented by a shame-ridden self-hatred that also aggressively alienates others. Freud suggests that this is the consequence of a taboo on hating the lost person or way of life, resulting in an internal split that precludes the possibility of moving through grieving and integrating learning from losses.

This can create what Bollas (2018) describes as a borderline psychotic state of mind where:

> The borderline split allows no communication between the opposing parts. The dissociative self ... is distanced from a traumatized part of the personality, but this is not out of sight—indeed, it is in full view. Unlike the borderline, the dissociated self is walking hand-in-hand with its traumatized other half, like a soldier rescuing a comrade in the field of battle. However, the net effect will be a lack of communication between the two sides; the observing self is strangely indifferent to the self that is wounded.

This outlines a framework for beginning to understand the mental health risks and fears stretching into the future. If these predictable effects are a feature of what I am describing as the risks of *societal* long Covid in the population, their amelioration, and protection from their effects lies in the hands of the body politic.

The coronavirus pandemic and its context

At the start of the pandemic there was no vaccine to protect humankind, and few precedents for hospital treatment of those who caught it and suffered from the after-effects of blood clotting, respiratory failure, and organ malfunction that have characterised what has come to be called "long Covid". Long Covid provides a metaphor for the disadvantages in health care through failures in dependency and the dependability of institutions such as the NHS in the UK. It is also a metaphor for the many failures in democratic government, in grasping the nature of the threat to the health of the nation leading to appalling and life-threatening consequences for so many of the population in the way this crisis has been managed.

It could be argued that it was the shock of the pandemic that was so completely unforeseeable, that governments across the world and not least in the UK could not have been prepared. However, in 2015 Microsoft founder and billionaire philanthropist Bill Gates was one of the speakers at the Vancouver TED conference, where he spoke about the Ebola crisis in West Africa. He observed that we are not prepared for the next epidemic. "If anything kills over ten million people in the next few decades, it's most likely to be a highly infectious virus rather than a war—not missiles, but microbes," he warned. What was needed, according to Gates, was a system to mobilise hundreds of thousands of health workers at short notice, and of course, tests, vaccines, and treatments, the stock-in-trade of Big Pharma and hospitals. This perception is echoed in the work of Gilbert and Green (2021) in describing the delayed opportunity to develop pandemic vaccinations until after the crisis struck:

> Those of us working in the field had expected something like this for years. At the beginning lots of people were asking "why did we not see this coming?" The answer is that we did see it coming, and we had started preparing, but we had not been able to persuade anyone to spend the money that we needed to do what was required.

The failures of the body politic

In *The Guardian* on October 2, 2020, Jonathan Freedland wrote:

> The serial incompetence of Boris Johnson's government is not an accident. It may look like haplessness, but that is to mistake the symptom for the cause. Instead this government's ineptitude is a function of both the character of the man at the top and the defining creed of his administration.

In support of this argument, he cites the scrapped and faultily relaunched contact-tracing app that Health Secretary Matt Hancock had hailed as a crucial weapon in the fight against the pandemic. Critical days were wasted before a clearly inevitable national lockdown was imposed in March 2020—a delay that Professor Neil Ferguson, then on the Sage committee, estimates to have cost 20,000 lives. What added insult to the injury of this neglect was that multimillion-pound contracts were handed to insider Tory friends and backers to supply personal protective equipment that turned out to be useless against Covid. The result was that the UK managed to produce the highest death toll in Europe along with the severest economic slump in the world (Freedland, 2020).

Freedland's conclusion is that "this is not just bad luck, an unfortunate coincidence that saw a global health crisis collide with a set of ministers sadly unsuited to the task." His view relies on an analysis of the collision of neo-liberal economics, white-male supremacy, and an ideology that attacks, by dismissing any form of dependency or vulnerability in other people, and deals with anxiety by exporting it towards other people and institutions. The neo-liberal approach to politics favours free-market capitalism, deregulation, and reduction in government spending. It was this philosophy that had urged what Johnson's key advisor, Dominic Cummings, had sought through Brexit. His strategy was to change the structure of politics by purging expertise and tearing down what works, including diplomacy, to attack interdependence with European nations.

In mid-October 2021, the joint Health and Social Care Committee and the Science and Technology Committee of the UK House of Commons, which contain MPs from all parties, produced detailed findings in the long-awaited report—"Coronavirus: Lessons learned to date". The committee said it ranked as "one of the most important public health failures the UK has ever experienced". It describes how the "veil of ignorance through which the UK viewed the initial weeks of the pandemic was partly self-inflicted", and specifically among other criticisms: "Our committees heard that the UK did not take enough advantage of the learning and experience being generated in other countries, notably in East Asia" (*BBC News*, October 12, 2021).

This intertwining of ideology with populist ambition meant that Tory policy-making, under the guise of decentralising, created an even fiercer centralised control of policy among a few trusted ministers and advisors. This also had involved, during the run-up to the key Brexit vote, the attempt to prorogue Parliament so that it could not have adequate time to digest, let alone process in 2019 Brexit legislation that was the most significant constitutional change in the past 100 years. The ruthless manipulation of Parliament, the deliberate creation of a crisis that was judged by the Supreme Court to be unconstitutional, created fear of failing to deliver a Brexit that the British people were exhausted by and by that stage just wanted to be finalised. Here was the technique, well established among dictators, of divide and rule, of creating a crisis that would amplify fear, and then the longing for strong leadership that would resolve the problem and make it seem to go away.

Andy Cowper, editor of *Health Policy Insight* and a columnist for the *British Medical Journal*, writing in *The Guardian* on June 28, 2021, gave his assessment of the state of the NHS following the political scandal in which the UK health secretary, Matt Hancock, was sacked for breaking his own government's social distancing rules by being filmed in a clinch with a female advisor, with whom he had been having an extramarital affair. Cowper describes his track record: PPE (personal protective equipment) procurement shortages; the care home scandal in which patients had been transferred out of general hospitals to care homes without being tested, despite Hancock lying to Parliament that they had been; the decision to set up the failed test-and-trace programme on a centralised and outsourced basis, with no penalty clauses for poor performance.

Meanwhile, NHS staff had been working in appalling conditions in vastly overcrowded Covid units with a lack of PPE, during which time hundreds of health workers died. Nevertheless, Hancock insisted that the government's offer of a meagre 1% salary increase was a "pay rise", despite inflation running at 1.5%. Beyond this staffing undervaluation and under-recruitment, a lack of NHS investment has left NHS England with an underlying deficit; a £9bn capital and maintenance backlog, a high and long-standing level of staff vacancies; and a backlog of more than five million people waiting for treatment for the first time in the NHS's history. This backlog was already bad before Covid, indicated by an independent analysis from 2020, showing that, even pre-pandemic, the NHS would have needed to treat an extra 500,000 patients a year for four years to get back to its standard of eighteen-week maximum waits for hospital care (Cowper, 2021). The broader context is that the NHS has gone through a period of the lowest sustained funding growth in its history. Further analysis by the Health Foundation shows that from 2015 to 2019, NHS funding grew by 1.6% a year: well under half the historical average (ibid.).

The defensive dynamics of managing fear by creating it in others

How then can we analyse the ideology and emotional relatedness of such government policies in action, given the considerable unpreparedness for any crisis, let alone a pandemic? My hypothesis is that such policies were based not just on attacks on any possibility of ordinary neediness by members of a population dependent on tax-paid health care, but a deliberate ideology born of hatred of dependency, vulnerability, and a mocking of the basic needs of people for dependency. The aim has been to create a climate of fear, and further, as with Brexit, to accuse others of promulgating "Project Fear" about consequences. Further, I would argue that such an anti-caring, anti-dependency mocking of what was sometimes decried in the right-wing press as a "nanny state", was in fact born of a state of fear in the groupthink of UK leaders, begging the question; where did such fear come from and why is it allowed to dominate our politics by an electorate that votes for it through the ballot box? It is easier to see where the first came from, following research on the number of Conservative leaders whose emotional development was stunted by the boarding school experience (Khaleelee, 2016; Schaverien, 2011). It is harder to unearth where electoral dependency on such leaders comes from, other than from the zeitgeist of individual survival being a key value of electors who seek leaders who are ruthless in achieving it for themselves. Such uncaring views also mock the possibility of offering more than token charitable donations of surplus vaccinations to third world nations, thereby denying the need for global responses on the basis that none of us is safe until we are all safe.

Further evidence about exported fear can be found in Johnson's key advisor Dominic Cummings's account of his rule-breaking dash to relatives in the north when his wife had Covid symptoms. This was clearly the result of a panic attack in the face of the stressful work in which he was engaged, seeking procurement for emergency medical supplies that should already have been in place. His argument in his press conference in the Number 10 Rose Garden was that his own situation deserved exceptionalist treatment, given what he was doing for the country, a stance he upheld until he was finally sacked.

It has been suggested that the challenge of the need for global collaboration in facing the problem of Covid is but a rehearsal for the greater challenges in facing mankind's dependency on fossil fuels that have led to the drastic risks to global climate. Here we have a complex systemic issue where the attempted cure, that targets one aspect of transmission of a virus, also reveals other unhealthy dimensions of unregulated global trade. These include damage to the eco-system, plus an unregulated carbon economy that undermines sustainability and accelerates what some writers have described as *ecocide* (Hoggett & Nestor, 2021). Sally Weintrobe (2021) has suggested an analytic framework for the neo-liberal ideology of *uncare* and *exceptionalism*, that could equally be used to describe the failures of the global community in addressing Covid.

"*Psychological Roots of the Climate Crisis* tells the story of a fundamental fight between a caring and an uncaring imagination. It helps us to recognise the uncaring imagination in politics, in culture … " Sally Weintrobe argues that

> Achieving the shift to greater care requires us to stop colluding with Exceptionalism, the rigid psychological mindset largely responsible for the climate crisis. People in this mindset believe that they are entitled to have the lion's share and that they can "rearrange" reality with magical omnipotent thinking whenever reality limits these felt entitlements.

I began this chapter describing the battle with Covid as a war. Like all wars, especially the world wars of the twentieth century, the multiple causes are to be found in the ideological, colonialist, and dominant/dominating forces across the world in the history that began upstream of any actual outbreak of this warfare. Upstream from the spread of Covid have been neo-liberal economic colonising forces through globalisation of international trade and travel that have been the ideal carrier of this potentially deadly disease. Further, the colonising ideology of unregulated market capitalism and neo-liberal, white-male dominated ideology has undermined the organs of government that provide dependable institutional frameworks within which democracies demonstrate their care for individual members of society.

Since the Health and Social Care Act of 2012, part of the consequence of this ideology has been that in the UK, the Secretary of State for Health and Social Care no longer carries a duty of care for the health of the nation. This responsibility is now delegated to local authorities and health trusts who do not have control of the purse strings. This means a division between responsibility and resourcing and a further politicisation of dependency of health as an unwanted dimension of governmental responsibilities. This political dynamic is further evidenced by the postponement of a promised White Paper on the structure and financing of social care, including the fast-growing needs of elder care, as it will be politically unpopular now so many of society have swallowed the politics of *uncare* and individual, rather than collective social responsibility.

Nowhere is this conflict more poignant than in the battle for personal, social, and political recognition that has shaped the experience of the Black Lives Matter movement in the USA and other countries that can surely be described as a world war against the scapegoating and abusive servitude of more vulnerable minorities. It was from this struggle with unresolved trauma from slavery and the American Civil War, made alive through the successive election of presidents Obama, then Trump in the USA, that the quotation from Claudia Rankine at the head of this chapter arrives to speak its painful relevance across the present. Hers was the experience of being dominated by unresolved history being kept alive and haunting present struggles for recognition. This struggle was repeated in the way the government in the UK ignored calls for recognition and special protection for the more vulnerable BAME staff who statistically were shown to be more at risk from Covid and who sustained more deaths. Ironically, it was reported to me that in one Covid ward management had created priority for rationed PPE to be used by BAME staff. In consequence white staff proposed that it was the vulnerable yet "protected" BAME staff who should do the barrier nursing of highly infectious patients!

If this is true for the righteous warfare for recognition of black peoples, where "You can't put the past behind you. It's buried in you," how much is the same true of the global Covid-19 pandemic that has "turned your flesh into its own cupboard".

In analysing the overlap between the pandemic and the unregulated economy sustained by neo-liberal ideology, psychoanalyst Christopher Bollas (2021) comments on Trump's America:

> As the president fuelled white nationalism and the far right, drumming up support from his fan base, the word "virus" became a signifier that bifurcated to identify two seemingly unrelated phenomena: the transmission of a biological virus

and the transmission of false news. Covid entered the American body and killed people, while Trump created a social virus, a malignant mutation of previously adequate social structures, as he spread psychically destructive communications that were meant to enter the American body politic or mind. The convergence of both viral forms of communication created a mentally confusing pathogen. As they travelled around the country, both were psychically invasive, breeding fear on a scale that the American community had not experienced before.

If justice and inclusion of minorities are to be included in just health policies, then the Covid pandemic, as Bollas suggests, creates an overlap between fear of lack of social structures and the virus as an invasive force attacking the body and its immune system.

The social group, its *skin*, and its response to the pandemic

In describing learning available from the experiential framework of group relations conferences, Pierre Turquet wrote (1975) of "Threats to Identity in the Large Group". He describes the struggle of the individual to join a large group and make a contribution. The experience is "essentially one of search" and "Essential to this joining process is that the singleton should find a boundary or skin which both limits and defines him." He goes on to suggest that there are two skins, "one is external, the skin of my neighbour, the other internal (my own skin)" (p. 96). The groupthink of shared beliefs and attitudes provides one clear example of how ideas give a group a sense of its own containing safe skin.

Global Covid responses can be linked with another previous medical crisis, namely the outbreak of HIV/AIDS across many societies in the 1980s and particularly, but not exclusively around the gay communities. Social anthropologist Mary Douglas (1992) describes individual and grouped responses to this threat. She outlines four approaches to the experience of being a body in an epidemic:

- The body as porous—open to unpredictable invasion: this view ranges between unrealistic paranoia and realistic self-protections including recommended hygiene and social distancing.

- The body as strong and self-sufficient—with efficient immune system that copes with infections: this view risks omnipotent denial of interdependency.
- The body protected by personal immune "skin" as well as by a community "social skin": while this view appears as an attempt to salvage a sense of social interdependency at a time of lockdowns, it can also appear as a naive survival solution if followed at the expense of all other protections.
- The body as a machine with its own protective envelope that is assisted by medical technology: this view again, taken as a sole solution, carries the risk of idealising medical intervention and ignoring societal recommended protection.

These shared beliefs create subgroup "social skins" (Morgan-Jones, 2022; Turner, 2007) for responses to the virus, each with a different shaping to its internal and external boundaries. Douglas points to four stances in relation to the large group dynamics of society: a) the isolate, b) the individualist, c) the dissenting enclave, and d) the central community, and explores the dynamics between them as they relate to the distribution of four stances on the body. This analysis provides a development of the kind of thinking that Turquet (1975) pioneered in large group dynamics. It suggests how people move between being over-socialised and being isolated in an incoherent way (Hopper, 2003). It is hard to work with different sources of authority and be both an individual and also a member of a large group with its different subgroupings, each carrying a tempting identity and creating the possibility of rapid and confusing shifts in affiliation between them. The risk is that people can hold two radically different positions at the same time and use denial as a mechanism to deal with contradictions. This echoes the technique of dissembling used by politicians.

Part of the dynamics of society under the stresses and threats of a pandemic is to create inter-group aggressive rivalries between one set of solutions and another. This is illustrated by a number of societal splits beyond the four described above:

a) There are those determined to downplay risks of infection and to idealise lifting of lockdowns to return to normal economic living.
b) There is the conflict between those pro-vaccination and the "anti-vaxxers".

c) There is the idealising clapping in the UK and other nations of health workers, while complaining about support for increasing their pay that may require increasing taxation.
d) There are also many examples of denial of the risk of infection to BAME group members, and how to, and even whether to, protect them through organisational policies.

In sum, each approach suggests how urgent it is for people not to become locked in a single solution, but rather to take a common-sense view in the meaning of integrating different perspectives. However, this demands emotional and social labour in talking them through, and inspired leadership and dialogue on behalf of society, in working through the emotions associated with this confusing and uncertain management of contrasting fears.

The chapter now moves from the failed containment of fear through the missing dialogue in the body politic, to the practical dimension of containment of fear through health organisations and the understanding of their specific tasks.

The tasks of health workers and their organisations

A valuable approach to understanding health responses to the pandemic is to explore the organisational experience of health workers. In the UK two months of Thursday evening clapping for our "brave key workers" in the health and emergency services was a way through which they were encouraged in taking the risks with their own safety and exposure to infection in the face of limited supplies of protective equipment and low pay. It was also a way that isolated communities of people could represent their solidarity against their own fear of infection. This was against a backdrop of starvation of resources over ten years of austerity policies, and excessive input from management control aspiring to reduce a huge deficit caused by the 2008 financial crisis and the mismanagement and deregulation of banking and investment services. In fact, this approach to recovery was shaped by right-wing neo-liberal ideology and the determination to shrink the state and discourage failures in society from being resourced by a welfare and health system at the heart of the pandemic.

So, if the provision of health care as a system reveals the current human values of the body politic, what might be the way social experience shapes the meanings of embodiment and health? This chapter now turns to systems psychodynamics to explore this question and to ask how the primary task of the health system can be seen from different perspectives, particularly how the espoused values of society are embodied in various approaches to describing the primary task of hospital and emergency workers:

- *Normative Primary Task (for institutional survival):* "We are caring and curing. We do this for society."
- *Existential Primary Task:* "Our purpose is to know our patients and their needs" (the hope).
- *Phenomenal Primary Task:* "We are running all day to not forget tasks and people and to stop them dying" = managing expectations (= survival of staff—not a health service but a sickness and death denying service).
- *Hermeneutic Primary Task:* "We embody the meaning of illness and disease that cannot be fathomed. We do this for society and respond to its demand to create faith in a safe world."

We can see from this brief summary of definitions of primary task that what is required is a flexible and all-encompassing approach that can move freely between these perspectives, as well as transcending them to find purpose and meaning in them. Together, they embody the hope of society for a caring and dependable service meeting healthcare needs even in the face of the radical uncertainties of the pandemic. They also seek confirmation from political leadership that can value and resource this task performed on behalf of society.

Conclusion

This chapter has explored meeting points between the different failures of dependency and the way society groups around ideologies of health in facing existential fears of survival. The fear of surviving a dangerous and highly infectious virus, and the failures by the body politic to provide trustworthy management of the crisis, have created a double fear. Both fears urgently demand emotional containment through being discussed empathically, openly, and accompanied by societal and policy agendas that provide a sense of leadership that is addressing emotional uncertainties and mental health vulnerabilities nationally and internationally. I have sought to trace the sources of fear to the unknowns about the virus and about the lack of resources within the UK NHS across previous years. I conclude that behind these policies and management of the pandemic lies an uncaring ideology of exceptionalist entitlement that demeans fear, dependency, and neediness. This includes in its way of addressing it, the export of fear and extreme anxiety back into the wider population, seeking instead to play up achievements such as the heroism and flexibility of health staff and the ingenuity of the people who invented and manufactured vaccines as containers of fear without taking responsibility for government's part in under-resourcing the NHS, and in proliferating unregulated travel and trade that were so effective in spreading the virus, among many failures. I suggest that it is the particular interplay of complex multi-system factors in this pandemic that demand perspectives that include the individual, the social group, and the organisation, and their wider perspectives that are worth investigating further to understand how to live with Covid and endure the challenges of long Covid on many fronts.

References

Benjamin, W. (1940). On the concept of history. http://members.efn.org/~dredmond/ThesesonHistory.html (last accessed April 12, 2020)

Bollas, C. (2018). *Meaning and Melancholia: Life in the Age of Bewilderment*. London: Routledge.

Bollas, C. (2021). Civilisation and the discontented. In: H. B. Levine & A. de Staal (Eds.), *Psychoanalysis and Covidian Life: Common Distress, Individual Experience* (pp. 3–21). London: Phoenix.

Cowper, A. (2021, June 28). Hancock has left the NHS in crisis. Don't assume Javid will save it. *The Guardian*.

Douglas, M. (1992). *Risk and Blame: Essays in Cultural Theory*. London: Routledge.

Freedland, J. (2020, October 2). This government's incompetence is no accident. It was inevitable. *The Guardian*.

Freud, S. (1917e). Mourning and melancholia. *S. E., 14*: 237–258. London: Hogarth.

Gates, W. (2015). TED talk: Warning of future pandemics & epidemics. www.rev.com (last accessed October 12, 2021)

Gilbert, S., & Green, C. (2021). *Vaxxers: The Inside Story of the Oxford AstraZeneca Vaccine and the Race against the Virus.* London: Hodder & Stoughton.

Hoggett, P., & Nestor, R. (2021). First genocide, now ecocide: an anti-life force in organisations. *Organisational and Social Dynamics, 21*(1): 97–113.

Hopper, E. (2003). *Traumatic Experience in the Unconscious Life of Groups: The Fourth Basic Assumption: Incohesion: Aggregation/Massification or (ba) I:A/M.* London: Jessica Kingsley.

Khaleelee, O. (2016). Boarding school, Brexit, and our leaders' judgement. *Organisational and Social Dynamics, 16*: 271–276.

Morgan-Jones, R. J. (2007). "Retainment" of staff: the challenge to the system in managing presence and absence of staff for the work task. *Organisational and Social Dynamics, 6*(1): 22–41.

Morgan-Jones, R. J. (2010). *The Body of the Organisation and Its Health.* London: Karnac.

Morgan-Jones, R. J. (2022). The language of the group skin: what gets under the skin, attacking the capacity of teams to think. In: T. M. Ringer, R. Gordon, & B. Vandenbussche (Eds.), *The Collective Spark: Igniting Thinking in Groups, Teams and the Wider World.* Gent, Belgium: Grafische Cel Sint-Lucas—LUCA School of Arts.

Rankine, C. (2005). *Citizen: An American Lyric.* London: Penguin.

Schaverien, J. (2011). Boarding school syndrome: Broken attachments a hidden trauma. *British Journal of Psychotherapy, 27*: 138–155.

Turner, T. S. (2007). The social skin. In: M. Lock & J. Farquhar (Eds.), *Beyond the Body Proper: Reading the Anthropology of Material Life* (pp. 83–106). Durham, NC: Duke University Press.

Turquet, P. (1975). Threats to identity in the large group. In: L. Kreeger (Ed.), *The Large Group: Dynamics and Therapy.* London: Constable.

Weintrobe, S. (2021). *Psychological Roots of the Climate Crisis: Neoliberal Exceptionalism and the Culture of Uncare.* London: Bloomsbury.

CHAPTER 7

Power, fragility, and recovery

by Winnie Fei and Zhang Jian Li

Epidemics and crises

The emergence of Covid-19 is arguably the biggest global public crisis of the past century, wreaking havoc around the world, starting in 2020, killing millions of people and dealing a major blow to the global economy. A lot of hidden problems were exposed under Covid-19: the opposition between ethnic groups divided country, political party; religious conflict, the East and the West torn, etc. The vaccine didn't play a decisive enough role in containing the virus. The virus continues to mutate and become much more pathogenic and infectious, and global eradication of the virus is nowhere in sight. At present, the most serious consequence is ideological confrontation, the conflict between East and West; man's primitive nature comes to the fore at times of psychic disturbance. Jung (1959) was keenly aware that the greatest danger to mankind is the unpredictability of mental reactions; paranoia and fear, such as that induced by a pandemic, generate a 'psychic epidemic.'

Hypoimmunity

We could understand that the crisis of this virus is an invasion and attack on the body's immune system: this is the fragility of the human body. According to traditional Chinese medicine, if a person is as vigorous as a healthy baby and has a strong resistance, the invasion may not defeat him. However, it seems that immunodeficiency was occurring in humans well before the novel coronavirus attack, and we want to understand, in this case, what is going on to cause our own deficiencies?

The ancient Taoist book *Zhuangzi* (2010) recorded stories from Chinese mythology of long ago. At first, the state of the world was chaos (Hun Dun). During this time, pure and opaque Qi were mixed to give birth to the "god of chaos", who lived in a place called the Tianshan Mountains. Hun Dun was huge, with no facial features; Hun Dun relied on his feelings to enjoy songs and dances, to distinguish between good and evil. Because he contained within him the essence of heaven and earth, the energy of the birth of the universe, he moved very slowly and painfully. There were two gods living next to Hun Dun: Shu was the emperor of the South Sea, Hu of the North Sea, and Hun Dun of the central region. Shu and Hu often met each other in Hun Dun's land and Hun Dun treated them very well. Shu and Hu discussed how to repay Hun Dun's friendship. They said, "People all have eyes, ears, nose and mouth to see, hear, eat and breathe, but Hun Dun has nothing. Let's try to open the seven orifices for him." So they spent two days chiselling out his eyes, and on the third and fourth day they chiselled out his nostrils, and on the fifth day they chiselled out his mouth, and on the sixth and seventh they chiselled out his ears. After seven days, Hun Dun finally possessed the seven orifices. But the energy in his body also drifted outward from these seven openings, just like a deflating ball, which melted into one body with heaven and earth and died.

Hun Dun dies after being chiselled out. After he perceived the external world, he lost wisdom and spirituality. Only with "no desire" can we see the secret of Tao. "Shu" and "Hu" both mean rush, they are the opposite of the very slow Hun Dun. To open the seven orifices means to become "eager" and "smart", which is connected with thinking and weighing things up. Therefore, "opening the seven Orifices" runs counter to "Tao". The word "knowledge" here means *speculation* (in the Bible it is the *fruit of wisdom*) and this clever development destroyed the pure nature of people.

Now, they no longer have strong immunity and become vulnerable to the attack of the outside world, at any time threatened by death; or it refers to human nature—the nature of inaction and nature, death.

Jung (1959) made a systematic and profound study of Chinese Buddhism and Taoism culture, and Chinese culture was deeply permeated into his academic theories. He even quoted the original texts of the *Tao Te Ching* and the *I Ching* for a long time, and carried out profound psychological interpretation. However, as Chinese, we may not inherit our traditional culture very well, because we are affected by the great impact of Western rationalism for the past one to two hundred years. There is no doubt that "science" and "democracy" are global hard currency, but we are already like ice at the beginning of spring, and the loss of traditional beliefs is like water in the ice.

As Jung (1959) had a collective unconscious to nourish consciousness, and the collective unconscious was more characterised by emotions and beliefs, as this traditional, classical, so-called theory combined with the science, so the charm of traditional beliefs and emotions gradually evolved into indifference, away from the fullness of the symbol of emotional life, away from the unique Chinese spirit of heaven and earth. There are more and more "rational" beings with "refined self-interest", who are a group of spiritual entities without ideals and beliefs. Chang'e has disappeared from the moon with the discovery of gravity, Nuwa no longer needs to repair the sky. Under the guidance of science, human beings are becoming more and more conceited, but myth is the prototype of human spirit, and history is the homeland of human spirit. In adopting and valuing above all the Western rational scientific method, China has let go of and devalued its spiritual Eastern Confucian foundations and thereby has created a void in the national psyche. What we need to address is not only the threat of Covid-19 to human lives and the impact on the economy, but also the need to build a value system that explores human consciousness.

The breathless Covid-19 and denial of life

The symptoms of coronavirus, a lung infection that makes breathing difficult, are similar to breathing hard when people are afraid. There's a denial of life, an unconscious fear that you're "not good enough", that saps life's power all the time. In Confucianism, the ultimate goal is to become a flawless sage, which unconsciously forms a very common tendency to pursue perfection. Therefore, a kind of caution comes into being. One worries that every action and every decision may make others unhappy or uncomfortable, so one avoids saying anything risky and doing anything likely to offend others, even if constructive. If someone is dissatisfied, this results in self-blame. Making oneself and the other conform to the norms of the group has therefore produced a surface harmony which covers over other important traits both positive and negative in the individual. The lack of real connection between people limits the possibility of real growth within each other. In this way, generation after generation, those who have an independent spirit and dare to speak out have been a minority. In the ten years of the Cultural Revolution, all of them were brutally and mercilessly strangled. Since then, the spiritual life of the Chinese people has rapidly retreated and declined, remaining on the surviving level of being alive.

In the Book of Job, we also find an external judgement of character. The core of the argument between Job and the three Oriental friends is that Job does not admit that the external disaster was caused by his sin, but the three Oriental friends arbitrarily insist that he should confess, otherwise how did he end up in this situation? In other words, in Eastern thought, people are responsible for all the disasters in life, and if your fate is bad, it must be because of the bad things you have done; if not in this life, then in a previous life. So the plane of disaster in Eastern thought does not have the plane of God from Job, the mystery. That is, disasters don't necessarily come from sin, like Jesus, who was sinless, or Job, who suffered, not because he sinned, but because God was behind their suffering. After Job's suffering, God declared that "my servant Job" had spoken better than the three men from the East, and that he would make a sin offering for them before God could forgive them. Job, in his own heart and in truth, debates the Eastern philosophy. In his fragility, Job speaks with truth, the three friends speak with philosophy and experience, and Job triumphs.

Courage to admit fragility

A novel coronavirus attacks the human race, and the death toll soars. In many places strict lockdown, quarantine, to control the rapid spread of infection. People's vulnerability, in the face of a small virus, fully exposed. Isolation slows down the pace of busyness and makes us feel isolated, which makes us realise the importance of love. Vulnerability makes us realise the value of happiness and courage to life. Psychologically speaking, fragility is the core of all our emotions and feelings. Fragility connects the needs of the true self. However, the danger brought by vulnerability makes people feel great fear. The denial and cover-up of vulnerability often leads to a deeper dilemma: "weakness".

Weakness is a state of feeling inadequate and deficient. Weakness makes us unable to achieve the situation and goals we desire to achieve. Subjectively speaking, a weak but sane person will almost inevitably perceive his own weakness, resulting in feelings of inferiority, worthlessness, and uselessness, followed by depression and frustration. In a world of confused values, everyone is profoundly affected by pride, arbitrariness, and deep-rooted egotism. Everyone wants to be admired for being strong and good. Once it is found that this desire cannot be achieved, the feeling of weakness continues to cover a person's existence. People will feel like a deflated ball, in the heart of the seeds of bitter poison. In this case, some people will choose to "lie down" and give up, and some people will choose to use all means and shortcuts, or even moral corruption, which has become a serious problem in contemporary Chinese society with the loss of spiritual belief.

In fact, fragility is not weakness. We say a baby is fragile, but not weak. With their vulnerability and needs exposed, they naturally become conduits for affection and love. Emotional energy flows from high to low like water. Psalm 8:2 says, "Out of the mouth of babes and sucklings you have built up power because of your enemies, to silence the enemy and the avenger." The power of the supreme divinity is expressed through the most vulnerable child, the fragility connects to the true self, and the true self connects to the divine. This is the law of life.

Owning up to your vulnerability can lead to feelings of shame, fear, and smallness. But courage is the ability to show weakness. It may be painful to expose ourselves, but it is not nearly as painful as to avoid it with our lives. Admitting our weaknesses may be dangerous, but not nearly as dangerous as giving up love, belonging, and joy—it is the experience of revealing our thoughts, feelings, and experiences to others that makes us vulnerable, but it is only by being able to explore the darkness that we can connect to the infinite light.

Recovery: full humanity

In Chinese schoolbooks, there is a story called "The Oil Peddler", in which there is a conversation between an old oil peddler and an aristocrat. Chen Yaozi, the Duke of Kangsu, was so good at shooting that no other man in the world could match him, and he boasted about his skill. Once, when he was shooting arrows at home, an old man selling oil put down his burden and stood there looking at him carefully for a long time without leaving.

The old man nodded slightly when he saw that nine out of ten arrows had hit their target. Chen Yao asked the old man, "Do you also know archery? Am I not very good with my arrows?" The old man said, "There is no other secret, it's just skill." Hearing this, Chen Yaozi said angrily, "How dare you despise my archery ability!" The old man said, "I know that from my experience in pouring oil." Then he took out a gourd and put it on the ground, covered the mouth of the gourd with a copper coin, and slowly poured oil into the gourd with an oil spoon. The oil poured into the gourd through the hole of the coin, but the coin did not get wet. So he said, "I also have no other secret, it is only skill." Chen Yaozi smiled and sent him away.

There is an excellent article in *Zhuangzi*. "Paoding dissecting the ox" also tells a similar story: Paoding butchering the ox for King Hui of Liang. The place that the hand touches, the place that the shoulder leans on, the place that the foot steps on, the place that the knee rests on, where the knife enters, is huo huo ground, in harmony with the rhythm of life: accord with "mulberry Lin" dance music rhythm, accord with "jing Shou" music rhythm. King Hui of Liang said, "Hey, good! How can you be so skilful?" Paoding laid down his knife and answered, "What I pursue is Tao, and I have surpassed the general skills. At first, when I kill a cow, I see a whole cow. Three years later, no whole cow was seen again. Now, I touch the cow with the spirit, not with the eyes, the senses are stopped and the spirit is in action. According to the natural physiological structure of the cow, cut into the gap between the bones and muscles of the cow body, along the gap between the bones, according to the original structure of the cow body, the place where the veins and meridians are connected and the place where the bones and muscles are combined have never been touched with the knife, let alone the big bone! A good cook changes his knife once a year. He cuts the flesh with his knife (just as he cuts the rope with his knife). The average cook had to change his knife once a month. He had broken it by cutting through bones. Now my knife is nineteen years old and I have slaughtered thousands of cattle, but the blade is as sharp as if it had been sharpened on a whetstone. There were gaps in the joints, and the blade was thin. Insert a thin blade into a hollow joint, wide enough, so there must be room for the blade to move! For nineteen years, therefore, the blade looked as if it had been whetted from a grindstone. Even so, whenever I met the joints of bones and muscles, I saw that it was difficult to cut, so I carefully raised my vigilance. My vision focused on a point, and my movement slowed down. I moved the knife very gently, and huo huo, the bones and meat of the cow were suddenly untied, just like the soil scattered on the ground. I stand up with it, and look about me for it, and feel content for it, and wipe it clean, and put it away." King Hui of Liang said, "Good! I listened to Paoding's words and understood the principle of keeping in good health."

Paoding and the oil peddler are ordinary people, but they have mastered the small things in daily life. Therefore, Taoism asserts that man's path to divinity lies in the vulnerable points of daily life. The finer the details, the more extraordinary the quality; this is not only the way of the craftsman to demonstrate their skills, but also the way of life and the highest spirit in contact. And those who have received the Tao are even above the emperor. This is about giving power back to ordinary people. Especially in Chinese society, since the Qin Dynasty, thousands of years of dictatorship and centralisation, where is the power of ordinary people? If only the lives of emperors and dignitaries are important, what is the value of ordinary people's lives?

Lacking power, their lives are especially humble and fragile. However, in Taoist thought, the most ordinary people and occupations are the path to the highest Tao. Accept fragility, expose fragility, embrace fragility, treat fragility with a focused and undistracted heart, and one will meet with the Tao and god. The power of recovery and healing comes from the acceptance and openness of oneself, discarding the ingenuity and utilitarianism, and restoring the essence and purity of human nature without comparison. Being open to fragility comes from inner humility and honesty. More vulnerability means a higher level (in the evolutionary chain).

As Covid-19 slows the world down, we might want to reflect on the nature of life. The pandemic has posed a huge challenge to mankind and it's also reshuffling the deck worldwide. Perhaps, being able to understand the law and the Tao of life can make the present slowness a blessing in the future.

References

Fang Yong (Translation annotation) (2010). *Zhuangzi*. Beijing: Beijing BaiFan.

Job, The Holy Bible, *New International Version*, Grand Rapids, MI: Zondervan, 1989, p. 569.

Jung, C. G. (1959). *Archetypes and the Collective Unconscious*. Xu Delin (Trans.). Beijing: International Culture Publishing, 2018.

CHAPTER 8

Vulnerability and resilience in a time of Covid

by Tim Dartington

The pandemic has reminded us of our vulnerability, individually and as a society, especially if we are finding it difficult not to use denial as a defence against the uncertainties of Covid. This is a struggle that affects the ordinary citizen and politicians alike, and it is testing our resilience, given reports of increased mental distress, domestic disturbance, and the devastating impact on those on the wrong side of the widening inequality gap in our social and economic structures.

In this time of an extraordinary if involuntary social experiment, we need to be philosophers as well as epidemiologists. We all have an underlying condition, called life, and it is universally fatal, but the trouble is, we still do not altogether believe that. According to Freud, death is not inevitable in our unconscious reasoning. "Our unconscious … does not believe in its own death; it behaves as if it were immortal" and "It is indeed impossible to imagine our own death; and whenever we attempt to do so we can perceive that we are in fact still present as spectators" (Freud, 1915b).

At some level we think we are not going to die, and in some ways there is a similar wilful ignorance that we think we can live a life without risk. We are never going to get that reassurance, but at the same time we may want to do everything we can to minimise that risk in our own minds.

For someone who is extremely fearful of dying, the advice is to be extremely careful, but there are limits to that precautionary advice. Also, we know that we are unreliable in calculating risk, more fearful of flying while we are more likely to die on the roads. We make our own judgements whether the virus or the vaccine is more dangerous to our health. Our response to the Covid threat then ranges from the ultra-cautious to the cavalier.

Wearing face covering became obligatory on public transport in the UK but it has not been strictly enforced, perhaps because of a tradition of tolerating dissent or a nervousness towards any response that smacks of authoritarian controls. On buses and trains there were always some people demonstrating a freedom of expression (literally, when we can see their faces). We may be both angry at their irresponsibility and, I suggest, covertly appreciative of their independence.

Levels of infections continue to cause concern in the UK, as government looks for an easing of all restrictions. In the summer of 2021 funerals have been muted, mourners restricted, while 60,000 supporters were singing their hearts out in the European football final at Wembley Stadium. A preferred form of celebration across the country was then to throw beer in the air—the droplets an unconscious enactment of the virus perhaps.

After fifteen months of living with the pandemic, an OPUS Listening Post[1] (also refer to Chapter 12 of this book) gave the opportunity for participants to reflect from their perspective and experience as citizens on these themes, that are so difficult to think about, both practically and philosophically.

A mother told how her six-year-old daughter was reluctant to take her teddy bear into school, even though they were having a teddy bears' picnic and this was allowed. "She was saying to me, 'Mummy, I think

---

[1] Listening Posts are a methodology developed by OPUS (an Organisation for Promoting Understanding of Society) to reflect on societal dynamics by way of group discussion. See www.opus.co.uk. This event with forty-two participants was held online on 19 June 2021 and was convened by Tim Dartington, Olya Khaleelee, and Carlos Remotti-Breton.

you've made a mistake.'" She had great difficulty persuading the child that it was safe to bring the teddy into school because of the virus. She was reminded that she herself always had a very close relationship with death, having been very sick as a child and come close to dying, and this fear had been reawakened in her during the pandemic.

We heard also of a psychiatrist, dedicated to his patients, who had a long-standing fear that he would die away from his home, and people would see that his house had not been vacuum-cleaned recently. One can imagine the stress of always having to have one's affairs in order, not knowing the timing or manner of our death.

A recent UK immigrant, having arrived from the Far East, contracted the virus in the first wave. She thought she might die in a couple of days, or a week, so there was time to think about it and she wrote out the financial information that her family would need. She said that she felt peaceful at that time, as she saw what she meant to everyone in her life. She might be an alien in this country, but that was okay. At such a time she did not feel that she had to achieve something else.

Whatever the specifics of our experience it is in the context of an ongoing if largely inarticulate debate between heroic and stoical responses to what we are facing as an existential crisis of meaning, of identity and purpose. How we respond to vulnerability in others and in ourselves can be seen to lie somewhere on a continuum between heroic, a fight response—whatever the problem we can defeat it—and stoical, an acceptance, a working with what we cannot avoid or delay or get rid of, however difficult or distressing. Neither response is right or wrong— we need both—one more than the other at different times; and that is the difficulty, because these positions, the heroic and the stoical, may seem to be in conflict with each other. It is difficult, if not impossible, to integrate these responses.

Evidence of a heroic response could be the galvanising energy of mutual-aid Covid groups and extraordinary neighbourliness, a whole group collecting to do the gardening for an elderly woman! At the same time, key workers—like those working for London Transport— have been attacked and spat on: acts of destructive hatred, fuelled by fear.

NHS colleagues have resisted the title of hero. A Listening Post participant commented: "They hated that label because they couldn't talk about the overwhelming fear and the resentment and the anger and the other feelings they were carrying into the workplace—because they had been put on a pedestal and sooner or later you'll be knocked off, and they all knew that was coming." There are moments when we are aware of the enormity of what we are trying to do as we intervene in the lives of others. We need to pause and acknowledge what is happening. The stress on ICU nurses over the last year has been described in many ways, very often referring to their roles as involuntary intermediaries between a dying patient and loved ones banned from attending the bedside.

Boris Johnson talked of the care he received from the nurse who gave him one-to-one care when he was, as he later said, near death. This is the heroic model of health care, conducted by front-line staff, fighting an unseen enemy. That nurse has since resigned, exhausted and angry about the failure to support those who have been supporting us through the last year.

We need to acknowledge how we manage vulnerability, by denying it in ourselves, and not acknowledging how we fear the vulnerability of others. Denying vulnerability in ourselves is obvious enough, putting a brave face on it. Professionally, we are not going to be much use to others if we are breaking up ourselves.

Conversations with friends and colleagues have swung violently between extremes of complaint that our authorities, including governments, are not being clear in what they are asking, and at the same time, resentment at the unwarranted intrusion they are making into our lives.

A Listening Post participant who had been a refugee as a child in the US spoke of the desire to breathe freely and embrace an American identity, and of the return to a focus on the societal after the deeply individualistic times of the Trump presidency.

In the UK there is often reference back to Margaret Thatcher as prime minister and her reported view that there is no such thing as society: what she said in a magazine interview was, "There are individual men and women and there are families. And no government can do anything except through people, and people must look after themselves first. It is our duty to look after ourselves and then, also, to look after our neighbours" (*Woman's Own*, 1987). We may think that Covid has brought that way of thinking to the fore. We have seen a shift away from trust between government and citizens, an acceptance of untruthfulness and deceit in a society that feels oppressive to those excluded from its privileges.

The Listening Post discussion explored the fear of speaking out. "It is scary, when to speak out and when to stay silent. Taking political action sometimes feels risky. Not taking action [on climate change] and staying silent is the greater risk."

"How much can I actually say? If I say too much of what I feel, which is that I'm finding it really difficult. I wake up every morning feeling very anxious now."

"I'm also worried about our social response to the Covid crisis. This leads me to a lot of dark places. ... And then I start to think, what do people really think of me and are they a friend or are they a foe."

A common response is that it will take time to get used to this new reality. What then do we mean by resilience in this context of conflicting emotions, a wished-for independence and fear of dependency? Resilience—bouncing back after a mishap—is not as straightforward as it seems. Convalescence after illness has dropped out of our vocabulary, with an insistence that we be up and running as soon as possible according to a recovery model. Assimilation to the new normal is problematic and positivity is another word for denial, for looking always on the bright side.

We may think it is too easy to get depressed in these circumstances, when we are required to be cheerful in the face of adversity. We have also to be wary of the seductions of win–win thinking. This is the political language of resilience: embrace change, explore the importance of self-management in role, endorse the politics of salvation rather than revelation, develop coping mechanisms to face the challenge of individualistic social systems. Gordon Lawrence (2000) made this distinction between salvation and revelation—where we remain available for experience, even when we are feeling a bit mad, what in others we would call psychotic; and we can work to develop and scrutinise our own observations about what is happening, and even act on these insights to make things better.

A Listening Post comment: "We were experiencing the tension between the collective, all of us trying together in the pandemic to do the right thing, and the individuals who want the freedom to express their different points of view and take their authority to do that."

If our responses remain essentially individualistic—up to the individual to make the best of their circumstances—rather than systemic, a societal capacity to adapt to change and not be stuck with outdated responses that no longer work, we do not have to address more vigorously the systemic inequalities, including institutional racism and class difference.

If we emphasise the systemic, in the sense that as a society we have a continuing interaction with our environment to survive and thrive in the world, this would also require a philosophical and ethical approach, with some sense of the good life we aspire to, of a society that does not punish its members for their vulnerability.

From a psychoanalytic perspective, it was suggested in the Listening Post that our experience of the past eighteen months has been of collective trauma, embedded in an historical, psychological, and social culture. It may take a long time to work out what it all means, to take on board the impact, including that on relationships between the generations in thinking about life and death and mortality.

For those brought up during the reconstruction of a free society in the austerity years following World War Two, itself following the Great War that was going to end all wars, we are recognising the weakness of the argument for the inevitability of progress. We are observing unimaginable inequalities within advanced societies and between these societies and the rest of the world, as well as the early ravages of climate change affecting our global chances of survival.

The notion of collective trauma was supported by reference to the lockdown experience of children of Holocaust survivors, or the remembrance of the Irish famine. These thoughts were linked to the fear of deprivation and showed in the tendency for panic buying and hoarding during the first weeks of lockdown.

While there was a looking back to history, there was also a concern, expressed directly by those with children, to address the environmental issues which we seem to have failed on, and this in turn led us to get in touch with a "devastating shock of what the virus is doing and the lies of politicians". A report from a social dreaming matrix[2] (also refer

---

[2] A social dreaming matrix provides a space to enable the sharing of dreams and associations for their social rather than individual meaning. See www.socialdreaminginternational.net.

to Chapter 3 in this book) where Brexit was represented as "a wonderful gift from underground" and which turns out to be a bone, suggests ways that reality may come to the surface to be seen for what it is.

For someone who left urban living for the countryside some years ago, the Covid situation was an opportunity to live in a family bubble, walking the fields for exercise. Moving to a rural environment he had been an "incomer" to the local population but now he shared their apprehension of tourists, with the underlying fear that they would bring the virus from the metropolis. They had time to think of their vulnerabilities, and also what was going on in the wider world, where they could keep in touch with friends by Zoom.

The concept of vulnerability feels different in different societies. Our political position depends on what is preoccupying our minds. We might look at the ways we are defending against whatever threats we are perceiving. And these fears can be manipulated, as we know—with Brexit and the Trump presidency as provocative examples in the years before the pandemic.

"In the Middle East and the Indian subcontinent people may ask, why are you so afraid, when we have to go out and make some kind of a living?" This Listening Post question challenged the intuitive isolationism in our thinking. We are living in a society that is largely vaccinated and we realise that nevertheless the risks are far from equal. We may want to examine our place in the system and our own privileges and disadvantages, but this is a very incomplete exercise, someone said, and that is one of the discomforts. Your family is healthy but what about the key workers, who get ill? You would like to know more if you can, but do you really know the conditions in which they are living? And why do they earn as little as they do, and how come we cannot afford to pay more to the nurses we have been applauding during the pandemic (who are now exhausted and disillusioned)?

An aspect of citizenship is caregiving to those who are at greater risk. A factor in our suspicion of government is the divergence between the particular, personal experience, and the generalisable statistical data, that politicians refer to when they speak of following the science. However, their interpretation of data remains highly political, influenced by economic forecasts, as well as health warnings, and subject also to ideological bias along a liberal/authoritarian fault line.

Governments are less compassionate, generally speaking, than families or individuals, because they have to take account of the lowest-common-denominator considerations of the common good. At the same time, individuals and families can be as prejudiced and illogical as any government—as we know from the lack of wisdom in so much social media.

Optimism assumes a good outcome but hope in itself does not necessarily make that assumption. The Greek concept of *eudaimonia*—translated crudely as happiness and more strongly as flourishing—has been revived in the mindfulness practices that are part of the well-being programmes that are getting increased credibility as an alternative to medicine by prescription. A stoical stance is not to focus on what others are doing for better or worse but to give attention to one's own actions.

Individual personal experiences cannot be simplified, but are always raising questions of identity and citizenship. Think for example of talking with a mixed-heritage son: if he sees himself as black or "politically black", is this killing off half of his heritage? The father says, "There is so much splitting, while we try to understand the whole person." Or we may ourselves be thinking about Covid in an autistic way.

"Covid has given me the opportunity to take a breather." We know this expression—taking a breather—usually after a period of intensive exercise. In meditation and mindfulness practices, there is the concept of the pause, a minute or two of calm, stepping back mentally from the stresses of the moment. The trouble is, when we are stressed, that is easier said than done; our heads are buzzing, often with not always helpful repetitive thoughts, "I am very familiar with the defence of being busy and I've spent the whole of this period [of the pandemic] being over-busy … it is difficult to talk about what you actually feel about what's going on at the moment." How much is this a shared experience and how much is it about oneself?

"I learned the defence of being busy at boarding school … I am getting in touch with the anxieties that I had then … The physical fear at the beginning, specially for those in the vulnerable age group, may have gone, but it has left behind something that feels really difficult to process without being over-emotional … I like the idea that we need to pause and that it is difficult. I find reading novels much more difficult. Being so anxious we can't pause sometimes."

Towards the end of the Listening Post a participant identified one of the themes as not knowing, and the feeling that we don't know enough to make decisions for ourselves. And when we want to know, there are so many angles of view. There is so much information that is confusing or difficult that we have to put together.

"It's about being most of the time with contradictions and having much difficulty making any kind of sense of all the contradictions we have around us."

It is difficult to tolerate questioning. "You know it's socially constructed in some way and that there is no objectivity." It was said that those who had done the Covid research were not allowed to speak anymore and those whose who questioned what they were told have been lumped with right-wing political extremists, for example, the AfD (Alternative für Deutschland) in Germany.

"We are so naked, so denuded, and so vulnerable."

One of the most painful observations from early work at the Tavistock Institute with disability groups had to do with the concept of social death, an abandoning isolation that may precede a physical death. Eric Miller and colleagues argued for a balance between horticultural and warehousing models of care (Miller & Gwynne, 1972). What was called horticultural then has gained new credibility with the recovery model now in social care. The isolation of residents in care homes and their high mortality during the pandemic bring to mind the dangers of the warehousing model.

Lockdown encourages us to be fearful of strangers: a forced reclusivity that eats away at our social identity. We are set rules of social behaviour that has deliberately enforced social distancing, not just from strangers but from friends and family as well as strangers. Nevertheless, there is a selfless gene, it seems, of generosity to the stranger.

There is a tension in thinking who is a stranger in the situation we are in. It has become convoluted, how we connect with others, and define connection and strangeness. "A stranger is someone who is not yet a friend." We may want to note our own xenophobia, giving a cautious welcome, if at all, to migrants and refugees from war and pestilence. The prefix xeno- used to apply both to stranger and guest, as it was proper in ancient Greece to offer hospitality to a stranger—according to some sources, because the stranger might turn out to be a god in disguise.

We may have family in different countries and compare notes of what our different governments allow. We can have light-touch conversations with strangers we meet along the way. "I talk to people on the road all the time." This Irish woman then told of the time last Christmas when an elderly woman in her village died. Her sons had emigrated years before and returned for the funeral, which they absolutely needed, wanted, demanded, despite the restrictions, and a lot of people went to the funeral. As a result, the numbers of people contracting Covid increased, schools were closed, and a lot of people became sick: one of the sons, who had come and organised the funeral, himself died.

We might think here of a hierarchy of need, and the need was to go against all the rules and regulations, in order to mourn a much-loved mother.

A woman speaking from New Delhi in India, after experiencing two Covid waves, reflected how she was drawn inward but after a year something shifted. Her urban neighbourhood, where she lived, was more visible, in contrast to her work on rural development, and she was getting involved locally, more than in so to say normal times.

While we are more intimate with strangers, we may become estranged from friends. "I have friends who would have come to blows had they not been protected by Zoom." The speaker described how we may experience differences of opinion, perhaps about international conspiracy or the tyranny of pharmaceutical companies. Or we think there is an imprisonment of the citizen that has been constructed by the political authorities, and global corporations that control our lives at a distance. The oppression of Zoom makes it very difficult to work through such ideas, what is real and what is fantasy in our own position and the impact on our relationships. There is no safe quiet space where you can differ gently. We miss the opportunities to repair, to touch again and find common ground.

Object relations theory, in the context of the British or Kleinian school of psychoanalysis, diverges from Freud's belief that people are motivated primarily by sexual and aggressive drives, suggesting instead that we are motivated by the need for a meaningful contact with others—our need to form relationships. This is how the psychoanalyst Wilfred Bion put it from his understanding of group behaviour:

> If we think of a group as an aggregate of individuals all at the same level of regression, the task of the individual is to establish

contact with the emotional life of the group, as formidable to the adult as the relationship with the breast seems to be to the infant. (1961)

It would be difficult to overestimate the need for connection. This is how desperate we are to connect, despite our protestations of individual autonomy. Social isolation historically has always been a punishment, as it is in prisons—and in solitary confinement within prisons—or an extreme spiritual practice for ascetics. Even to be ordinarily reclusive may be taken as a sign of eccentricity.

We are experiencing the challenge to our capacity to connect, exacerbated by the pandemic and the macabre league tables in our minds of countries thought to have done well by their populations and those abandoned to their fate.

In the Listening Post there was therefore unsurprisingly much talk of the desire for connection, but also the suggestion that we are avoiding the desire for touch—a more divisive concept, perhaps, as for some that would be taking too much of a risk. Some aspects of isolation have provided relief from the fear of contagion, from personal intimacy and sexual contact, a fear of intercourse. Creating a baby is difficult, raising a baby can be exceptionally difficult: and creating a project may also be hard work, taking years of effort with no guarantee of success.

"We can't be resilient without having a community. And the ability in a community to relate and help others." The opportunity of being isolated gave people the opportunity to look at transitions (like that of going back into the world of work) that were difficult—"relating is really difficult". "I may have a row with my daughter, but I know I'll always be her mother and there will be time to recover." In a place of transition, what do we want to keep, what we will have to let go? And what do we have to face returning to?

Someone of the older generation does not think that there will be good news again in her lifetime: she despairs of national politics, of both the political parties in the UK, and of international politics, the shame of Afghanistan after the failed turkey shoot in Iraq. We have moved on a long way from Francis Fukuyama's assertions that liberal democracy and global market dynamics had brought us to the end of history.

Is it even a comfort to think we are entering a new Dark Age—the relief of giving up on the myth of progress? In this context, melancholia might seem to be appropriate.

So, the question about our capacity for resilience might be posited: How can we retain a sense of hope without succumbing to a false optimism? Resilience is not a soft option. Unspeakable decisions, like those that put the health of the economy against the health of the people, are best left, we think, to the politicians, who will surely get it wrong—such is our lack of trust in their judgement—or left unspoken, in a general haze of not-knowing.

Death-dealing illnesses without a known cure—once, it was TB, then cancers, lately dementia—now Covid-19—are provocative to our modern sensibilities, which demand that every tragic event has to be ascribed to human agency—so that the default position about any tragedy is that if another cannot be held to account, consciously or not, then the fault has to be one's own.

How does this work out in a pandemic? Heroic responses are interventionist, often dramatic, the triumph of hope over despair; this is the culture of intensive care units, and the artificial ventilation of the most seriously ill. Or we may see expressions of denial, that the virus is a hoax, or a conspiracy, or an enemy we can overcome through an effort of will. No one can doubt the importance of this strategy, and the story of the UK prime minister's own illness and subsequent recovery offers eloquent commentary on what it may mean in practice. The story is told in heroic terms.

Dominic Raab, then Boris Johnson's deputy, said: "I'm confident he will pull through because if there is one thing that I know about this prime minister, he is a fighter and he will be back leading us through this crisis in short order."

The impact of the Covid-19 pandemic on our systems of care has therefore followed a predictable pattern. Attention was focused on the capacity of the health services to cope, meaning the capacity of hospitals to cope—the rationale of the lockdown being the importance of flattening the curve, managing the demand on hospitals to provide inpatient services for those in extreme danger from the virus. The wider impact on our collective capacity to live with some equanimity in society is a work in progress.

As often happens, participants at the Listening Post seemed to appreciate the opportunity to take their discussion to small groups, and then there was a struggle to find common ground in the concluding session, with debriefing from these groups and a wish to generate common understanding about what we think is happening in society. The dialogue was full of ambivalence in our response to the pandemic. While the first outbreak made for heroic responses, later waves have led to more depressive responses—though there has also been despair. Participants then described how they were struggling to integrate conflicting emotions and how this leads to erratic behaviour, embracing strangers and spurning friends. This was the impact of collective trauma, where we are all in it together but feel separate and alone.

In Listening Post methodology, the dynamics of the discussion are relevant to exploring its meaning. An individual speaks passionately about an issue in his mind, but it is difficult for others to understand and there is not widespread interest in following his argument, and so he is isolated, as if he is the source of contamination. Small groups that report back their discussion are seen to be following the rules—and then there is the group that does not conform—demonstrating a discordant freedom of choice, like the anti-vaxxers? Someone from the "silent group" commented that "I couldn't put two words together about what we said."

However, the last word goes to a Listening Post participant:

> This is the phenomenon of coming out of a "bubble" and into "society" and finding stuff that we have not been hearing in our bit. We suddenly hear something quite different—as if it were coming in a kind of post-apocalyptic way out of my bunker—what is the world going to look like? Some of it will be neatly packaged and some of it will just blow my mind.

References

Bion, W. R. (1961). *Experiences in Groups*. London: Tavistock.
Freud, S. (1915b). Thoughts for the times on war and death. *S. E., 14*: 273–300. London: Hogarth.

Lawrence, W. G. (2000). The politics of salvation and revelation in the practice of consultancy. In: *Tongued with Fire: Groups in Experience*. London: Karnac.

Miller, E. J., & Gwynne, G. V. (1972). *Life Apart: Pilot Study of Residential Institutions for the Physically Handicapped and the Young Chronic Sick*. London: Tavistock.

Woman's Own (1987). Interview with Margaret Thatcher.

Part III

The fourth humiliation of humankind

Photo by Halina Brunning, 2018

CHAPTER 9

The virus as symbol for the fourth narcissistic blow to humankind

by Claudia Nagel

The symbolic meaning of the virus

Covid-19 is still a rather unknown virus yet has proven itself to be a long-term threat to humankind. Only enormous precautions, including the standstill of public and economic social life or widespread vaccination, seem to be the actual choices of the moment to contain the virus and its spread. Although not proven, it still seems possible that the virus entered the human world through a Wuhan animal market. The cohabitation of human beings with wildlife is apparently not as easily manageable as previously thought. A little virus, a small part of nature, has taken over and now governs the rulers of the world's largest countries. Hence, we can see the virus as an elusive rupture that might entail a new notion of our relationship with nature and the earth. The virus and its effects demonstrate the frailty and fragility of humankind which, we are only now beginning to understand, can easily be completely disrupted. It seems that the virus is speaking to us and teaching us that we, the humans, are not the rulers of nature. In that sense, the virus can be attributed a symbolic function. None of our technologies, global networking, or globalisation are helping us. Rather the contrary.

Furthermore, our moral capacity is being deeply questioned on several levels. I will explain this in detail a bit later.

I proposed in April 2020 that we can understand the effect of this virus (and maybe others later) as an expression of the fourth blow to human narcissism—that we are not the rulers of nature (Nagel, 2020).

Briefly, it was Freud who, in Lecture XVIII in *Introductory Lectures on Psycho-Analysis* (1916–17), talked about the three blows to human narcissism at the hand of science. He was building on Bois-Raymond's eulogy on "Darwin and Copernicus" that he gave in Berlin after Darwin's death in 1882 (reprinted in *Nature* in 1883) (see Horgan, 2015).

The first blow was dealt when we learnt with Copernicus (and before that, Alexandrian sciences) that the world and thus humankind is not the centre of the universe. The second was introduced with Darwin discovering that human life emerged from animal life. And the third was described by Freud: we and our egos are not even the master of our own (mind and soul) house, the unconscious is the final ruler. Although this also says something about Freud's narcissism, it illustrates that our anthropocentric worldview has already suffered some deep cracks. So, now a tiny little virus adds to this and shows us again that we are not the masters of nature and the earth—neither technologically, nor morally.

In the second and next part of this chapter, I will reflect on our wish to be the rulers of the earth. In the third part I will consider questions about the humiliation, about the nature of nature and humankind, particularly from a philosophical, especially moral-philosophical, perspective. In the fourth part I will explore why the only right way to act is in accordance with the ethics of humanity, and in the fifth part I will work out a framework for the ethics of care as a trait in humanity that is key to our future survival. I will focus on the role of leaders of organisations since they should guide and provide us with examples of what to do. I will look at their specific role and how they, and thus all of us, can contribute to bringing the ethics of care to life.

The illusion of being the ruler of the earth

Before Covid-19 there was a belief that we had already won our struggle against nature, that we had conquered nature and tamed its most ferocious and animalistic forces. Before Covid-19 we (I mean to say here: most of the Western world, this is the world I live in, the rest

I only know superficially) thought that we had subjugated the earth. We have not only explored, but exploited nature as if she were infinite. We have developed a global network through which people, goods, news, technologies, and science travel around the world. We have seemed to follow what has already been said in the Bible: "Be fruitful, and multiply, and replenish the earth, and subdue it: and have dominion over the fish of the sea, and over the fowl of the air, and over every living thing that moveth upon the earth"—without any consistent questioning of how far we can go. It seems as if there is no built-in brake in us humans that can control an "overheating of the engine" finally leading to its destruction. The boundless belief in our endless power certainly has traits of megalomania—feelings of personal omnipotence and grandeur. This is possibly one of the reasons why actions against climate change on the individual as well as societal level have never really worked out so far.

And now a tiny little creature brings societal and economic life to a complete standstill. Not only that, but it caught us rather unprepared. It spread easily over the whole world in no time, at great cost to life, and it still seems to be difficult to manage. Several vaccines have been developed—a huge research achievement—but it is not yet clear how they will cope with the mutations of the virus. Still, medicines have not yet been found—more than one and a half years after the virus was first detected—because the virus is such a tricky thing. To stem the spread is extremely difficult and makes the virus an enemy which some nations even try to combat as if they were at war.

The nature of nature

This notion of the virus representing a narcissistic blow to us human beings introduces a number of questions:

- What makes this insight so painful that we feel humiliated?
- What is nature, does it fight back, and does it have morals?
- What is it to be human—compared to the "rest" of nature?

When humankind feels humiliated, we must think about how to react to this emotional challenge. These questions need to be asked to better understand the consequences and our response to this narcissistic blow.

Why do we feel humiliated?

The spread of the virus and the standstill of society have been engendering overwhelming feelings of disappointment, helplessness, anxiety, denial, fury, and anger. These feelings result from the uncertainty around how to deal with the virus.

Yet there is another level of uncertainty on top of this. The loss of dominion, the loss of the security that comes from the knowledge that nature and the world is managed; belief in technology and science has been scattered into pieces. We have taken a blow to our belief that we can manage everything, that we as human beings are the overarching heroic force that is capable of subduing everything around us—other human beings as well as nature. The loss of this conviction has caused us to feel narcissistically injured—sometimes on a conscious, sometimes on an unconscious level. But now nature has "taken over" again. Some people even say that nature is fighting back against us humans since we did not listen and act soon enough regarding climate warnings and climate change.

Another layer of humiliation is added by what the virus has demanded of us, which is to retreat from our civilised, value- and culture-based moral duties and to act beyond moral choices. This challenge is part of the fourth narcissistic blow to humankind. The virus has imposed and still imposes difficult choices on us—on the doctors triaging treatment, as well as the triage of whom to vaccinate first. These difficult choices in a science-driven world have been unimaginable—at least in the Western world. What would help us make the decision for triages such as this? What shall we do? Or, as the philosopher would ask: what ought we to do? This is a question for moral judgement, and one would hope that these choices are somehow moral. But thinking it through leads us to the fact that no moral choice is possible; it is inherently impossible to be moral here. No human life is worth more than any other—no moral categories exist, whether by age, gender, skin colour, illness, money, power, or other criteria—none can apply. The German constitution (and the constitution of other nations) states: "Die Würde des Menschen ist unantastbar", which translates into "Human dignity is inviolable"—this also means that no life is worth more than another. This basic demand can also be found in the UN Declaration of Human Rights (Art 1: All human beings are born free and equal in dignity and rights. … Art 3: Everyone has the right to life, liberty and security of person). Unfortunately, we have had to observe, how, for example, Italian and American doctors were forced to exercise triages and how they felt the tragedy and pain in doing so, an almost unbearable and deeply traumatising experience for them.

A further layer of humiliation can be found in the etymological roots of the word. Interestingly, the words humiliation and human(e) originate from the same proto-Indo-European root word, which the Latin word "humanus" also stems from, "(dh)ghomon" or "dhghem". It literally means "earthling", an "earthly being" as opposed to the gods (https://etymonline.com/word/human). The word "humble" is also connected with this root word via the Latin "humus". So, being humiliated as well as being human(e) and becoming humble are connecting us with the earth—"we are made from earth and will return to earth".

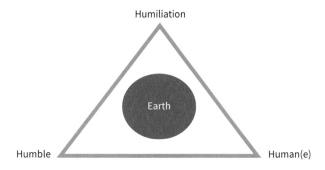

Figure 1. Earth as linking pin for humiliation

With the earth at the root-base for humiliation, humbleness, and humaneness the question of what the earth is, and by the same token what nature is, becomes prevalent. Even more so when we think about "nature fighting back", it is clear that we speak from a symbolic perspective. The same accounts for when we talk about the lesson the virus is teaching us or what kind of lesson nature wants to give us.

For both, if taken literally it would imply that nature and/or the virus act on the basis of reason and agency. It would mean that we ascribe nature and/or the virus the qualities of a subject. This leads to the following question:

What is nature?

Nature (in philosophy, where psychology once belonged) has two basic meanings: 1, the essence of something; 2, any observable material, organic or inorganic, being not made or created by humans (e.g. Vossenkuhl, 2002), and as such often used as a material counterpart to human beings and their actions; to freedom, mind, history, culture, and society. It seems plausible to say that nature is not a subject which could act out of free will, reflection, and reason. Schelling (1775–1854) is one of the rare (nature-) philosophers to have developed a different theory in which he understands nature not only holistically, but also as subject. This subject creates out of itself as *natura naturans*. Similarly to Goethe, he conceptualises nature as creating her own voices through which she can express herself—the highest voice being human reason. Nature produces itself, and in so doing follows fundamental principles (see Helferich, 1992). This is still an unusual perspective.

Today's nature philosophy does not discuss (to my knowledge) whether nature can act morally. What is discussed instead is whether animals can act morally. Non-human animals can now be understood as moral creatures, since elephants, rats, apes, cats, and dogs can act morally and might have moral-laden emotions, as Rowlands (2012) puts it. What is also discussed is, what kind of obligation do we as human beings have towards nature? (e.g. Krebs, 1993). Whichever way we take our thinking—human reason as the highest voice of nature or nature as a counter pole to humans, and as such having limited agency—the question remains: what makes us human and by that (hopefully) humane?

What makes us human and, by that, humane?

What is it that makes us humans human compared to non-human nature?

One of the important differences between human and most non-human animals as part of nature (this is today's conviction) is the cognitive capacity to imagine the future, to plan into the future and in so doing, to reflect on the consequences of actions, to look for and choose between alternatives and to have the capacity to change plans.

Looking into the (near or far) future is always connected to the basic question of "what do I do next?" and by that, "what shall I do?" or "what ought I to do?" (in the sense of Kant). This posits that there is an "I" which asks that question, that the I can reflect itself, and that there is the potential to act (Butler, 2003). Coming from this core question, our human existence is inherently embedded in a social context and is undoubtedly moral. Without the Other, the question would not make sense, since it is (of course, not only) the imagined Other which limits our actions in the way that there are norms, rules, and regulations.

The question the I asks implies the outer Other as creating or being the boundary for actions, and it also refers to the inner other to which we are accountable. The inner other can be the conscience, the superego, God, or the representation of an external judge. Giving an account of what we do entails judgement and values. In general, and based on experience, we can say that most humans think about how to lead a good life and how to behave in a good way. Moral action based on these reflections presupposes the concept of freedom and voluntariness. Out of these grow responsibility and accountability.

An action is said to be moral if it is evaluated according to the individual conscience of the person acting, while ethical means that the action is based on a system of morality and morals (Anzenbacher, 1992). An action can therefore be called ethical depending on, and changing with, the norms stemming from the system of morals and morality. As a philosophical discipline, ethics goes back to Aristotle, who took up older approaches such as those of Plato or Socrates. The term "ethics" comes from the Greek "ethikos" and means moral or moral through custom. The Greek "ethos" means custom or habit. Guided by the idea of a meaningful human life, that is, a morally good and just life, philosophical ethics tries to make universally valid statements about good and just action in a methodical way—and without appealing to political and religious authorities or to what is tried and tested. It is about answering the questions "What should I do? Who do I want to be, how do I want to live? What is a successful, a happy and fortunate existence?" complemented by questions such as, "In what social and political environment do we want to and should we live?" (Höffe, 1999).

Jung (1995, §825–857), however, asserts that ethics and morals are innate, since without the ability of the psyche to experience guilt there can be no sense of guilt. Jung understands ethos as a "special case of the transcendent function" which connects the unconscious with the conscious. Only in the conscious, reflective examination of one's own actions can what appears to be moral conduct be changed into ethical conduct.

In contrast, Freud (e.g. 1930a) views morality as a strategy, in which culture, indirectly also serving the pleasure principle, attempts to defend itself against the destructiveness of aggression. Culture virtually installs the superego in the individual to serve as his conscience to constrain the ego; this leads to the development of a sense of guilt and the need for punishment, and thus to the reduction of aggression. Freud considers the quest for the highest good, the purpose in life, as emerging from the pleasure principle, which takes priority over everything else. This would, however, completely instrumentalise reason and cannot become practical as pure reason in the sense of Kant. In turn, this would form the first result in the levelling of an independent meaning of morality (Anzenbacher, 1992).

Kohlberg has developed an influential model on how moral thinking develops. It comprises three levels: pre-conventional, conventional, and post conventional, and develops from obedience and punishment orientation through self-interest and conformity to social contracts and universal ethical principles (e.g. Kohlberg, 1976). At the end of this development stands the individual as an independent subject who follows their free moral choice based on universal ethical principles. This theory of moral development is based on the morality of justice and rights. It has been furthered by Gilligan (1982), who introduced the moral concept of caring. She differentiates between justice and caring as alternative perspectives, since all human relations can be characterised in terms of equality and attachment, and that inequality, separation, and complacency pose moral problems. The basic questions of "acting unfairly" and "not helping somebody in a time of need" mirror these positions as well. By including care, she integrates the female perspective into moral philosophy and ethics.

Table 1. Characteristics of the moral demands of care and justice

	Care	Justice
Framework	Attachment	Equality
Postulate	Help in times of need	Fairness
Prerequisite	Social context Socialisation/education	Freedom Voluntarism
Dominant feelings	Affection and empathy	Need for justice
Reason for moral problems	Separation/indifference, complacency	Inequality
Gender attribution	Rather female	Rather male

The reflection of justice and care, of equality and relatedness, are attributed to us humans as central to our way of being, to "our nature" so to speak. As already mentioned, both need freedom and voluntarism as well as socialisation and education. By that we can now claim that humanity is built upon these central human aspects. They demand that we become more humane by continuously self-reflecting and self-developing with the goal of leading a good and thus, a fulfilled life.

Without wanting to judge whether animals can act morally, we can say that our capacity for moral action and ethical reflection differentiates us at least from many aspects of nature (I do not want to follow the anthropocentric nature-philosophy that claims only humans are moral beings). Today we can also assume that nature as such is not a subject in itself and is thus neither good nor bad, it just is. Nature cannot justify pain. Thinking about, for example, the Christian God as "representative" of the subject of nature, we have difficulty finding a justification for pain and suffering (the question of theodicy). Job's quarrel with Yahweh in the Bible is a good example, where at the end Yahweh indirectly surrenders while expressing that he was not able to justify his doing so.

A deduction from the fact that nature just *is* must be that illness and death also simply exist, as a part of life and that there need be no reason for pain and suffering—it just exists, as does life. Life "has no object other than life itself. Life here is a possibility, a potentiality that never exhausts itself in biographical facts and events, since it has no object other than itself" (Agamben, 2001, p. 122). With that we can also say that the life of the virus has no other object than to live!

Humanity as an answer to the virus and the fourth blow

The appearance of the virus and its symbolic meaning as the fourth narcissistic blow can have a meaning for us—and most media and many authors at the beginning of the pandemic claimed the need for profound change to a life less driven by money, consumption, and success, more healthy, more local, and more profound. With the duration of the pandemic, this vision has been lost and has ended up as a much simpler discussion on how to design hybrid workplaces—which allow working from home as well as working on-site. Let alone that this proposition might only apply to a fraction of the worldwide workforce, other roles more often demand a physical presence: think of doctors and nurses, and those in farming, public and freight transport, building infrastructure, gardening and forestry, mining rare earth materials, among many others. This banal question reduces the answer to an avoidance or a neglect of our role for and in nature.

The virus presents a "rupture", totally contingent, unpredictable and (so far) uncontrollable (Di Nicola, 2018). A rupture is a painful moment, a moment when something unexpected and fundamentally different happens. A rupture needs to be reacted to, as no reaction would itself also be a reaction. When we understand this rupture as an "event" (in the language of the French philosopher Alain Badiou), it may lead to an opening for new possibilities. Then novelty and real change are possible. When the predicament is mishandled, it could lead to trauma, a closing down of the possibilities. Di Nicola (2018) applies this to the individual, but I would like to widen his perspective to groups, organisations, and to society. To transform the rupture into an "event" with an opportunity for change, we have to (self-)contain, stay true to this event and integrate it. Without containment and integration the rupture can become a trauma, which will be difficult to heal and will close the door on further development.

What is most vital is to rethink our relationship to ourselves as humankind and to nature as such. If finally, we cannot and shall not subjugate nature, then we have to think about how best to play our part in nature within the possibilities of our human nature and its qualities. The questions are, therefore: What can we contribute? How can our specific nature serve Mother Earth as well as ourselves?

As demonstrated, we humans are moral beings, and have by that the obligation to act ethically. From the standpoint of humanity, the foundations for our moral reasoning are care and justice.

Ethics based on justice claim inviolable human dignity, equality, and freedom as core values. Much has been said about this aspect of humanity. It focuses on the development of the individual and their language, emotional, cultural, social, and creative capabilities, and, on the other hand, on the creation of legal and social systems fostering human dignity in all areas of life (education, work, public administration, as well as the penal system) (e.g. Höffe, 2002). The rise of identity politics has been one translation of this moral request—the turn to identitarianism has become the unfortunate perversion into moralism with the subsequent loss of morals (yes, I agree, this would need a longer discussion).

Interestingly, Butler (2003, p. 94) designates the limits of reason as a sign of our humanity. Only in our relatedness with "the Other in me" can the ethical relation to the other develop, and only by being open and influenced by the other and by thus being vulnerable can ethical reflection start. In her Adorno Lectures 2002 Butler claims, in agreement with Nietzsche and Freud, that bad conscience drives the individual into (moral) narcissism, which makes relations with the other impossible and thus destroys our liveliness. Being related means being alive. If we could interpenetrate everything with reason, we would not only deny being open, related, and dependent, but also we would no longer be psychological beings who love, feel pain, and can be enchanted as well as hurt. Although we want to protect ourselves against being hurt, we would become inhumane if this protection was complete. I want to follow Butler (and Adorno) in understanding humanity as relatedness with the other, as the acknowledgement of our own fallibility as well as our vulnerability. In doing so, ethical actions include the other, the care for the other, and the care for relatedness. Our survival depends not on our concordance, but on our connectedness (Gilligan, 1988), or as Plato puts it, "gods and men are held together by communion and friendship ..." (Plato, 508a).

Humanity of care and connectedness/communion and its link with the earth

Connectedness and care are based on the insight of vulnerability and fallibility. Only when I can see myself as committing errors and being hurt can I care for another (human) being. Care implies love and other positive emotions as the basis for connectedness, that is to say, empathy, appreciation, warmth, containment. Care and connectedness can be integrated in the above-mentioned connection between humiliation, humaneness, and humbleness since they belong to the nature of being human and humane. It symbolically closes the circle of being human around the earth as core.

Figure 2. Humanity of care and connectedness closes the circle

The lesson

Is it not interesting that in times of a worldwide outcry or request for connectedness, the only way of connecting we see is either virtually via the internet or—if existent—with the core family around the so-called home office. Being (more) human(e), and humanity as reflected in care and connectedness, should be the core driver for all that we do—if we want to survive together with the earth and nature.

There are two ways for us to translate care and connectedness: we need to take care of nature and connect with it, and we need to take care of humankind and its connectedness which can as well be transliterated into creating a sense of community. The climate protection debate and nature ethics already reflect in depth how we should take care of the earth and nature.

Hence, here I would like to focus on how positively to impact the interhuman psychodynamics of care and connectedness in daily life and in leadership.

Organisations are the institutions where most people spend most of their daily lives, even more than with their family or friends. By organisations, I mean all types of organised social systems created for working on a task—from an association, NGO, or political party to a corporation or a public administration body. Organisations are inherently social, and thus a place where people meet and connect. They pervade all areas of human life and have many different faces. When thinking about creating more humanity, it thus makes sense to focus on organisational leaders and leadership as they have the biggest impact on organisations.

How to build more connectedness—containment and authentic leadership

Before the pandemic, American people working in organisations, for example, spent 5% of their working time at home; by spring 2020 this figure grew to 60%. This development did not continue, but it is assumed that in a future hybrid work environment, 25% to 30% of working time will be spent at home. The advantage, that apparently many managers only recently discovered, was that the workforce consists of real people in real homes with real children and the need to cook dinner or to get the washing machine running (*The Economist*, 2021).

This seems to have created a better understanding of the human needs of working people. However, more and more voices are of the opinion that creative thinking, problem-solving, and innovation are difficult and less productive when groups are limited to online interaction. On the other hand, remote working can bring people together across time zones and countries and supports the development of mutual understanding. It is therefore important for leaders to connect both worlds—the virtual and the real—and create connectedness and a sense of community and care. Elsewhere I have explored the need in times of crisis to create organisational hope and identity via containment, authentic leadership, and staying in role and task (Nagel, 2021a). This also applies here.

The biggest enemy of real connectedness (not fantasised, imagined, or defensive) in organisations and groups is anxiety and fear. Primarily it is acted out in different basic assumption mentalities, a notion developed by Bion (1962) and further developed in the realm of psycho- and socio-analysis by several different authors (Turquet, Lawrence, Bain & Gould, Hatcher-Caro, and Nagel; for an overview see Nagel, 2021b). The antidote to group defences such as basic assumptions is containment—from the leader and from other organisational members. Containment is creating a safe space for transforming negative emotions. This safe space can develop within the relationship of two people, in a group, in an organisation, or even via structures and processes. The capacity for containment is part of the human life-long developmental process, and not only applies to containing others, but also to oneself. Both, containing another and self-containment, are closely linked to *negative capability* (Simpson & French, 2006)—the capacity to bear ambiguities, ambivalences, and the accompanying emotions of stress and anxiety of the unknown without falling apart or rushing into a split (-decision) in later life. This negative capability is extremely important for leaders since they continuously find themselves in ambiguous and ambivalent situations where they must make a decision and where no decision is itself also a decision.

Containment and being held by being in a safe space are a life-long necessity and are the factors that differentiate healthy and destructive relationships. This capacity to contain depends on a receptive and open attitude, forgoing immediate action, not letting pressure and thus anxiety take over, and allowing for thoughts and things to develop.

Leaders can build psychological safety by creating the right climate, mindset, and behaviour within their teams to deal with negative emotions and difficult moments. They can also act as catalysts, empowering and enabling other leaders on the team—even those with no formal authority—to help cultivate psychological safety by role-modelling and reinforcing the behaviours they expect from the rest of the team. The result is that people dare to share what they think and feel around work-related issues (in a socially acceptable manner) without fear of being punished. In sharing what they experience and feel, a sense of community can develop. Creating containment in a virtual world seems to be a real challenge, and in the actual discussion difficult social conversations should take place in face-to-face meetings.

Authentic leadership may consist of charisma or idealised influence (attributed or behavioural), inspirational motivation and intellectual (and spiritual) stimulation, and individualised consideration. Others see in it not a particular leadership style, but a "root construct … (which) fosters high levels of trust which in turn encourage people to be more positive, to build on their strength, to expand their horizons of thinking, to act ethically and morally and to be committed to continuous improvement in organisation performance" (Helland & Winston, 2005, p. 49). This therefore allows for effective leadership. One of the keys to effective and authentic leadership is hope as an overall common process. The aim of effective leadership is to attain shared organisational goals that are beneficial for all stakeholders (Helland & Winston, 2005).

When claiming authentic leadership, however, two aspects need to be considered and adapted. Authenticity in leadership shall not mean getting stuck in a non-adaptive, rigid leadership style—new experiences and a new context will change the person and require adaptation in leading authentically (Ibarra, 2015). Furthermore, authenticity in this context does not mean to "authentically" act out all emotions and thoughts that come to the mind of the leader. Self-containment is a crucial attribute, as is the request to stay in role and task.

The next figure summarises in an overview the described contributions from leaders, followers, and integrational and external contributors that can create care and community together with containment for increasing humanity, and thus provide an answer to the fourth narcissistic blow.

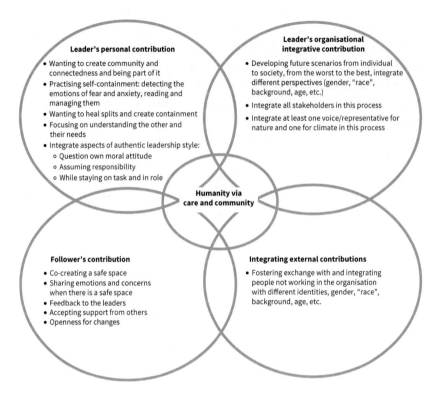

Figure 3. Necessary contributions for a humanity of care and communion in organisations. Adapted from Nagel (2021a)

Conclusion

In trying to understand the ignominy caused by the virus as a symbol of the fourth humiliation, it becomes noticeably clear that we human beings need to think deeply about how to react. Being part of nature, the virus forces us to reflect on how we can humbly contribute to the nature of which we are part. One of the major advantages of humans is that we have the capacity for moral action and ethical reflection, and by that, for humanity. Ethics of care and justice are at the core of finding answers to how we react to the virus, particularly the ethics of care in focusing on community and connectedness. I have here focused on leaders of organisations since they have the most outreach in the everyday lives of many people.

References

Agamben, G. (2001). For a philosophy of infancy. *Public*, *21*. https://public.journals.yorku.ca/index.php/public/article/view/29996 (last accessed April 4, 2022).

Anzenbacher, A. (1992). *Einführung in die Ethik*. Düsseldorf, Germany: Patmos.

Bion, W. R. (1962). *Learning from Experience*. London: Karnac.

Butler, J. (2003). *Kritik der ethischen Gewalt. Adorno Vorlesungen 2002*. Frankfurt, Germany: Suhrkamp.

Di Nicola, V. (2018). Two trauma communities: A philosophical archaeology of cultural and clinical trauma theories. In: P. Capretto & E. Boynton (Eds.), *Trauma and Transcendence: Suffering and the Limits of Theory* (pp. 17–52). New York: Fordham University Press.

Economist, The (2021, April 8). From desktop to laptop. The shift of a hybrid world of work will have an impact on managers.

Freud, S. (1916–17). *Introductory Lectures on Psycho-Analysis* (XVIII: Fixation to the traumas: The unconscious). *S. E., 15*: 273–285. London: Hogarth.

Freud, S. (1930a). *Civilization and its Discontents*. *S. E. 21*: 59–148. London: Hogarth.

Gilligan, C. (1982). *In a Different Voice. Psychological Theory and Women's Development*. Cambridge, MA: Harvard University Press.

Gilligan, C. (1988). *Mapping the Moral Domain: A Contribution of Women's Thinking to Psychological Theory and Education*. Cambridge, MA: Center for the Study of Gender, Education, and Human Development, Harvard University Graduate School of Education.

Helferich, C. (1992). *Geschichte der Philosophie*. Stuttgart, Germany: J. B. Metzler.

Helland, M. R., & Winston, B. E. (2005). Towards a deeper understanding of hope and leadership. *Journal of Leadership and Organizational Studies*, *12*(2): 42–54.

Höffe, O. (1999). *Lesebuch zur Ethik. Philosophische Texte von der Antike bis zur Gegenwart*. Munich, Germany: C. H. Beck.

Höffe, O. (2002). Humanität. In: O. Höffe. *Lexikon der Ethik*, 6th edition (pp. 120–121). Munich, Germany: C. H. Beck.

Horgan, J. (2015). Copernicus, Darwin and Freud: A Tale of Science and Narcissism. Freud did not originate his famous description of Copernicus and

Darwin as deflators of humanity's anthropomorphic worldview. https://blogs.scientificamerican.com/cross-check/copernicus-darwin-and-freud-a-tale-of-science-and-narcissism/ (last accessed April 4, 2022).

Ibarra, H. (2015). The authenticity paradox. Why feeling like a fake can be a sign of growth. *Harvard Business Review, 93*(1/2): 53–59.

Jung, C. G. (1995). Zivilisation im Übergang. *G. W., 10*. Solothurn, Germany: Walter.

Kohlberg, L. (1976). Moral stages and moralization: The cognitive-developmental approach. In: T. Lickona (Ed.), *Moral Development and Behavior: Theory, Research and Social Issues*. New York: Holt, Rinehart and Winston.

Krebs, A. (1993). Haben wir moralische Pflichten gegenüber Tieren? Das pathozentrische Argument in der Naturethik. *Deutsche Zeitschrift für Philosophie, 41*(6): 995–1008.

Nagel, C. (2020). COVID19 presents us with the fourth narcissistic blow to humankind—not only leaders need to recollect their human qualities. http://nagel-company.com/files/blog/essays/COVID19_as_the_4th_narcissistic_blow_to_humankind-Claudia_Nagel_April_2020.pdf (last accessed April 4, 2022).

Nagel, C. (2021a). Leader or victim or both? The role of containment in times of crisis. Presentation at the VI international conference of the Association for Psychoanalytical Coaching and Business Consulting, "Energy of Business". Moscow, May 12–13, 2021.

Nagel, C. (2021b). On the psychodynamics of hope and identity in times of crisis: Why they are needed when basic assumption victimism/supremacism prevail. *Organisational and Social Dynamics, 21*(1): 56–77.

Plato. *Gorgias*. Revised edition. W. & C. Emlyn-Jones (Trans.). London: Penguin Classics, 2004.

Rowlands, M. (2012). *Can Animals Be Moral?* New York: Oxford University Press.

Simpson, P., & French, R. (2006). Negative capability and the capacity to think in the present moment: Some implications for leadership practice. *Leadership, 2*(2): 245–255.

Vossenkuhl, W. (2002). Natur. In: O. Höffe (Ed.), *Lexikon der Ethik*, 6th edition (pp. 185–186). Munich, Germany: C. H. Beck.

CHAPTER 10

Covid—an intrusion of the Real

by Simon Western

Introduction

The Covid pandemic is the biggest single disrupting global event since World War Two. It exposes our human fragility in devastating ways, and at the same time opens a new space of possibilities, revealing our collective capacity to respond to disruptions in ways previously unimaginable. The social lockdowns, mask wearing, state financial interventions, and speed of vaccine production have been unprecedented.

This chapter will make connections between the Covid-19 pandemic and other disruptions in our life-worlds. These disruptions seem very different, such as the climate crisis or the technological revolution, yet they are intimately connected and have commonalities. Most importantly, they all require a similar leadership, and a social, political, and organisational response.

The chapter has three parts. First, it sets out a view of the Covid pandemic that situates it as a "modernity problem". Second, it discusses and makes connections between the triple disruptions of our times; the technological revolution, environmental crisis, and social-global disruptions, making a case for Eco-Leadership to address these disruptions. It concludes by discussing the P.I. age, claiming that P.I. (precarious-interdependence) is the master signifier of a new epoch. The P.I. epoch demands a shift away from the modernist mindsets in which we are entrapped. Only by developing new mindsets, new ways of thinking, and discovering emergent ways of how humanity relates to our "being-in-the-world" (Heidegger, 1927) and "being-of-the-world", will we be able to adapt and regenerate.

Covid—a modernity problem

In 2019, at the beginning of the pandemic, I wrote an essay (later published in Western, 2020) that proposed that Covid was an "Event" (Badiou, 2007), an intrusion of the "Real".

> Covid is an intrusion of the (Lacanian) Real into our imaginary worlds, destabilising us in ways that are unfolding. The Real in psychoanalytic terms is something beyond language, an essence that cannot be symbolised. It is beyond knowledge but exposes a truth that speaks to our condition and demands something from us. Alain Badiou writes that an Event (*événement*) is "a multiple which basically does not make sense according to the rules of the situation". Covid-19 is such an Event, because its causation is multiple, and it undoes our twentieth-century fantasy that science and mankind have conquered nature, or as French psychoanalyst J. A. Miller writes, "I would say that capitalism and science combine, they have combined, to make nature disappear." (Western, 2020, p. 2)

The combination of science and capitalism can be also read as modernity. The modern ethos, the cultures and the subjectivities it produces, has attempted to make nature disappear in the sense that it separates nature from the human race. It divides nature from humanity, and until we understand how to undo this misstep, we will be condemned to repeat pandemics, wars, and environmental carnage.

The project of modernity can be defined as a project of divide, control, and extraction. Modernity set out specifically to control nature. The wildness of nature, and the wildness of human nature were to be tamed, civilised, and controlled by applying the new modern faith of science, capitalism, and reason. Modernity naturalised division and control, whereas in pre-modernity things were connected and entangled. When there was trouble in nature, it was related to trouble with the gods, and trouble in the human sphere. To have an impact in one area, all three areas had to be addressed. Paying homage to the gods, changing human sinful ways, or perhaps offering sacrifices, would hopefully impact on the wrath of nature. The pre-modern world was an enchanted world, and while we can scoff at the "magic" and irrational and unscientific ideas, there was also a wisdom that was lost as we gained more information and more knowledge in our race to be modern. This lost wisdom is our connectedness and interdependence with the environment, the material world, and our shared humanity with others. T. S. Eliot understood this well and expressed it in his poem "The Rock" (1934), a critique of modernism:

> Where is the Life we have lost in living?
> Where is the wisdom we have lost in knowledge?
> Where is the knowledge we have lost in information?
> The cycles of Heaven in twenty centuries bring us farther from
> GOD and nearer to the Dust. (Eliot, 1963)

Darwin and others categorised and divided animals and plants into species, and social sciences did the same with people. This path led to eugenics that still influences psychological and sociological thinking today (Pilgrim, 2008). Modernity divided humans into ethnic species, classes, and many other subcategories. The nation state, for example, is taken for granted as a norm yet is a fairly recent invention (Anderson, 2006). Nations were created, dismantled, and divided through wars and with pencils and rulers on maps. The division usually was decided on the basis of resources, power, political advantage, and convenience by imperialists and colonialists. The Middle East was carved up between Britain and French colonialists in 1916, when representatives of Great Britain and France secretly reached an accord, known as the Sykes–Picot Agreement, and the fallout continues today. Interestingly, even the most stable and long-established states such as the United Kingdom continue to be in dispute and flux, with Northern Ireland, Scotland, and Wales in constant tension over independence and governance issues, and the UK in constant tension in its relations to Europe and others. The idea of a stable state is a fantasy, as is the idea of stable boundaries in other categories and spheres. In the economic sphere, Taylorism oversaw the division of labour and close control of the worker in the factory, applying scientific rigour to work, giving birth to the Fordist production line and mass production. These economic changes led to social changes such as urbanisation, mass consumption, and new political, social, and subjective ways of living and being. The modern subject became a divided self (Laing, 1960), an alienated being detached from human nature. Extractive capitalism used the "natural" environment and human beings as a limitless and throwaway resource. The plantation, slavery, the workhouse, and the factory were connected, and management methods used today were derived from this past (Steiner, 2019). The Covid pandemic is a part of this evolving narrative, arising not only from an aberrant virus, but also from the results of modernity and its pervasive ethos. The Covid pandemic arose due to dense urbanisation, crowded markets with live animals, our extractive dietary and food organisation processes, loss of biodiversity, and mass air travel.

We are now having to face what has been denied and repressed. A world where extraction and exploitation, division and control, progress and growth have left us facing an environmental crisis that will cause monumental damage both to human lives, and to our multi-species kin.

Modernity was born from extracting natural resources without limit, extracting slaves from Africa, extracting labour from the poor, and always dividing humans from "nature", and in doing so, extracting vitality from our souls. Modernity brought great advances in health care, and a rise in living standards for billions, alongside terrible wars and living conditions where the poor suffered and continue to suffer unimaginably. Great gains were made, but the cost and damage done has been beyond measurement.

A fantasy of domination and omnipotence

The fantasy of our "domination" and control has been subverted by the pandemic, and the climate crisis reveals a fragile Anthropocene, and desperate displacement of people, water, and carbon, and a huge loss of biodiversity. The pandemic is not separate from this environmental crisis, it is another part of the lesser told story that undoes the modernity faith. This different story tells us that we are entangled, enmeshed, connected, and interdependent, rather than being above, separate, divided, and in control (Haraway, 2016; Latour, 2013; Tsing, 2015). There is an urgent need to liberate ourselves from modernity.

> We live in times where the Real of nature is re-appearing in traumatic ways, undoing human omnipotent fantasies. The macro ecosystems of the climate crisis are imposing themselves, and micro ecosystems have unleashed a viral contagion that is shaking the world. (Western, 2020, p. 3)

Covid-19, portrayed as the latest example of untamed nature inflicting itself upon our civilised selves, is the dominant "modernity" narrative we are told. The other is that the "bad other" misused our scientific brilliance to create the rogue virus in a laboratory. Both narratives divide and situate humans outside nature, either being traumatised by wild nature, or by interfering with the "natural" order of things. The dominant media/political narratives point to the solution that we apply—"more of the same", that is, more "capitalism-science" (Miller, 2012) to control nature once again. Yet despite the vaccination programmes, we are beginning to realise that the problems we are trying to solve are not linear or solvable. We are configuring the problems with such a limited modernist worldview that we have become stuck. We are in a cul-de-sac of thinking. Donna Haraway urges us to think, saying, "Think we must, we must think," and yet warns us that "It matters what ideas we use to think other ideas. It matters what thoughts think thoughts. It matters what knowledges know knowledges. It matters what relations relate relations. It matters what worlds world worlds. It matters what stories tell stories" (2016, pp. 34–35). The thinking, the stories, the relations, and the knowledge we have entrapped in our modernist ways of being, and the challenge we face is to find new ways to think, relate, and tell new stories.

Modernity mindsets cannot cure the world of this virus or the other environmental or other intrusions of the Real that are impacting upon us. This is because the problems we face are only symptoms of our entrapped ways of thinking and being.

The brilliance of science that so quickly developed vaccines does not escape the political and human capacity for sabotaging our potential success. Leaving huge swathes of unvaccinated populations, whether because profit prevents poorer nations getting vaccinated, or conspiracy theories prevent the muddled minds of distrusting vaccine resisters. There is no such thing as pure neutral science. Bruno Latour (2012) embraces sciences not science; the rhetoric we heard from politicians during the pandemic "We are following the science" was problematic: the question of which science arises. Scientists from different backgrounds debated and argued, scientists from the same backgrounds debated and argued, politicians and economists, social scientists and empirical hard scientists contested what to do, what the research and data meant. Different countries and different politicians and different scientists drew different conclusions. There is no higher unified authority to tell us the answer (Haraway, 2016, p. 41): this is a modernist expectation, hierarchy, experts, knowledge in a pyramid. Yes, we must listen to the (plural) science/s, and make contingent decisions as best we can. We must also think in new ways.

Science cannot be unified or divided from politics and power. This doesn't diminish the importance of science, it gives us more data to understand why mistakes are made, why we cannot rely on "science" because politics are entangled in decision-making. There are many sciences, not one omnipotent neutral, outside force called "science". Who gets the vaccines? Which vaccines get media praise, and which vaccines get distorted and undermined by the media, or by competing pharmaceutical corporations? What interests are at play? These are power games being played out under an umbrella "listen to the science" mantra. Science, like everything else, is entangled, connected, and interdependent.

The Covid pandemic is a warning; it is an amplifier of what already exists. It warns us to lose our attachment and devotion to human omnipotence, and to traverse the fantasy that the ethos of modernity can save us. There is an urgent demand to start developing new narratives that recover our lost sense of belonging to this planet, and to learn to live with precarity, fragility, connectedness, and interdependence in new ways.

Covid—a hybrid ecosystem

The Covid-19 pandemic is a network of actants, a hybrid and complex ecosystem consisting of technology, the social, and the environment. Castells (2011) describes our age as the "network society". Castells is right to point to the impact of the digital age of networked information, yet the networked society we live in transcends the digital platforms he identifies. Bruno Latour and actor-network theory taught us that human and non-human actants combine to create networks (Latour, 2005). The non-human Latour refers to consist of technology, machines, material objects, and the natural environment. Together, this ecology of "things" creates dynamic interdependent ecosystems. If we look at Covid through this lens we see that:

> Covid-19 evolved within a network consisting of animals and humans, viruses and marketplaces, urban density and social etiquettes, political actions and decisions, economic practices, globalised trade, mass travel and digital information networks and emotional and affective networks (Ahmed, 2013). Collectively these and other actants became a stable enough network, enabling the pandemic to occur. (Western, 2020, p. 4)

The Covid ecosystem is entangled in the triple ecosystem disruptions we face in all areas of our lives.

Triple disruption—one ecosystem

In the first edition of *Leadership: A Critical Text* (2007) I wrote that we face a triple disruption.

1. Technological revolution
Digitalisation, the internet of things, artificial intelligence, quantum computing are examples of a technological revolution that will continually and exponentially disrupt our life-worlds and the planet.

2. Social disruption
Geopolitical, political, and economic pressures and globalisation are macro disrupters. Social changes are also impacted by technological

and other societal shifts such as the demographics of health, diet, and ageing. Cultural and collective social changes such as the rise of consumerism alongside individualism and psychological, emotional, and relational changes are also disruptors. One of the greatest challenges we face today is social inequity; the gap between rich and poor has grown. Black Lives Matter protests reveal racial discontents, all of which undermine our humanity and our ability to develop sustainable and caring societies that can address the challenges we face.

3. Environment emergency
Local and global impacts from pollution to flooding, wildfires, and droughts are increasing, and global warming is irreversible according to the latest Intergovernmental Panel on Climate Change Report (https://www.ipcc.ch).

Modernity approaches these triple disruptors as divided entities and tries to solve them with linear problem-solution mindsets. There are massive shifts in acknowledging the challenges and realising the systemic interrelatedness of the challenges. Yet still our practices and problem-solving capacities return to existing modernist patterns. Our abilities to collaborate across siloed scientific and political boundaries remain very primitive and underdeveloped. Our biggest challenge is not to see the triple disruptions as separate entities that require connecting, to cross boundaries; but to see them as one hybrid, entangled and interconnected, interdependent ecosystem. The Covid pandemic was a result of this hybrid ecosystem and working to prevent and contain pandemics in the future will demand ecosystem responses. The environmental crisis drives technological and social changes, and technology and society have created the environmental crisis. This reciprocal circularity must be acknowledged and worked with in all the challenges we face.

Eco-Leadership

A shift in mindsets, narratives, and worldview is required, which will lead to new forms of organising and new forms of political, social, and economic leadership. The theory and practice of Eco-Leadership, developed over the past decade (Western, 2010, 2018, 2019), puts ecosystems at the heart of organising, and it addresses the triple disruptions as one ecosystem. Eco-Leadership is the most recent leadership organisational discourse, arising to adapt to the triple disruptions we face. The illustration below maps the four dominant leadership discourses. The Controller, Therapist, and Messiah discourses are all products of the modernist mindset. The Eco-Leadership discourse is an emergent new way of conceptualising leadership and organisation, and it can be applied to businesses, public and non-profit organisations, as well as to political and social leadership. Social movements have pioneered Eco-Leadership; one such example comes from researching the "occupy" movement, which I named as autonomist leadership (Western, 2014).

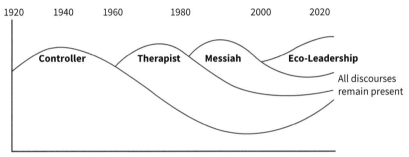

The four discourses of leadership. (Originally published in Western, S. (2019). *Leadership: A Critical Text*. 3rd edn. London: SAGE as Figure 8.1, p. 154.)

Eco-Leadership is an emerging discourse. It is a theory and practice of leadership embodying four qualities and three principles of practice.

The four discourses of Eco-Leadership

(Originally published in Western, S. (2019). *Leadership: A Critical Text*. 3rd edn. London: SAGE as Box 31, p. 270.)

1. Connectivity and interdependence
Eco-Leadership is founded on connectivity, recognising how the network society has transformed social relations, and it also recognises our interdependence with each other and the environment. Eco-Leadership

focuses on internal organisational ecosystems (technical, social, and natural) and the external ecosystems in which organisations exist. Eco-leaders pay attention to distributing leadership internally and making their organisations more autonomous, creative, participatory, and self-managing. Externally, Eco-Leaders look to take advantage of opportunities and adapt to disruptions, through their connectivity and interdependence with wider ecosystems, that go way beyond the usual stakeholder maps.

2. Systemic ethics
Eco-Leadership is concerned with acting ethically in the human realm *and* protecting the natural environment. Systemic ethics goes beyond company values and individual leader morality, which conveniently turns a blind eye to the wider ethical implications of their businesses, for example, ignoring the downstream impacts of social inequity such as poor treatment of supply-chain workers, and impacts of pollution and environmental damage.

3. Leadership spirit
Eco-Leadership acknowledges the importance of the human spirit. It extends its values beyond material gain, paying attention to community and friendship, mythology and spirituality, the unconscious and non-rational, creativity and imagination. It draws upon the beauty and dynamic vitality within human relationships, and between humanity and the natural world. The human spirit is evoked in myriad diverse ways, and is not locked into a particular spiritual, religious, or humanist belief.

4. Organisational belonging
To belong is to be a part of the whole, it is to participate in the joys and challenges faced by communities. Businesses and corporations, like schools, banks, and hospitals, belong to the social fabric of community, and cannot operate as separate bodies. Eco-Leaders commit organisations to belong to "places and spaces", developing strong kinship ties. "Place" refers to local habitat and community, and "space" to the virtual and real networks that organisations also inhabit. Organisational belonging means ending a false separation, realising that

company interests and societal interests are interdependent. Organisational belonging is to rethink organisational purpose and meaning.

The three principles of practice for organisations (Western, 2019)

1. Social purpose
Creating shared value. Aiming to create shared value for wider society, beyond shareholder profit/organisational growth … this also drives employee engagement, motivation, innovation, retention, and recruitment.

2. Participative organisations
Leadership everywhere! Distributing leadership, maximising individual and team potential. Creating a feeling of belonging, responsibility, autonomy to act plus a convivial, generous, courageous, adaptive, learning, and dynamic culture. Mobilising the potential of each individual and the whole organisation.

3. Eco-mindsets
From machine to eco-mindset. Internally—from top-down control to influencing ecosystems. Sharing collaborative cultures, connecting across boundaries. Externally, Eco-Leaders observe technological, environmental, and social ecosystems, seeing new opportunities and adapting to disruptions.

Applying Eco-Leadership qualities to the Covid pandemic, there is a huge shift away from the current emphasis of relying on "science capitalism" to solve the problem; a different mindset to attempting to return as fast as possible to economic growth and an extractive modernist way-of-being that caused this and the other disruptions. Placing connectedness, interdependence, leadership spirit, systemic ethics, and organisational belonging at the heart of the challenges, changes the whole picture. We reconfigure the challenge away from a linear problem to solution, and discover that the challenge we face is not an aberrant virus, but actually how we "live and die" together with our multi-species companions on planet earth. The principles of Eco-Leadership act as a guide for each organisation to (i) reimagine its purpose to deliver shared value to the wider ecosystem, (ii) encourage participation within the organisation and beyond it, to create a participatory and engaged network of belonging, that will innovate and adapt to change, (iii) to develop eco-mindsets that work to connect, to see patterns, and to re-engage with technological, environmental, and social ecosystems in ways that align to the challenges we all face.

Conclusion—living in a P.I. age

I am indebted particularly to Donna Haraway, Bruno Latour, and Anna Tsing, amongst others, for their insights that have helped me develop my thinking in the past few years. They push me to realise just how endemic and pervasive the modernist mindset is. Despite trying to think beyond functional, linear modernist ways, beyond binary and closed systems, beyond the open-system theories which I have found too limiting, and beyond anthropocentric ways, I find that I and those around me fall short. The biggest challenge we face trying to engage in new ways to understand organisational, social, and political change is to think with eco-mindsets. When working with organisations to help them develop Eco-Leadership cultures, this requires the capacity to think outside the reductionist and linear pathways of modernist sensibilities.

The challenge to think in new ways is vastly underestimated. Hannah Arendt wrote that "thinking is to train one's imagination to go visiting" (cited in Haraway, 2016, p. 126), and to achieve this we must engage our imaginations and our bodies in different ways. To develop eco-mindsets is to move beyond repeating new mantras such as "from ego to eco"— a favourite phrase from integral thinkers and psychology informed approaches, that misses the point completely. We need to shift from psychology focused thinking to ecological and relatedness focused thinking. It is to shift the focus away from mechanistic thinking (Controller leadership) and from psychologising the problem (Therapist leadership). It is to depart from the "politics of salvation" (Lawrence, 2019) and from seeking Messiah leadership. All these approaches are entrapped in the modernist discourse. To move from ego is to situate humans at the centre of the problem and make it a psychological-altruistic (and impossible) task. Perhaps some Zen Buddhists or Hindu monks who spend their lives working to rid themselves of ego can achieve this mighty goal, but for the rest of us we must live with our egos. Our ego can be a force to drive change for the better and can also be a dysfunctional force. From a Lacanian psychoanalytic perspective, the task is to put our ego challenges and our individual and collective symptoms to work for a better world. Psychology and the insights of psychoanalysis are part of the hybrid ecosystems that we need to address. Their applications to our thinking are useful if we connect them to environmental and ecological ways of thinking (Bateson, 2000). Applying biomimicry as solutions, in other words learning from nature, is part of the ecosystem of thought we need, but we also must not apply biomimicry as if nature is teaching us—because this yet again puts a division between nature and us. We are nature, and until we think about the human-technological-environmental ecosystems as one, we will continue to make the same mistakes. The real challenge for humanity is to think beyond the limits of the past century. We need to think beyond the modernist mindset of binaries, boundaries, control, anthropomorphism, progress, and growth. Developing eco-mindsets is the challenge we face; this includes understanding human psychological and social engagement as part of our multi-species and non-human ecosystem.

"We must think, think we must" (Haraway, 2016)

In the psychoanalytic literature, there are many insights into thinking, yet they mostly stay within the modernist mindset. Some later works of Bion and Lacan stray into esoteric territory but aside from this, most psychoanalytic system approaches reflect the modernist mindsets from which they emerged. Psychoanalysis since Freud has strived to situate psychoanalysis within the modernist project, craving for recognition from within an empirical scientific, academic tradition. Psychoanalysis still calls its seminars "scientific meetings" which makes me think of the phrase from Shakespeare's *Hamlet*, "the lady doth protest too much, methinks"! Lacanians are more circumspect and critique empiricism and scientism within psychology, but Lacan's attachment to science speaks through his theories and his "mathemes", his formulas that mimic other sciences, perhaps revealing his desire to be recognised in this scientific tradition (Lacan et al., 2018). In the Tavistock tradition, the attachment to modernist ideas of hierarchy, division, and stable boundaries is reflected in the language of splitting, such as "good and bad breast" and BART (boundaries, authority, role, and task) that guides group relations and organisational consultancy work. These are examples of the modernist approach, where division, binaries, hierarchy, and attachment to clarity of boundaries, inform and limit the different thinking that is so urgently needed. The patriarchal ideas seen in the maternal and paternal metaphors, and in the role of the father, the law of the Father, and the Oedipus complex also emerge from the modernist mindset. Psychoanalysis is well positioned to bring its insights, and develop new thinking beyond the limits of modernity, and some of this work has been pioneered by Lacan, by Deleuze (1977), and Deleuze and Guattari (1988), but much more is needed. The first step is for those of us working with psychoanalytic theory to see the discourses that entrap our work. In a recent paper (Western & McDonnell, 2022) we discuss a shift away from the use of BART in group relations conferences and its replacement with NIPI as an acronym to guide the work: NIPI stands for networks, identity, power, and influence. NIPI takes the focus away from identifying authority as a hierarchical position power held by the director and staff, and it challenges the idea that clarity of role task and boundary offer containment and are ideals for working conditions. These ideas are from the twentieth century. NIPI opens a new lens to understand the psychodynamics of group relations work in terms of fluid networks, shifting identities, and how the networks we live in are influenced by both informal and formal power. This moves the work into a new paradigm, aligned to the earlier references to Eco-Leadership and what Bauman calls liquid modernity (2013).

There is (and never was) an outside

Nature, in modernity terms, is something that humans sit outside of, something they look at with love and fear. There is a boundary between us and it. Nature becomes an object to overcome or utilise as a resource for production or enjoyment. Modernity had created a "disenchanted world", a world where the material world including "nature" had lost its pluralistic enchanted spirits. In the Abrahamic faiths, *environmental stewardship* originates with the creation stories, where God gives humans dominion over the fish of the sea, the birds of the air, and the animals of the land (Genesis 1:1–2:4).

Modernity and capitalism re-inscribed this stewardship with its extractive-controlling ethos. Nature was to be controlled and tamed, to be used as an unlimited resource. The stewardship was understood as controlling wildness/sin—in nature and human nature. Colonisation of "wild and untamed countries and peoples" was justified in these terms. A new morality, supported by the Church, justified the domination of nature and the domination of "uncivilised" people, made it the duty of the civilised to control and civilise the uncivilised, and to extract from people and nature what was required to build this new world. Indigenous genocide and environmental catastrophe go hand in hand. Communist and capitalist utopians shared the same modernist beliefs and aims—but with different methodologies (Gray, 1995). Religious faith was translated to a new modernity: secular faith, with science, enlightenment, and reason, stepping into the God void (Taylor, 2009). We must relearn that there is no "outside of" nature, and never was. The warning of Covid was to return the Real of nature to our denaturalised modern world. Yet it is to return nature not from the outside but from within the ecosystems and webs of life we share.

If we treat Covid as untamed nature, as an alien force that requires controlling, then we miss the point. Covid is another manifestation of technology, society, and the environment combining as a "nature-humanity-technology" ecosystem precisely in the same way as the environmental emergency is a product of this triple combination of disruptors. Covid amplifies our existing predicament. It highlights the need for a move in mindsets and narratives to shift our ways-of-being-in-the-world. "We must think, think we must" (Haraway, 2016). To think means to access vulnerability without allowing it to paralyse us, or to throw us back into controlling ways. In a recent paper (Western, 2021), I wrote that the "Meaning of Greta" (Thunberg) was to reveal to us our vulnerability and yet to transcend it, to put our symptom to work for the greater good. Greta brought her vulnerability to the world stage and used it as a signifier for what needed to change. I also discussed how she represents the world being turned upside down, that is, by a child berating world leaders to act like adults, and at the same time she challenges the world to turn itself upside down again and realise the terrible predicament that modernity has brought to us. A paradigm change is needed.

The P.I. age

P.I. is the master signifier for our times. Precarious interdependence means facing a new world reality, engaging with the world in new ways. Our challenge is to learn to live in a P.I. age, to accept that precarious interdependence is the present and future reality. Our desires to be controlling and omnipotent, to remove fear and risk are futile. Our desires to overcome lack, to constantly grow, and always to seek progress leads to a dystopian future.

The triple disruptions that unleashed Covid, climate change, and social inequity have created a precarious world for humans and our multi-species companions. We can no longer be external to nature; we must realise that we are nature. We must learn to live in a P.I. world. It always will be a precarious and interdependent world. It always has been, yet modernity offered the fantasy salvation of creating a "civilised" world outside of nature. Our thinking must traverse this fantasy. There is no salvation, only adaptive and regenerative living in a P.I. age. There is no separation, no autopoiesis, only what Haraway calls "sympoiesis" or making-with.

> Sympoiesis is a simple word; it means "making-with." Nothing makes itself; nothing is really autopoietic or self-organizing. In the words of the Inupiat computer "world game," earthlings are never alone. That is the radical implication of sympoiesis. Sympoiesis is a word proper to complex, dynamic, responsive, situated, historical systems. It is a word for worlding-with, in company. Sympoiesis enfolds autopoiesis and generatively unfurls and extends it. (Haraway, 2016, p. 58)

Haraway argues against technofix dreamers and at the same time against the growing cult of doom and despair that creates paralysis. She argues that we need to "stay with the trouble":

> Staying with the trouble requires making odd kin: that is, we require each other in unexpected collaborations and combinations, in hot compost piles. We become with each other or not at all. (2016, p. 4)

The P.I. age undermines the dominant narrative away from modernity as a master signifier that unleashes its chain of signifiers such as division, reductionism, rationalism, extraction, linear, control, individualism, capitalism, consumerism, science, progress, growth. Covid is a return of the Real, a timely reminder of why we need to think in new ways. It has amplified this urgent demand that pre-existed the pandemic and will outlast it.

References

Anderson, G. (2006). The idea of the nation-state is an obstacle to peace. *International Journal on World Peace, 23*(1): 75–85. http://jstor.org/stable/20753518 (last accessed September 2, 2021).

Badiou, A. (2007). *Being and Event.* London: A. & C. Black.

Bateson, G. (2000). *Steps to an Ecology of Mind: Collected Essays in Anthropology, Psychiatry, Evolution, and Epistemology.* Chicago, IL: University of Chicago Press.

Bauman, Z. (2013). *Liquid Modernity.* Oxford: John Wiley & Sons.

Castells, M. (2011). *The Rise of the Network Society (Vol. 12).* Oxford: John Wiley & Sons.

Deleuze, G. (1977). *Anti-Oedipus.* London: A. & C. Black, 2004.

Deleuze, G., & Guattari, F. (1988). *A Thousand Plateaus: Capitalism and Schizophrenia.* London: Bloomsbury.

Eliot, T. S. (1963). *Collected Poems, 1909–1962.* New York: Harcourt, Brace & World.

Gray, J. (1995). *Enlightenment's Wake: Politics and Culture at the Close of the Modern Age.* Abingdon, UK: Routledge Classics, 2007.

Haraway, D. J. (2016). *Staying with the Trouble.* Durham, NC: Duke University Press.

Heidegger, M., (1927). *Being and Time.* New York: State University of New York Press.

Intergovernmental Panel on Climate Change Report (2021). https://ipcc.ch/report/sixth-assessment-report-working-group-i/ (last accessed May 20, 2020).

Lacan, J., Miller, J. A., & Sheridan, A. (2018). *The Four Fundamental Concepts of Psycho-analysis.* London: Routledge.

Laing, R. D. (1960). *The Divided Self: An Existential Study in Sanity and Madness.* London: Penguin Classics, 2010.

Latour, B. (2005). *Reassembling the Social: An Introduction to Actor-Network-Theory.* Oxford: Oxford University Press.

Latour, B. (2012). *We Have Never Been Modern*. Cambridge, MA: Harvard University Press.

Latour, B. (2013). Facing Gaia. Six lectures on the political theology of nature. Gifford Lectures at the University of Edinburgh, Edinburgh, UK.

Lawrence, W. G. (2019). The politics of salvation and revelation in the practice of consultancy. In: *Tongued with Fire* (pp. 165–179). London: Routledge.

Miller, J. A. (2012). The real in the 21st century. https://lacanquotidien.fr/blog/2012/05/the-real-in-the-21st-century-by-jacques-alain-miller/ (last accessed May 20, 2020).

Pilgrim, D. (2008). The eugenic legacy in psychology and psychiatry. *International Journal of Social Psychiatry*, 54(3): 272–284. doi: 10.1177/0020764008090282.

Steiner, P. (2019). Slavery and modern management—Caitlin Rosenthal, *Accounting for Slavery. Masters and Management* (Cambridge, MA, Harvard University Press, 2018). *European Journal of Sociology*, 60(3): 500–503. doi: 10.1017/S0003975619000390.

Taylor, C. (2009). *A Secular Age*. Cambridge, MA: Harvard University Press.

Tsing, A. L. (2015). *The Mushroom at the End of the World*. Princeton, NJ: Princeton University Press.

Western, S. (2007). *Leadership: A Critical Text*. London: SAGE.

Western, S. (2010). Eco-leadership: towards the development of a new paradigm. In: B. W. Redekop (Ed.), *Leadership for Environmental Sustainability*, Vol. 3 (pp. 50–68). London: Routledge.

Western, S. (2014). Autonomist leadership in leaderless movements: anarchists leading the way. *Ephemera: Theory & Politics in Organization*, 14(4): 673–698.

Western, S. (2018). The eco-leadership paradox. In: *Innovation in Environmental Leadership* (pp. 48–60). New York: Routledge.

Western, S. (2019). *Leadership: A Critical Text*. 3rd edn. London: SAGE.

Western, S. (2020). Covid-19: an intrusion of the real the unconscious unleashes its truth. *Journal of Social Work Practice*, 34(4): 445–451.

Western, S. (2021). The Meaning of Greta: A psychosocial exploration of Greta Thunberg. *Organisational and Social Dynamics*, 21(1): 78–96.

Western S., & McDonnell, B. (2022). N.I.P.I. not B.A.R.T.: Designing a group relations conference for our Precarious-Interdependent world. *Socioanalysis, Journal of Group Relations Australia*, 23: 61–82.

For more information on eco-leadership see www.eco-leadership.institute

CHAPTER 11

Questions of denial—Covid as a catastrophe

by Andrzej Leder

One of the most important lessons the pandemic taught us is about the force of the denial in our societies. First, the simple fact of the expanding illness was denied. Then, the obvious measures of protection—like mask wearing—became a subject of ideological war; an important faction of Western societies denied the positive influence of the protection a surgical mask provides. And finally, one of the greatest achievements of the human mind—vaccination—provoked a virulent aggression, drawing about 30–40% of the population of the most developed countries into a suicidal refusal of vaccination against the virus.

This behaviour is a symptom of the wider, structural process, the denial of the authority of science and reason as sources of confidence in our societies. For many, the rational understanding of the world is sterile; they need a Manichean vision of the powers of evil responsible for their malaise, and of a brutal hero, avenging their implied innocence. Such a *desire* and *phantasma*[1]—I use this term in the Lacanian

---

[1] When I use terms stemming from psychoanalysis, especially Lacanian, in their technical meaning, they will be written in italics.

sense—are provoking the question: what is really denied in this structural move? My text will try to develop this question. Are we dealing with some crucial feature of our times? If yes, what are the conditions of possibility for this kind of mental structure?

* * *

In their book about the language of psychoanalysis, Jean Laplanche and Jean-Bernard Pontalis are profoundly working on the Freudian concepts of defence mechanisms. One of the most interesting entries refers to the mechanism of disavowal or, as I will call it in this text, denial (Laplanche & Pontalis, 1974, pp. 119–120).

The original German term describing this complicated defence mechanism is *Verleugnung*, a construction where the root *-Leugnung, das Lüge* (denial, a lie) and the prefix *ver-* are connected. The prefix *ver-* in German has a double function. In its deep root it matches the late Indo-European *per-*, whose meaning is to transcend a boundary, transgress something. However, the second meaning of the prefix *ver-* is to show a wrong move by the subject, who gets away, gets lost, overshoots; like, for example, in the reflexive verb *sich verspäten, sich verloren* (being late, being lost).

If we connect the sense of the word "to lie" and this "overshooting" meaning buried in the prefix *ver-*, we can think about a self-deception which is so extreme, overdone, that it carries the subject into a mist of *phantasma* and destroys his capacity to connect with the reality principle. I think that Freud chose this term, *Verleugnung*, to underline this aspect of profound self-deception—at the limit of a delusion—of this defence mechanism. It is important to keep this aspect in mind when we think about denial.

In the early stages, the concept of denial in psychoanalytic theory was connected with the difficulty that a child has to accept the lack of a penis in his mother. However, as Laplanche and Pontalis (1974) perspicaciously remark: "absence is not perceived as such" and thus "the object of disavowal [denial] would not be a perception … but rather a theory designated to account for the fact" (pp. 119–120). This issue is of crucial importance. Denial operates in a very cunning way. It does not change our crude perception, the images on our retina are not repressed; however, it changes our perception deeply, as it perverts the understanding of these images perceived by our retina. These considerations bring Laplanche and Pontalis to such a question: "Does not disavowal … bear upon a factor which *founds* human reality rather than upon a hypothetical 'fact of perception'?" (p. 120, original emphasis). I would posit that in denial it is precisely the capacity to understand the meaning of what is perceived that is obliterated. Factors underpinning human reality are not "facts of perception" but existential necessities. Even if they are not perceptible, they are obvious: a human being has needs and desires, depends on others, but also can be grateful. Denial distorts such obvious factors. As the crystal shard in the eye of Kai, the hero of Andersen's tale *Snow Queen*, it turns goodness sour and gives a gloss to evil. It deforms every human feeling and attitude.

Thus, denial plays an enormous role in the affective economy: if the subject were to understand the meaning of the perceived facts, he (or she) would have to confront the whole range of difficult connected feelings. If the subject replaces an understanding of the perceived scene with a fetishistic narrative of his perception, he can retain *jouissance*,[2] and dismiss any kind of difficulty. Denial is the basic defence mechanism for perversion.

But what do we mean by a fetishistic narrative? In his foundational text "History beyond the pleasure principle: Some thoughts on the representation of trauma", Eric Santner offers this definition: "By narrative fetishism I mean the construction and deployment of a narrative consciously or unconsciously designed to expunge the traces of the trauma or loss that called that narrative into being in the first place" (1992, p. 147).

The essence of Santner's rationale is to ascribe to narrative fetishism the desire to retell the traumatic event—for example, the injuries of war—but without the difficult feelings necessary for its authentic working through. This attitude aims not to forget, but to remember, however without undergoing any process of mourning: "Fetishism, as I am using the term here, is by contrast (to mourning) a strategy whereby one seeks

---

[2] The question of the translation of the Lacanian term *jouissance* into English is always controversial. Some authors don't attempt it and use only the French form. I will use this approach.

voluntarily to reinstate the pleasure principle without addressing and working through those other tasks" (p. 147).

Santner explores the capacity for mourning, or its lack, after a traumatic historical event: "Both mourning and narrative fetishism as I have defined these terms are strategies whereby groups and individuals reconstruct their vitality and identity in the wake of trauma. The crucial difference between the two modes of repair has to do with the willingness or capacity to include the traumatic event in one's efforts to reformulate and reconstitute identity" (p. 150). Narrative fetishism will thus not require the subject to work through her or his identity.

Santner finds an example of the narrative fetishism in *Heimat*, an eleven-part series directed by Edgar Reitz for German television in 1984. As a response to the shock provoked by the American series *Holocaust*, broadcast in 1979, it pushed real represented events—examples of anti-Semitic violence—into the background and deprived them of affective importance, as the viewers' emotions were captured instead by the history of love, of sympathetic German heroes. The distribution of cathexis was distorted, the viewer very much enjoyed "the love story", while the horrifying facts were denied any emotional *gravitas*. This attitude is characteristic of the perversion, legitimising *jouissance* in spite of perceived facts.

* * *

It is important to see how this mechanism of denial (*Verleugnung*) is the inverse of repression (*Verdrängung*), whereby facts themselves are hidden while the affective responses they provoke cannot be prevented from flooding back into consciousness. The former is characteristic of perversion, the latter of neurosis. The neurotic response is accompanied by the appearance of a repressive law which prevents access both to the traumatic event and to *jouissance*.

An excellent literary example of how repression works can be found in W. G. Sebald's *On the Natural History of Destruction*, a book dedicated to the non-memory, or simply the repression of the memory of how German cities were devastated by Allied bombing during the last years of World War II. In discussing the literary and personal testimonies of these traumatic experiences, Sebald argues: "A number of the letters and accounts that reached me did deviate from the basic pattern of family reminiscence, showing traces of uneasiness and distress still emerging today in the minds of their writers" (1999, p. 85).

However, the traumatic facts and scenes never appeared in these texts. All one could see were the traces of the "dreadful truth" as it made "its way to the surface" without ever fully coming to light.

The "zero hour", the discursive figure in post-war Germany meaning "a totally new beginning"—to which Sebald so often refers as the non-memory of everything before 1945—can be comprehended as synonymous with the neurotic repression of the memory of past events. This non-memory was imposed by the first chancellor of the Federal Republic of Germany, Konrad Adenauer, playing the role of the "father figure" to prevent the perverted *jouissance* of narrative fetishism during the first years of the post-war period. German society's obsessive freneticism in embracing consumption and productivity is clearly connected with the repressed memory of traumatic events. As Freud suggested in "Mourning and melancholia" (1917e), the impossibility of mourning runs parallel to the over-cathexis of the "new order".

In the reaction of people worldwide to the Covid-19 pandemic the defence mechanism of denial, which is the basis of perversion, appears as much more important than repression, characteristic for the transference neuroses. Why do I support this thesis? It comes from the different relationship of denial and repression when considering the temporal dimension. Repression operates on memory, on the past. Denial operates in the present. If a perceived fact, here and now, is so striking, so obvious, that it cannot be ignored, but, at the same time if the emotional rection connected to it is unbearable, it will be the subject of denial, of disavowal. Its understanding will change dramatically and—at the expense of "factors founding human reality", as Laplanche and Pontalis describe it, a parallel rationale will start to develop; distant from the reality principle, but fitting the subjects' desires and cathexes. Denial will push subjects' minds away from the "factors founding human reality", and particularly the supreme faculty of our mind—reasoning.

The massive spread of the Covid-19 illness was such an obvious fact. At the "present moment", just in front of our eyes, people started to die. Our retinas could not get rid of the images of coffins taken out from hospitals in the middle of the night by military trucks. But we could develop a "fetishistic narrative" satisfying the need for security and sometimes even *jouissance*, despite the horror and mourning.

For some, the fetishistic narrative was a tale of someone's guilt. Accusing somebody is a good way to experience an intense emotional discharge and is capable of transforming the feeling of helplessness into an active hatred. Thus, for many Americans (and some Europeans), the virus was intentionally developed and released from a laboratory by China. Trump voters were especially eager to believe this, as Donald Trump personally suggested such a narrative. He played the role of the "perverted father figure", permitting the prohibited enjoyment of hatred. Similar accusations directed against the USA appeared on the Russian internet and wherever Russian boots reached.

In parallel came the attack on masks as the means of protection. The narrative of stolen freedom was capable of changing the hard feeling of "being subject to sanitarian mass action of mask wearing" into the *jouissance* of a freedom fighter. This *jouissance* and vindictive feelings were at the root of aggressive acts against people wearing masks and those who encouraged it.

Another kind of narrative fetishism appeared as: it is a kind of influenza, you don't have to take it seriously. Present in the first reaction of some political leaders—like Boris Johnson before he became ill himself—it has evolved into a completely independent and pretty dangerous account. Medical and "big pharma" lobbies would have been trying to frighten people, showing them mannequins under respirators, so as to sell more of their products, especially vaccines.

Vaccines, an enormous success by international laboratories, became at the same time the most hated element in the effort to stem the flu plague. In the violence of attacks against vaccinating medical stuff, in the gloomy and cruel character of rumours concerning "deadly consequences" of vaccine use, and the perfidy of the intentions of their manufacturers, the deep character of denial, disavowal, *Verleugnung* appears. Perfectly caught by Freud, it leads to such a self-deception that our reason becomes paralysed by some kind of *praecox Gefühl*, described by ancient psychiatrists as a feeling of facing madness.

Why do I, after Santner, call this a kind of narrative fetishistic? They are not simple rationalisations. Telling them is like playing with a fetishistic object. Lust makes the eyes of the narrator shine and his/her heartbeat accelerates. The narrator is excited, repeats words and sentences as if touching some material object—silk stockings or a loaded gun. Likewise, as with material objects, the fetishistic narrative cannot be critically analysed or falsified. What would it mean anyway, to "falsify" the fetishistic power of a material object? It cannot be understood, it can only be felt and experienced. As we cannot "persuade" a perverted person not to get excited in the presence of the fetish, as we cannot prove that it is a usual object, we cannot rationally change the opinion of an anti-vaccine believer. There is too much *jouissance* in his tale.

This is why I believe that Santner's concept of narrative fetishism perspicaciously catches the specificity of the theories professed by Covid-19 deniers. Nevertheless, it is a catastrophe of reason. Reason is disarmed in the face of a fetish. A fetish is not another person, it has neither the feelings nor the memory of Others. A fetish is an object of *jouissance*.

Psychoanalysts frequently said that the nineteenth century in the West was an epoch of hysterical and obsessional neurosis, while the first half of the twentieth century, with two world wars, was a time of trauma; and during the second part, the narcissist personality was predominant. The interesting aspect of this observation could be summarised by the following question: if the changing features of our culture can be defined by the predominant personality structure, what kind of personality would we expect today? What does the abundant presence of *denial* as a defence mechanism tell us?

Let us try to understand what one really means when one says that hysteria or obsession were so important at a given time. Hysteria and obsession are the transference neuroses, reactions to an oppressive, rigid conscience, *superego*, connected with internalised parental figures. An oppressive *superego* was (and still is) typical of societies where social and familial ties are very strong, even overwhelming. Where social roles are strictly defined, where paternal authority cannot be questioned, where some *desires*, contents, and attitudes are totally repressed, *repression* becomes the most important defence mechanism. Such was the bourgeois society of the late nineteenth century.

At the social level the transference neuroses can be well described with the Lacanian term of the *desire of the Other*. The character of the *belle epoque* was completely determined by the attitude towards the *Big Other*—an incarnation of the social imaginary (Taylor, 2004)—and the position the subject could adopt in relation to it. This is the sense of the term *transference neuroses.*

But the traumatic deeds of the first half of the twentieth century destroyed the legitimacy and unambiguity of the nineteenth-century social imaginary.[3]

One of the "victims" was the modern concept of progress. After the paroxysm of the student revolts of the 1960s—which can be read as the consequence of the repression of previously experienced traumas—a completely different attitude started to develop. It was well expressed in the formula of "the end of history" announced by Francis Fukuyama. The focus of the 1980s and 1990s was on the global relationship of everything to everything else. In philosophy, this was the time of postmodern revision of "big narratives", organising the imaginary of Enlightenment Europe. In politics—the neo-conservative revolution. In economics—the uncontested domination of neoclassical theory and the accelerated globalisation of production.

Consciousness did not focus anymore on the movement of changes in time, that is, on progress, but on a co-existing, parallel-in-time diversity which fills the present moment, inflating it into a multidimensional space. However, the diversity which is perceived here and now, which is cut off from the past and present, gives rise to a growing sense of excess and overloading. This diversity was experienced as a potential abundance, seemingly available if only one were to hold out one's hand. Seemingly, because in fact it calls for constant choices synonymous with the inaccessibility of the majority of possibilities; it involves a deep feeling of resignation. Excess covers emptiness.

The reaction would be a withdrawal of *libido* from objects.

With this characteristic it is easy to recognise important features of the narcissistic personality. Christopher Lasch (1979) gave a profound analysis of the evolution of American society towards the predominance of narcissism. One could summarise his thesis in a short sentence: the decomposition of the rigid structures of hierarchical society and puritanical family life, mainly in the 1960s and 1970s, promoted a

---

[3] The layer of social consciousness and unconsciousness is used interchangeably with the concept of the imaginary—a term used by Charles Taylor—or that of the symbolic field, a notion derived from Lacan's psychoanalysis.

personality-type consistent with clinical definitions of "pathological narcissism". For Lasch, "pathology represents a heightened version of normality" (1979, p. 38). The link between the rigidity of the nineteenth-century predominantly puritan culture and twentieth-century narcissism in Lasch's rationale becomes obvious when we read Louis Menand's comment on the hot discussion about the culture of narcissism:

> Lasch was not saying that things were better in the 1950s, as conservatives offended by countercultural permissiveness probably took him to be saying. He was not saying that things were better in the 1960s, as former activists disgusted by the "me-ism" of the seventies are likely to have imagined. He was diagnosing a condition that he believed had originated in the nineteenth century. (2002, p. 206)

The epoch of transference neuroses, we could add.

Even if the withdrawal of *cathexia* from the relation with the others—and the *Big Other*—was characteristic of the narcissistic character of the late twentieth century, it was possible because of the undisputed hegemony of America and, to put it more broadly, of the West, in the globalising world. The abundance of fetishised commodities in the West was a direct result of remaining out of eyeshot, but nevertheless ruthlessly exploiting the global South (see Leder, 2014).

We must underline this issue. Even if the narcissistic personality is most often built upon a "narcissistic wound", it feeds on the permanent reaffirmation and recognition of its omnipotence and superiority. It can be permeated with anxiety and doubts; however, they are always linked to the main question: does the world acknowledge its "natural" supremacy? If yes, triumphalist euphoria is attained; if not, a vindicative wrath coupled with fear and despair appears.

If we apply, like Lasch or Žižek, this personality analysis to our culture in the last epoch of global Western hegemony—more or less from the last decade of the twentieth century up to the present—we can easily detect this cycle in political and cultural events. Our societies were reassured, when everybody seemed to recognise the "end of history" and the ultimate triumph of liberal democracy, by the market economy permitting permanent growth. However, when voices of protest or a violent resistance were appearing, words and acts changed radically, becoming vindictive and full of anger.

A series of events at the beginning of the twenty-first century destroyed the self-confidence of the West. From the annihilation of the World Trade Center on 9/11 2001, the Lehman Brothers' fall in 2008, through the more-and-more-evident growth of the economic and political strength of China, challenging the hegemony of the West, the protracted "war on terror" and the hatred of the Islamic world, repeated immigration crises—all these deeply affected the perception of the place of Western societies in the world. The global South emerged as a pivotal factor in the new image of the planet. However, maybe the most important issue was the progressive pauperisation of the Western middle class parallel to the shocking concentration of capital, as described by Thomas Piketty (2014). The vision of the next generation, the generation of children, living in worse material conditions than the previous one, became a source of fear and anger. And that generation of children, from their side, challenged the paradigm, indisputable up to this point: the paradigm of permanent growth at the expense of ecological and human consequences.

All these facts could no longer be repressed.

* * *

This stirring image on our retinas could become the trigger for deep reflection on our civilisation and reconsideration of the priorities and "obviousness" with which we were living. However, this would mean a profound and difficult moral experience, confronting us with the truth of extremely difficult feelings, of guilt, fear, and mourning the "lost paradise" of the consumer society.

Why those emotions? The Western mind would have to accept that our security and comfort of life has ended, and this thought would provoke a sense of hurt and injustice. What is more, the Western mind would have to accept that we are guilty, in relation to the planet and to other people living in the global world. This would provoke a deep feeling of responsibility. The Western mind would have to accept that we were wrong and that it is time to change. However, this kind of insight challenges the narcissistic feeling of superiority. Only a reason, capable of connecting to others, with their existential position, as Hannah Arendt (2003) stresses with Kant, would be capable of achieving this change.

However, it is unlikely that this kind of moral exercise will happen in the near future. The mechanism of denial has already been mobilised.

The Western mind does not want to confront the sense of the images it perceives. It is ready to develop a string of self-deceptive rationales, rather like sleepwalking. Hence, multiple *fetishistic narratives*, in Santner's sense, find their place in the symbolic sphere, forging the new *imaginary*. Many of them are concerned with the pandemic.

Social media, often accused of being the source of self-deception, truly are allowing the creation, ad hoc, of these kinds of narratives, perverting the understanding of the perceived facts and spreading through the web with the speed of light. However, aren't all the phenomena of social media more of a symptom than the cause of the increasingly oppressive power of *denial* as the main defence mechanism? Is it not that the politicians, who pick up such stories and desires, who take the role of the perverted father figure, are permitting *jouissance* despite the horrifying images on the retina?

And isn't this whole process hiding the dawn of *perversion* as the key personality structure of our time?

Let us see. It would be hard to stand face-to-face with the truly (in)human sense of the thousands drowning in the Mediterranean; or, as in Poland, people dying of cold on the Belorussian border. Is this not the reason why so many eagerly welcome the story of the "Islamic danger" to Europe, displaced into cherishing vindictive feelings towards immigrants?

Similar attitudes permitted the separation of parents and children in the detention camps on the southern US border, during Donald Trump's presidency.

Is it so difficult to accept the reality of the climate catastrophe, although nearly all scientists agree that we have less and less time left? Better then to accuse scientists of spreading "leftist manipulation", hiding the interests of the new ecological industry, than to move and change one's way of life.

Is it impossible to feel the fear and guilt connected with the pandemic? Better then to raise one's self-esteem fighting for the freedom not to wear masks, or express the anger by accusing Bill Gates of distorting vaccines with chips.

And so on, and so on ...

* * *

French philosopher Rémi Brague (2005) meditated on Thucydides relating the Peloponnese war. He asks the question: how much was Thucydides Athenian? Everyone knows, in the ethnic and political sense, that he was. However, for Brague, his "Athenicity" comes from another point. He writes:

> We know that Thucidydes, if he is Athenian, deserves praises of modern historians. Because he knows how to tell impartially and to acknowledge the wrongs of both sides. There is one moment, however, that he is acting in a resolute way as Athenian. And it is not some factual detail of his work, but the overall intention that drives it. (p. 44)

Why do I recall a philosophical text on a historian's writing concerning a war fought 2,500 years ago?

I think that meditating on Thucydides's writing about Athens's confrontation with Sparta, Rémi Brague, in a way not entirely compatible with his conservative vocation, perceived some crucial insights about the truth. "Not being satisfied with what is already on hand, this is a specifically Athenian attitude, while Spartiates are aiming to safeguard their ἑτοῖμα (I, 70, 4)" (Brague, 2005, p. 42), which means ready-made formulas, easy patterns; Sparta's traditional way of understanding the world, not confronted with crystallising reality, cherishing denial. Rémi Brague continues with strong words: "A refusal to take risks, absence of courage (ἀταλαίπωρος) is the very opposite of Athenian attitude" (p. 44). The courage is in thinking, it is necessary to add, as it would be impossible to deny the physical bravery of Spartans. The philosopher ends in a way crucial for us: "The perspective people have on their past is spontaneously 'Spartian'. On the contrary, Thucydides' is definitively 'Athenian'" (p. 44) . I would add: the perspective people have on their present is, unfortunately, Spartan.

Even if Athens had lost the war, showing how a democracy can commit suicide, European culture is inspired by that *polis*, its spirit is Athenian, as Rémi Brague writes. It is Athenian mainly because of this bravery in thinking, the most distant of recklessness, rather the foundation of civil courage. With psychoanalytical insights, we shall extend the validity of this concept: not only bravery in thinking, but also the resilience of feelings.

"An Athenian is capable of facing reality," writes Brague (2005, p. 51). In this sense Emile Zola, when in the fire of the Dreyfus affair he wrote *J'accuse*, or Raphael Lemkin, when already during and after WWII he was elaborating the juridical concept of genocide, were Athenian in spirit. This kind of bravery of thinking is especially important against the catastrophe of reason.

We need more of this kind of bravery.

References

Arendt, H. (2003). *Responsibility and Judgment*. New York: Schocken.

Brague, R. (2005). *Introduction au monde grec. Études d'histoire de la philosophie [Introduction to the Greek World. Studies in the History of Philosophy]*. (All quotations are author's own translations from the original French.) Paris: Champs Essais.

Freud, S. (1917e). Mourning and melancholia. *S. E.*, *14*. London: Hogarth.

Laplanche, J., & Pontalis, J.-B. (1974). *The Language of Psychoanalysis*. D. Nicholson-Smith (Trans.). New York: W. W. Norton.

Lasch, C. (1979). *The Culture of Narcissism: American Life in an Age of Diminishing Expectations*. New York: W. W. Norton.

Leder, A. (2014). The power of symbols, vulnerability of trust and securitization. In: H. Brunning (Ed.), *Psychoanalytic Essays on Power and Vulnerability*. London: Karnac.

Menand, L. (2002). *American Studies*. New York: Farrar, Straus & Giroux.

Piketty, T. (2014). *Capital in the Twenty-First Century*. Cambridge, MA: Belknap.

Santner, E. (1992). History beyond the pleasure principle: Some thoughts on the representation of trauma. In: S. Friedlander (Ed.), *Probing the Limits of Representation: Nazism and the "Final Solution"* (pp. 143–154). Cambridge, MA: Harvard University Press.

Sebald, W. G. (1999). *On the Natural History of Destruction.* A. Bell (Trans.). London: Hamish Hamilton, 2004.

Taylor, C. (2004). *Modern Social Imaginaries.* Durham, NC: Duke University Press.

CHAPTER 12

What the International Listening Posts are telling us about Covid

by Rob Stuart and Olya Khaleelee

Background

In the final days of 2019, reports started to circulate in the People's Republic of China of an outbreak of a severe strain of "pneumonia" in the city of Wuhan in the Hubei province. The story was picked up by Reuters staff on December 31 (Reuters, 2019) and a few days later, on January 3, 2020, the BBC was one of a number of Western news sources to report on a "mysterious virus in Wuhan" (Woolhouse et al., 2012).

There was little evidence at that time to suggest that this novel coronavirus, later called Covid-19, would be any different to the three to four new viruses on average that are discovered every year. That did not stop speculation in the media and online that this disease could be a new form of "severe acute respiratory syndrome" (SARS).

The World Health Organization (WHO) followed its established procedures for the investigation of new diseases, working closely with the Chinese authorities and its international partners. As of January 10, 2020 the WHO "did not recommend" any special health measures for travellers to Wuhan and the surrounding area (WHO, January 10, 2020): "WHO advises against the application of any travel or trade restrictions on China based on the information currently available on this event."

Then, on January 14 and 16, the situation changed completely as the first imported cases of the Covid-19 were confirmed in Thailand (WHO, January 14, 2020) and Japan (Schnirring, CIDRAP, 2020) respectively. Neither patient reported having visited the market in Wuhan where the virus was thought to have originated, raising fears of possible human-to-human transmission.

The news arrived too late to influence almost three billion Chinese travellers' plans for New Year's celebrations, which began on January 17. This event was described as the "World's Biggest Mass Migration" (Coffey, 2020). Somewhat inevitably, the city of Wuhan was placed under quarantine (Neilson & Woodward, 2020) only a few days later, on January 23, and by the following day, twelve Chinese cities had introduced travel restrictions to curb the spread of the virus (*New York Times*, January 24, 2020).

On January 30, the WHO declared the coronavirus outbreak a "Public Health Emergency of International Concern" (PHEIC) (WHO, January 30, 2020). Any hope that the declaration of a PHEIC would spur the international community to action was likely to have been severely dashed by March 11, when the WHO was forced to characterise the Covid-19 outbreak as a pandemic, after more than 118,000 cases in 114 countries, and 4,291 deaths (WHO, March 11, 2020):

> In the days and weeks ahead, we expect to see the number of cases, the number of deaths, and the number of affected countries climb even higher.
>
> WHO has been assessing this outbreak around the clock and we are deeply concerned both by the alarming levels of spread and severity, and by the alarming levels of inaction.
>
> We have therefore made the assessment that COVID-19 can be characterized as a pandemic.

Importantly, the WHO also noted in the same statement on March 11 that "several countries have demonstrated that this virus can be suppressed and controlled"—including China. It warned that "The challenge for many countries who are now dealing with large clusters or community transmission is not whether they can do the same—it's whether they will."

UK

In the UK, Public Health England (PHE) advice to travellers followed that of the WHO. Therefore, on January 10 it advised: "The risk to travellers to Wuhan is low, but they are advised to take simple precautions such as practising good hand and personal hygiene and minimise contact with birds and animals in markets in Wuhan as a further precaution" (PHE and DHSC, January 10, 2020).

A full two weeks passed before the Secretary of State for Health and Social Care, Matt Hancock, delivered his first statement on the novel coronavirus to Parliament on January 27. He said: "The risk to the UK population is 'low' and … while there is an increased likelihood that cases may arise in this country, we are well prepared and well equipped to deal with them" (Hancock, January 27, 2020).

However, just one day later, a rather more cautious Foreign Secretary, Dominic Raab, advised "against all but essential travel to China" (Raab, January 28, 2020). Little did he or Hancock know that the virus had already entered the UK on January 23 (Lillie et al., 2020).

Nonetheless, it was not until February 2 that the UK government launched its first coronavirus public information campaign:

> The campaign will advise the public to: always carry tissues and use them to catch coughs and sneezes, and bin the tissue; wash hands with soap and water, or use sanitiser gel, to kill germs. (DHSC, February 2020)

Another week drifted by before the UK government felt it necessary to declare "the incidence or transmission of novel Coronavirus … a serious and imminent threat to public health" (DHSC, February 10, 2020a).

On the same day, February 10, the UK government introduced its first piece of legislation to deal with the virus, although it only applied to individuals already identified by the authorities as being at risk of spreading the disease: "The Health Protection (Coronavirus) Regulations 2020 have been put in place with immediate effect to impose restrictions on any individual considered by health professionals to be at risk of spreading the virus" (DHSC, February 10, 2020b).

On March 1, with cumulative cases of the virus up 735% over the previous week (WHO Report, 2020), the health secretary finally announced his "battle plan" for Covid-19 (DHSC, March 1, 2020). The announcement also included news that Prime Minister Boris Johnson would chair a COBR ("Cabinet Office Briefing Rooms") meeting after the weekend. In the same announcement, the prime minister reminded the British public of "the importance of washing our hands with soap".

By March 18, all UK schools were ordered to close (PM's statement, March 18, 2020), followed by pubs, bars, and restaurants (Ministry of Housing, March 2020) and then, somewhat inevitably, on March 23, the prime minister was forced to give the British public "a very simple instruction—you must stay at home" (PM's statement, March 23, 2020). By the government's own admission, its strategy of containment of the novel coronavirus had failed.

Reflections

It is easy to forget how strange those early days of 2020 were. For many in the West, news of the epidemic in the East filtered through slowly. There was little information on which to base an opinion, so most people carried on with their daily lives in blissful ignorance. Little did they know that their lives would soon be turned upside down by the novel coronavirus.

Indeed, when OPUS held its "Dawn of 2020" International Listening Post meetings in the first weeks of January, the epidemic was not even mentioned. By the end of the month, however, the situation had changed significantly. Aided, no doubt, by news of the first local infections, the threat posed to all by the coronavirus was slowly starting to feel more real.

At the same time, governmental responses to the virus seemed muted. Although the UK was aware of the virus from as early as January 10, it was not until January 27 that Matt Hancock addressed Parliament and, in so doing, warned the British public of the likely impacts of the virus. It would be another month before Boris Johnson would chair his first COBR meeting in response to the pandemic.

By that time, on March 3 there had already been two deaths from the virus and a total of 309 confirmed cases of the virus in the UK. The following week, those figures would be 1,902 confirmed cases and

27 deaths—a 1,250% increase (WHO Report 2020) that surely could have been prevented, had the prime minister and his government acted sooner.

On March 17, Richard Horton, editor of the medical journal *The Lancet*, accused the UK government of "playing roulette with the public". He called for quarantines and the closing of international borders. "I can't help but feel angry that it has taken almost two months for politicians and even 'experts' to understand the scale of the danger from SARS-CoV-2 … those dangers were clear from the very beginning" (Burdeau, March 17, 2020).

It was not only inept leadership and inefficient bureaucracy that were responsible for the spread of the virus. We should not forget the role of individual citizens, for example, the woman from the Hubei province who boarded a flight just one day before the Chinese authorities quarantined the entire area (Ellery et al., February 13, 2020). She became the first confirmed patient to be treated for coronavirus in the UK.

Then there is the story of the businessman from Hove, who contracted the virus at a sales conference in Singapore on January 20–22. He travelled back to the UK via a ski resort in the French Alps and found time to visit his local pub on February 1 before eventually alerting the authorities to his condition and testing positive for the disease (*The Guardian*, February 10, 2020).

Given the catastrophic death toll in the UK and worldwide—at the time of writing, over 164,000 in the UK alone and over 6 million worldwide (WHO Coronavirus Dashboard)—we need to reflect upon what happened in order to learn from our mistakes. Luckily, the OPUS International Listening Post provides us with some insight into what people were thinking during the greatest pandemic of modern times—the first truly global pandemic.

Notes from the International Listening Post

Introduction

Listening Posts are a core part of the work of OPUS, a charity set up in 1975 to promote the reflective citizen: to develop an awareness that whether we as individual citizens take action or do not take action, we nevertheless help to shape the society in which we live. We therefore co-create society and we unconsciously mobilise specific leaders to fit our contemporary state of mind. This concept is based on the idea that, as with individuals and groups, society also operates with an unconscious—a collective unconscious—and that this phenomenon can be studied in the same way that an individual's mind can be studied on the psychoanalyst's couch. It is an intelligible field of study (Khaleelee & Miller, 1985).

Listening Posts are seen as a way of carrying out this study. They are based partly on Bion's ideas (1952) that the individual is a group animal and that groups function on basic assumptions about group survival. Other key influencers married psychoanalysis with the field of group relations. On the psychoanalytic side was Pierre Turquet (1974, 1975) exploring the dynamics of groups of different sizes including large groups, and Robert Gosling (1981) with his conceptualisation of the dynamics of very small groups.

Kurt Lewin wrote about the theory of groups as "wholes", while Ken Rice explored the development of the system theory of group relations, and Isabel Menzies clarified defensive structures of organisations. Eric Miller, who worked closely with Ken Rice, was head of the Group Relations Training Programme at the Tavistock Institute from 1959 and policy adviser to OPUS from 1975 until his death in 2002. He led the development of the Listening Posts with other colleagues, to take these ideas further. His postulate was that the wider group—society—is present in the mind of the individual and can be mobilised even within the small group when individuals are invited to reflect on their roles and experiences as citizens (Khaleelee & Miller, 1985).

The Listening Posts first operated within the UK during the 1980s and later were developed internationally by the OPUS director in co-operation with many others, particularly with our Italian colleagues. Now around thirty-seven countries participate in the International Listening Post project.

Emergent themes

Fear

The first major theme emerging from the International Listening Post is *fear*:

- "In the early days of the pandemic, there was fear and panic" [Ireland].
- "[With] large numbers of people dying, [and] many people losing close friends and relatives, the experience of death [was] closer and more real. This [led] to heightened levels of survival anxiety and regression" [UK].
- "We [were] fearful about getting Covid, often bordering upon 'panic in the pan(dem)ic'" [Ireland].
- "The pandemic puts us in contact with death, but one of the possible reactions to this is the repression of fear and anxiety" [northern Italy].
- "We deny, don't want to acknowledge our vulnerability: sickness, old age, weakness, death" [Lithuania].

All around the world, participants in the Listening Post reported increased levels of fear as a response to Covid-19. Fear is an understandable response to something as dangerous and uncontrollable as the virus. Interestingly, we may distinguish two types of fear. The first is "survival anxiety", which may be described as a conscious response to a perceived threat. The second is an "existential fear" of mortality, which may tentatively be described as an unconscious response to the human condition.

In the context of Covid-19, survival anxiety helps us focus our attention on the threat posed by the virus and adapt our behaviour accordingly, for example, by washing our hands or wearing a face mask. However, existential fear is less helpful as it may lead some to deny the threat of the virus, for example, by characterising it as "no worse than the flu". This type of fear also works against survival anxiety by undermining adaptive behaviour: if the virus poses no threat, why wash our hands?

Hypothesis:

- Covid-19 reminded us of our mortality and made us feel vulnerable.
- As a result, we noticed an increase of both survival anxiety and existential fear.
- Unable to come to terms with our own mortality, we denied the true scale of the threat and repressed our fears.

- We then failed to take effective action to prevent the spread of the virus.

On March 12, as the UK government pursued its disastrous policy of "herd immunity", Boris Johnson had these less than encouraging words for the British public: "I must level with you, level with the British public, many more families are going to lose loved ones before their time" (Kahn & Dunn, April 7, 2020). Three days later, UK supermarkets were urging their customers to "be considerate and stop panic buying" (*Sky News*, March 15, 2020).

Confusion

The second major emergent theme is *confusion*:

- "We needed to adjust ourselves for [the] bombardment of information" [Faroes].
- "[There was] a strong desire to deny, resist, and avoid the plethora of 'negative information from the media'" [Turkey].
- "It is increasingly … difficult to transfer beta elements into useful thoughts for thinking; for some reflection itself becomes difficult" [Canada].
- "We are faced with the limits of our thinking and the limits of our lives" [northern Italy].
- "[We are] unsure about everything" [USA].

Listening Post participants reported increased levels of confusion as a result of the media response to the pandemic. They were overwhelmed by 24-hour news bulletins, raw data ("R" numbers, infection rates, and ever-increasing death tolls), and Covid-19 "horror stories" intended to influence behaviour. They found themselves increasingly unable to think, process, and understand all the information:

- "One thing is coming after another and sometimes everything seems to be coming at the same time … [It] 'pulls me down if I think about it too much'" [Ireland].

One possible response to the media "bombardment" was to disengage from the news: switch off the television, turn off the radio, or disconnect the phone, shutting out the outside world. We did not want the virus to infect our minds any more than our bodies. This understandable approach had the adverse effect of increasing our dependency on governments and their scientific advisors to manage the pandemic on our behalf:

- "As citizens, there is an unfamiliar reliance on government, politicians, scientists, and medical advisors to manage our best interests during the pandemic" [Canada].
- "Those with political power 'steer the boat' in a stormy sea … the only possibility of salvation is perhaps to obey the commander, in order not to be shipwrecked" [Rome].

It was a risky strategy—more so in Western countries such as the UK and USA, where populist, neo-liberal governments were in power. Boris Johnson's advice on March 1, to "wash our hands with soap", may have been necessary but it was in no way sufficient. At that moment in time, Italy was already in lockdown. Yet, Johnson also seemed to boast that he "shook hands with everybody" (*The Independent*, March 27, 2020) at a hospital where patients were being treated for Covid-19. A little over three weeks later, he himself was in an intensive care unit being treated for the virus.

In the USA, President Donald Trump achieved new levels of notoriety during a press conference on April 24, in which he considered the benefits of injecting bleach into the body (BBC News, April 24, 2020) as a means of sterilising an infection. "It's a suggestion," he said. Clearly there is a danger in our (over)reliance on leaders.

Hypothesis:

- The media response to Covid-19 (24-hour news bulletins, raw data, and horror stories) quickly overwhelmed our ability to think, process, and understand.
- As a result, we started to feel lost, confused, and completely helpless.

- Unable to come up with any solutions of our own, we turned off the media and withdrew from society.
- Thus, our dependency on (sometimes unreliable) governments increased.

Grief

The third major theme emerging from the International Listening Post is *grief*:

- "People are dying, you only have to read the newspaper to see that, but there's no mourning for those people" [Milan].
- "These situations that we are exposed to cause deep wounds" [Turkey].
- "I do not think we will return to normality, every event leaves a mark" [southern Italy].
- "[I'm] 'finding it tough to keep going' and 'keep an even keel' …" [Ireland].
- "Now is like a marathon. I try to adapt but cannot be proactive … I feel tired … I would like to take a breath, to go out and breathe some fresh air … The sense of loneliness is heavy" [Milan].

Listening Post participants reported heightened levels of grief as a response to the pandemic. The pain of losing a loved one to the virus was compounded by social distancing and lockdown. It was no longer possible to meet with friends or family to mourn our losses.

Technological methods of communication (e.g. phone, text messages, social media, and video conferencing) were a lifeline for many, but could not replace real-life, face-to-face interactions. As a consequence, many of us experienced depression and even melancholy during lockdown—heavy feelings and a prolonged sense of grief that sometimes felt endless. It became difficult to maintain emotional contact with each other; therefore, when we suffered, we suffered alone.

- "[We are] willing to protect our bodies from physical death, [but in so doing] we give up an essential part of our humanity—the alive, real, bodily relationship—which leads us to social death" [Lithuania].

Hypothesis:

- Covid-19 has killed loved ones and devastated communities.
- We have experienced overwhelming levels of grief, sorrow, and loneliness.
- Unable to properly mourn the losses we have suffered (and with no end in sight), we have entered a state of melancholy.
- Thus, it has become more difficult to maintain emotional contact with each other and participate in social life.

Shame, blame, anger, and despair

A fourth theme emerging from the International Listening Post may be formulated around the closely related concepts of *shame, blame, anger, and despair*:

- "There was an overwhelming fear of some force that could and would shame you" [Ireland].
- "I do not want to stand out or turn myself into the topic of discussion or gossip, so I follow the herd" [Faroes].
- "I do not know if I have done something wrong and am about to be accused … It feels like a police car is driving behind me" [Faroes].
- "The fear of being punished was big in the group" [China].
- "It is as though a punitive parent has sent us to our rooms because we cannot be trusted: we have been locked in ('locked down')" [UK].
- "The anger for having been reduced to children who must obey the rules imposed from above, deprived of any decision-making possibility, coexists with resignation to a state of captivity and a consolidated dependence on those who hold political power" [Rome].

Such feelings are indicative of a "paranoid–schizoid" mindset, in which persecutory anxieties are prevalent and the psychic defences of splitting and projection are engaged as a means of preventing the total disintegration of the psyche.

Given governmental demands for individual citizens to act responsibly, many became obsessed with "doing the right thing". This led to strong feelings of shame when simple lapses of concentration such as forgetting to wear a facemask inevitably occurred, as well as heightened anxiety around being singled out for blame and becoming a social pariah.

A related point is the fear of punishment, and the unconscious, mistaken belief that lockdowns were imposed because we, as individual citizens, had "done something wrong". Of course, it is convenient for governments to allow this belief to continue, since it allows them to escape responsibility and the possibility of being held to account (or "punished") at the next general election.

The mainstream media has contributed to the "irresponsible citizens" narrative by highlighting instances of people frequenting bars and clubs or visiting the beach, for example. As a result, feelings of shame (i.e. "*I* have not been good enough") have been replaced by feelings of blame and anger (i.e. "*You* have not been good enough").

As the pandemic progressed, some of the strongest feelings of anger were directed towards governments. In times of crisis, we look to our governments for leadership; however, many of our leaders, particularly in the West, have appeared unable to manage the competing demands of safeguarding public health and protecting the economy:

- "Government choices on health and economy are compromises that don't satisfy anybody. Distrust of the politicians arises, as well as social conflicts" [Milan].
- "The government [is] blamed for not saving us from our fears and anxieties. Whilst constantly asserting that it is 'in control' and with everything 'well organised' the evidence does not support this and the virus progresses unabated" [UK].

In the UK, the British public was outraged when the prime minister's right-hand man, Dominic Cummings, inexplicably broke Covid-19 rules by apparently driving 200 miles to get his eyes tested (*The Independent*, May 25, 2020). More recently, Matt Hancock similarly stirred up public anger after a photograph emerged of him in a passionate embrace with his advisor (*The Guardian*, June 25, 2021).

After a year of living with Covid-19, social distancing, and lockdowns, it is perhaps no surprise that some Listening Post participants also reported feelings of despair:

- "I am in despair for my country. I can't see good things about hope. I do not think that we manage this process well as a country. I think we all struggle with uncertainty" [Turkey].
- "When it comes to society, I don't know whether there will be anything left to piece back together" [Poland].

Hypothesis:

- In the absence of containing leadership, it became clear that government expectations for individual citizens to "act responsibly" were unreasonably high.
- Therefore, citizens began to experience persecutory anxieties and a terrible feeling of not being good enough.
- Unable to prevent the spread of the virus, we started to feel as though we, as individual citizens, had somehow failed.
- Then we angrily blamed each other and felt despair as society began to fracture.

Breakdown of society

The fifth and final theme to be presented here is slightly different than the others presented above in that it is not psychological but rather sociological. It is *the breakdown of society*:

- "The pandemic dramatically exacerbates social and economic inequality and reveals the stark disparities in access to life-sustaining resources" [Canada].
- "As the pandemic started to progress, I saw unemployed people in the society and people struggling. I [felt] sorry and sad" [Turkey].
- "There are approximately 430 million fellow citizens who are migrants, completely neglected for basic education and health care" [India].
- "Being in power consists in building the advantage of one group at the cost of the others … other needs and emerging identities find neither reflection nor support at the systemic level" [Poland].
- "Inequality in capitalist society together with the Covid crisis [has] brought about a lack of trust in authority and the breaking apart and fragmentation of society into minority groups" [Israel].

- "Brazilians do not demand anything from the government. Instead, they take an every-man-for-himself stance" [Brazil].
- "Is this survival of the fittest? It feels like a post-apocalyptic war zone, where it's everyone for themselves" [South Africa].
- "The failure of major institutions … has led to regression to primitive levels of functioning characterised by splitting, projection, and retreat to a sense of pseudo self-sufficiency" [USA].
- "The current system has failed" [southern Italy].

Listening Post participants reported preoccupations and experiences that can easily be associated with a breakdown of society. These reports seem to indicate a loss of faith in governments and other social institutions that we believed (perhaps naively) were there to keep us safe. Those beliefs have been severely tested by the pandemic.

In normal times, governments and other social institutions such as councils, schools, churches and other places of worship, community centres, sports clubs, and even the local pub all serve as "containers" for our anxieties, where we may talk and share experiences, or else engage in comforting social rituals such as kicking a ball into the back of a net.

Unfortunately, the pandemic brought about a catastrophic loss of containment. Social distancing and the experience of being deprived of human contact during lockdown compounded our understandable emotional responses to the virus. The tragic result appears to have been social fragmentation into minority groups and/or a retreat to individualism.

It is our responsibility as more privileged members of society (here, an assumption is being made on the types of people that are likely to be reading this report) to recognise that no matter how shocking these findings may seem to us, for other, more disadvantaged members of society they reflect a sad reality of everyday life:

- "Some are comfortably waiting for the vaccine to be provided, but others, if not exposed to the virus, will starve to death" [Brazil].
- "It's easy to worry about the economy from a position of privilege … People at the bottom are going to lose out the most" [South Africa].

Covid-19 has only exacerbated pre-existing structural failings in society. The problems we are facing now as a result of the pandemic are not new but they are more visible and pronounced. We know that the virus has a disproportionate effect on people of lower socio-economic status and minority ethnic backgrounds. Is it not ludicrous and derisory to suggest, "We're all in this together!"? (Sensi, April 10, 2020).

Hypothesis:

- Covid-19 has had a devastating impact on people from lower socio-economic and minority ethnic backgrounds.
- The virus has unveiled economic disparities and gaps in social welfare provision.
- Faith in governments and society is at an all-time low.
- Therefore, individuals have turned away from government, from society, and from each other, prioritising their own interests above those of others.

Conclusions

The findings of the International Listening Post in 2021 are of great importance to the OPUS mission of promoting understanding of society. Although it was not possible to cover everything in this brief chapter, for those who are interested to find out more, the reports of twenty-two countries are available on the OPUS website and are highly recommended.

The emergent themes that were selected for this chapter focus predominantly on psychological experiences of the Covid-19 pandemic in relation to societal influences, in particular the role of governments and the mainstream media in determining our individual responses to the crisis. It should come as no surprise that there is an immutable link between the individual and society.

Neither should it be surprising that serious problems have been identified. For example, the failure of the UK government adequately to protect its citizens was due not only to a lack of competence, but also to a failure of neo-liberal ideology, including the imposition of the austerity period that preceded the pandemic and led to severe underfunding of the NHS and a lack of fully trained doctors and nurses. We see similar problems in countries all around the world that lack basic social welfare provision.

At a more macro level we can see that without trust, democratic governments cannot function effectively. Loss of trust means that containment for society as a whole fails, and citizens fall back or regress back to their next most meaningful grouping, whether that is the family, nuclear or extended, or their local community. One of the more positive outcomes of this regression has been that the normally dormant role of citizen has been mobilised in a conscious and productive way, so that neighbours have actively helped and supported each other during these difficult times.

Further, there are implications for climate change, temporarily forgotten in the panic of the pandemic but now impossible to ignore. For example, we know now that the pandemic cannot be resolved by individual measures alone, such as hand washing and the wearing of face masks, without the implementation of a global mass vaccination programme. Similarly, the climate crisis cannot be resolved by regular recycling and a reusable coffee cup. Global governments must take responsibility for the crisis at a systemic level. This was explored during the COP26 (Conference of Parties) international conference in Glasgow in the autumn of 2021.

There are also some interesting parallels to be drawn between the origin of climate change issues (making the atmosphere toxic) and the origin of the pandemic, which was apparently due to the close contaminating proximity of humans with animals (making humans toxic).

Finally, an equally grave possibility lies in changes in society, whereby distrust of government and a failure of containment will tend to mobilise more authoritarian leaders, leading to a greater dismantling of democratic structures. The question remains as to whether citizens, now more in touch with the power of their citizen roles, are able to use their authority proactively to rebuild their communities democratically from the bottom up so as to enable greater integration of wider society; or whether governmental failure is so profound and the fractures are so deep that this proves impossible to achieve.

References

BBC News (2020, April 24). Coronavirus: outcry after Trump suggests injecting disinfectant as a treatment. https://bbc.co.uk/news/world-us-canada-52407177 (last accessed August 19, 2020).

Bion, W. R. (1952). Group dynamics: a review. *International Journal of Psychoanalysis*, 33(2): 235–247.

Burdeau, C. (2020, March 17). Boris Johnson's talk of "herd immunity" raises alarms. https://courthousenews.com/boris-johnsons-talk-of-herd-immunity-raises-alarms/ (last accessed August 18, 2021).

Coffey, H. (2020, August 16). World's Biggest Mass Migration begins as China prepares to mark New Year https://independent.co.uk/travel/news-and-advice/chinese-lunar-new-year-mass-migration-spring-festival-flights-trains-a9288301.html (last accessed August 16, 2021).

Department of Health & Social Care (2020, February 2). Coronavirus public information campaign launched across the UK. https://gov.uk/government/news/coronavirus-public-information-campaign-launched-across-the-uk (last accessed August 18, 2021).

Department of Health & Social Care (2020a, February 10). Secretary of State makes new regulations on coronavirus. https://gov.uk/government/news/secretary-of-state-makes-new-regulations-on-coronavirus (last accessed August 18, 2021).

Department of Health & Social Care (2020b, February 10). Health Secretary announces strengthened legal powers to bolster public health protections against coronavirus. https://gov.uk/government/news/health-secretary-announces-strengthened-legal-powers-to-bolster-public-health-protections-against-coronavirus (last accessed August 18, 2021).

Department of Health & Social Care and the Rt Hon Matt Hancock MP (2020, March 1). Health Secretary sets out government "battle plan" for COVID 19.

Ellery, B., Smith, C., Ball, T., & Wace, C. (2020, February 13). Coronavirus hits London as infected woman flies in from China. *The Times*. https://thetimes.co.uk/article/coronavirus-in-london-as-infected-woman-flies-in-from-china-dvhx79m8t (last accessed March 29, 2022). https://gov.uk/government/news/health-secretary-sets-out-government-battle-plan-for-covid-19 (last accessed August 18, 2021).

Gosling, R. H. (1981). A study of very small groups. In: J. S. Grotstein (Ed.), *Do I Dare Disturb the Universe? A Memorial to Wilfred R. Bion* (pp. 634–645). Beverly Hills, CA: Caesura.

Guardian, The (2020, February 10). "Superspreader" brought coronavirus from Singapore to Sussex via France. https://theguardian.com/world/2020/feb/10/super-spreader-brought-coronavirus-from-singapore-to-sussex-via-france (last accessed August 18, 2021).

Guardian, The (2021, June 25). Matt Hancock apologises after photos show him kissing aide. https://theguardian.com/politics/2021/jun/25/matt-hancock-gina-coladangelo-grant-shapps-health-job (last accessed August 18, 2021).

Hancock, M. (2020, January 27). Wuhan coronavirus: Health Secretary's statement to Parliament. https://gov.uk/government/speeches/wuhan-coronavirus-health-secretarys-statement-to-parliament (last accessed August 16, 2021).

Independent, The (2020, March 27). Coronavirus: How Boris Johnson ignored health advice at his peril before Covid-19 diagnosis. https://independent.co.uk/news/uk/politics/coronavirus-boris-johnson-positive-test-health-advice-shaking-hands-hospital-hancock-a9430231.html (last accessed September 9, 2021).

Independent, The (2020, May 25). Dominic Cummings says he left Durham self-isolation to drive to Barnard Castle to "test his eyesight". https://independent.co.uk/news/uk/politics/dominic-cummings-statement-barnard-castle-durham-eyesight-press-briefing-speech-a9531766.html (last accessed September 9, 2021).

Khaleelee, O., & Miller, E. J. (1985). Beyond the small group: society as an intelligible field of study. In: M. Pines (Ed.), *Bion and Group Psychotherapy* (pp. 354–385). London: Routledge & Kegan Paul.

Kahn, J., & Dunn, K. (2020, April 7). U.K's Boris Johnson, who initially advocated herd immunity, becomes symbol of the strategy's danger. https://fortune.com/2020/04/06/uk-boris-johnson-coronavirus-icu-herd-immunity/ (last accessed August 19, 2021).

Lillie, P. J., Samson, A., Li, A., Adams, K., Capstick, R., Barlow, G. D., Easom, N., Hamilton, E., Moss, P. J., Evans, A., Ivan, M., PHE Incident Team, Taha, Y., Duncan, C. J. A., Schmid, M. L., & the Airborne HCID Network (2020). Novel coronavirus disease. Covid-19: the first two patients in the UK with person to person transmission. *Journal of Infection, 80*(5): 578–606. https://ncbi.nlm.nih.gov/pmc/articles/PMC7127394/ (last accessed August 16, 2021).

Ministry of Housing, Communities & Local Government, and the Rt Hon Robert Jenrick, MP (2020, March 20). Government announces further measures on social distancing. https://gov.uk/government/news/government-announces-further-measures-on-social-distancing (last accessed August 18, 2021).

Neilson, S., & Woodward, A. (2020, December 24). A comprehensive timeline of the coronavirus pandemic at 1 year, from China's first case to the present. *Business Insider.* https://businessinsider.com/coronavirus-pandemic-timeline-history-major-events-2020-3?r=US&IR=T (last accessed August 16, 2021).

New York Times, The (2020, January 24). Toll from outbreak climbs in China as infections reach Europe and Australia. https://nytimes.com/2020/01/24/world/asia/china-coronavirus.html (last accessed August 16, 2021).

Prime Minister's Office, 10 Downing Street and the Rt Hon Boris Johnson, MP (2020, March 18). Prime Minister's statement on Coronavirus (COVID-19). https://gov.uk/government/speeches/pm-statement-on-coronavirus-18-march-2020 (last accessed August 18, 2021).

Prime Minister's Office Downing Street and The Rt Hon Boris Johnson, MP (2020, March 23). Prime Minister's statement on Coronavirus (COVID-19). https://gov.uk/government/speeches/pm-address-to-the-nation-on-coronavirus-23-march-2020/ (last accessed August 18, 2021).

Public Health England and Department of Health & Social Care (2020, January 10). Novel coronavirus and avian flu: advice for travel to China. https://gov.uk/government/news/novel-coronavirus-and-avian-flu-advice-for-travel-to-china (last accessed August 16, 2021).

Raab, D. (2020, January 28). Foreign office advises against all but essential travel to mainland China. https://gov.uk/government/news/fco-advises-against-all-but-essential-travel-to-mainland-china (last accessed August 16, 2021).

Reuters (2019, December 31). Chinese officials investigate cause of virus outbreak in Wuhan. https://reuters.com/article/us-china-health-pneumonia-idUSKBN1YZ0GP (last accessed August 13, 2021).

Schnirring, L. (2020, January 16). Japan has 1st novel coronavirus case; China reports another death. CIDRAP News. https://cidrap.umn.edu/news-perspective/2020/01/japan-has-1st-novel-coronavirus-case-china-reports-another-death (last accessed August 16, 2021).

Sensi, J. (2020, April 10). Boris Johnson says we're all in this together, so why is the government penalising the self-employed? *Accountancy Today*, front page. https://accountancytoday.co.uk/2020/04/10/boris-johnson-says-were-all-in-this-together-so-why-is-the-government-penalising-the-self-employed/ (last accessed September 11, 2021).

Sky News (2020, March 15). Coronavirus: Supermarkets tell public to be considerate and stop panic buying. https://news.sky.com/story/coronavirus-supermarkets-tell-public-to-be-considerate-and-stop-panic-buying-11957735 (last accessed August 19, 2021).

Turquet, P. M. (1974). Leadership: the individual and the group. In: G. S. Gibbard, J. J. Harman, & R. D. Mann (Eds.), *Analysis of Groups* (pp. 337–371). San Francisco, CA: Jossey Bass.

Turquet, P. M. (1975). Threats to identity in the large group. In: L. Kreeger (Ed.), *The Large Group: Dynamics and Therapy* (pp. 87–144). London: Constable.

Woolhouse, M., Scott, F., Hudson, Z., Howey, R., & Chase-Topping, M. (2012, October 19). Human viruses: discovery and emergence. https://ncbi.nlm.nih.gov/pmc/articles/PMC3427559/ (last accessed August 13, 2021). https://who.int/news-room/articles-detail/who-advice-for-international-travel-and-trade-in-relation-to-the-outbreak-of-pneumonia-caused-by-a-new-coronavirus-in-china (last accessed August 16, 2021).

World Health Organization (2020, January 14). Novel Coronavirus—Thailand (ex China). https://who.int/emergencies/disease-outbreak-news/item/2020-DON234 (last accessed August 16, 2021).

World Health Organization (2020, January 30). Statement on the second meeting of the International Health Regulations (2005) Emergency Committee regarding the outbreak of novel coronavirus (2019-nCoV). https://who.int/news/item/30-01-2020-statement-on-the-second-meeting-of-the-international-health-regulations-(2005)-emergency-committee-regarding-the-outbreak-of-novel-coronavirus-(2019-ncov) (last accessed August 16, 2021).

World Health Organization (2020, March 11). WHO's Director General's opening remarks at the media briefing on Covid-19. https://www.who.int/director-general/speeches/detail/who-director-general-s-opening-remarks-at-the-media-briefing-on-covid-19---11-march-2020 (last accessed August 16, 2021).

Part IV

Our new Covidian world

Norwegian Landscape, 1900 by Edvard Munch
Credit: Universal History Archive/UIG/Bridgeman Images

CHAPTER 13

The Long Covid at an individual and societal level

by Anthony Berendt

> *The keeper's gibbet had owls and hawks*
> *By the neck, weasels, a gang of cats, crows:*
> *Some, stiff, weightless, twirled like dry bark bits*
>
> *In the drilling rain. Some still had their shape,*
> *Had their pride with it; hung, chins on chests,*
> *Patient to outwait these worst days that beat*
> *Their crowns bare and dripped from their feet.*
> —"November" (Hughes, 1960)

Introduction

> *Ladies and Gentlemen, the times are bad*
> *When worry's sane and not to worry mad.*
> —*Mr Puntila and His Man Matti* (Brecht, 1950)

If *The Long Covid* were the title of a novel or film, it might tell a story of hardship, fear, loss, endurance, hope, and deliverance, through and from a global pandemic. While Covid-19 and long Covid are physical diseases of individuals occurring in the context of a pandemic, the Long

Covid is a global experience, an ordeal, a test of endurance. How will it define us all, and how will it cast its shadow into the future, as, like the shapes in the rain in Ted Hughes's poem above, we "outwait these worst days"?

We can ask this question, but can we sensibly address it yet? Pandemics typically last for years (McMillen, 2016). From a global perspective, it is far from over, with just under 3 million new cases, and just under 50,000 deaths per week, reported in October 2021 (Johns Hopkins University, 2021).[1] While the industrialised, higher income nations are armed, above all, with their vaccination programmes, globally many people are still at risk. Despite 6.8 billion vaccine doses administered worldwide, only 3% of people in low-income countries, and 48.3% of the world's population, have received a dose (Our World in Data, 2021). More than 4 billion people are entirely unvaccinated. How many of these have natural immunity from encountering SARS-CoV-2 is unknown.[2]

Nonetheless it has been argued that "epidemics are as much social, political, and economic events as they are biological; the 'end', therefore, is as much a process of social and political negotiation as it is biomedical" (Charters & Heitman, 2021). Epidemics (and pandemics) typically end for some groups of people before they end for others; and they very rarely end with the complete disappearance or eradication of the pathogen. So, too, for Covid-19; we already see some nations, with high levels of vaccination, easing social restrictions despite continuing transmission. Of course, there are powerful economic and social drivers for society to return to its habitual activities, essential as they are to the current global economic engine of which we are all a part. Meanwhile the disadvantaged and vulnerable of the world, even some of those fully vaccinated, will continue to die because of Covid-19, long after those in power declare the pandemic to be over (Giubilini & Charters, 2021).

---

[1] After this chapter was first written, the Omicron variant swept the globe. Weekly deaths peaked at over 23 million in January 2022 and, by September 2022, had never fallen below 3 million per week (with the exception of March 2022 when deaths fell below 50,000 per week).

[2] In September 2022, 12.62 billion vaccine doses had been administered worldwide; 21% of people in low-income countries, and 67.7% of the world's population, have received at least one dose. More than 2.55 billion people remain unvaccinated.

Despite this, this chapter will consider, with reference in part to systems-psychodynamic ideas, what long-term changes might occur at an individual and societal level as a result of the Covid-19 pandemic. I will also discuss the clinical entity of "long Covid", and consider both how the various *physical* manifestations of infection with the SARS-CoV-2 coronavirus might be used as *metaphors* for responses at a societal level, but also—and much more importantly—how individual and collective responses to Covid-19 as a *disease* might mirror, in a true parallel process, the individual and collective responses to Covid-19 as a global *experience*.

In considering what these tell us about the future, we have to think not only about previous pandemics, but also about our world prior to December 2019. For it is not so much that Covid-19 will cast shadows on history, but that instead it acts as a source of illumination, showing us, in unforgiving and sharper contrast, the shadows we have been casting since long before Covid-19 struck.

Why do pandemics happen? In the past, we might have blamed malign supernatural forces or the wrath of God. Today, we point instead to multiple interacting factors that are of humanity's making: increasing encroachment of humans and their livestock into the natural environment, creating opportunities for microbes to jump species barriers from wild animals to domestic animals and/or humans; changes in farming, animal husbandry, and food production that may also favour this; the growth in number and size of densely populated cities where people live and work, often in crowded conditions; the development of extensive global networks of travel for people and goods (Ferguson, 2021). These are all behaviours demanded and maintained by our existing geopolitical economic systems, and they create ideal conditions for pandemic spread. The Covid-19 pandemic can be thus seen as a manifestation and consequence of civilisation as we have made it.

Covid-19 and long Covid

The natural history of infection with SARS-CoV-2 has proved highly variable, ranging from being entirely asymptomatic, or with mild symptoms, to causing severe, life-threatening involvement of multiple organs. The virus can disseminate widely in the body and gain entry to the cells lining blood vessels, triggering a range of inflammatory and coagulation problems (Parasher, 2021). These varied presentations and outcomes of disease reflect the variability of viral spread and host response.

It was initially assumed that as with many viral infections, survivors of SARS-CoV-2 infection—of Covid-19—would make a rapid and uneventful recovery, unless they had suffered specific complications such as clotting in blood vessels causing stroke, heart attack, or problems with blood supply to limbs, or major physical deconditioning following the need for prolonged intensive care. This supposition was reflected in official documentation about what to expect after Covid-19. However, within a few months of the declaration of the pandemic, it became clear that for some patients, recovery, even after what seemed to be minor infection, was not straightforward. Patients were experiencing persistent symptoms lasting many weeks, sometimes months, after their acute illness. Social media played a particularly important role in this aspect of the pandemic coming to light. In part this was because many patients had much more limited access to primary care doctors—whom they could otherwise have consulted about their symptoms—because of infection control precautions; in part because not all doctors were validating and supportive of these patients' continuing problems (whereas fellow sufferers were); and in part because social media allows the rapid creation of online communities for support and the exchange of experiences.

The symptoms of long Covid, as this syndrome came to be called, are highly variable in nature and over time (Davis et al., 2021). Most patients have multiple symptoms involving multiple organ systems. The most debilitating symptoms that patients report are fatigue, breathing problems, and cognitive dysfunction ("brain fog", poor attention, and difficulties in problem-solving, decision-making, and executive functioning). A whole host of other symptoms are experienced, including sleep disturbance; neuropsychiatric symptoms; memory impairment; and gastrointestinal, respiratory, cardiovascular, skin, genitourinary and musculoskeletal problems. Over time, the nature and balance of these may change, but at any one time, a patient is likely to be struggling with many different symptoms.

A study of patient narratives associated with long Covid highlighted the strangeness of these experiences, the chronicity of symptoms, and the relapsing and remitting nature of the condition, often within a context of isolation from medical interest and support. In this sense, long Covid has been described as "a 'patient-made illness', the first to emerge by patients finding one another through social media" (Callard & Perego, 2020 quoted by Rushforth et al., 2021), in the context of "the collective failure—arguably for good reasons—of clinicians to acknowledge, interpret, or act on their patients' stories and plights" (Rushforth et al., 2021). Similar issues arose during the HIV pandemic, when patients often had to act as their own advocates when institutions lacked knowledge and much of society was unsympathetic (Funtowicz & Ravetz, 1993).

There is much that remains uncertain about long Covid, with a range of hypotheses that include persistent viral infection, residual fragments of viral material, post-traumatic stress, and long-lived dysfunction of the immune system triggered by the initial infection. Research into causation and treatment continues. Long Covid (as defined by persistent symptoms at twelve weeks after infection) appears to affect a significant proportion of the population. Estimates of the prevalence of long Covid vary between studies, ranging from 2.3% to 37% of people post-Covid-19. While 1.2% of infections in twenty-year-olds lead to debilitating long Covid symptoms, the proportion rises to 4.8% in sixty-year-olds (Park et al., 2021). In England alone, there may be 2 million people with some, though not necessarily debilitating, symptoms at twelve weeks, with services being set up in response to assist in their rehabilitation. With holistic support, rest, gradual return to activity, and management of symptoms, many patients recover slowly over time (NHS England, 2021).

Long Covid as a metaphor for the pandemic

It is tempting to see long Covid as a metaphor for the pandemic as a whole. The world has had an encounter with a new and unknown adversary, SARS-CoV-2, in a full-blown pandemic. There was initial confusion. Just as for the individual developing long Covid, society was unsure what was happening, how serious it would be, what would happen next. Just as with the lack of validation of long Covid symptoms by people in power (medical professionals), the validation of society's experiences was lacking; insufficient attention was given to concerns, and lack of government action increased distress. And just as the long

Covid patient suffers from multiple complaints in multiple organ systems, including brain fog, fatigue, memory impairment, and difficulty breathing, society as a whole has often seemed unable to think coherently, behaves in parts as if fatigued by the pandemic, appears not to remember the lessons of the past, and feels suffocated in lockdown.

This metaphor may be interesting, but is it useful? Mechanistically, the symptoms of a long Covid sufferer do not *create* the features described at a societal level. There is no systemic link across from the myriad symptoms of the individual to how whole societies have responded to the Covid-19 pandemic. Nor does a psychodynamic link in the opposite direction seem plausible; we would have to suggest that the symptoms of people with long Covid are introjections of the global population's feelings of confusion, fatigue, and anxiety (to name just a few symptoms), a tenuous argument likely to be highly contentious and upsetting to most long Covid sufferers.

There is, however a different potential link, and one that more plausibly establishes a parallel process between everyone in the pandemic. Each individual, whatever their situation, is connected in the common experience of the pandemic, in the Long Covid—an individual and collective experience of uncertainty, and the anxiety it creates, in the face of an unknown threat. This uncertainty cannot readily be resolved, but must be endured, by individuals, groups, nations, and the world. Whatever our situation, our lives must accommodate the new context of the pandemic, the uncertainty it brings, and the affront it constitutes to the illusion of certainly that we mostly try, so hard, to create.

The systems-psychodynamic perspective

All models are wrong, but some are useful.
—George Box (statistician)

Sigmund Freud was nominated for the Nobel Prize for physiology or medicine in twelve different years (Nobel Prize nomination archive, 2021). He was never awarded it, reminding us that his ideas were important to some, but contested, from a scientific standpoint, from the outset. Despite this, his impact on psychology has been profound and pervasive. At the heart of objections to his theories was the view that they were based on a hypothesis, and had not been derived or proved through scientific methods. Yet they have been the basis of the successful treatment of many patients in the last century, as well as striking a chord beyond their use in medicine, one that continues to reverberate today. The controversy over Freud's theories can be seen as a conflict between different belief systems (the scientific method versus the theoretical discourses of the humanities) and different hierarchies of evidence, but it also throws into focus that there are different conceptions of truth, and that truth and usefulness are continua located on different axes; "true" is not always "useful"; "useful" is not necessarily "true" by everyone's reckoning.

The objections of the Nobel award committee did not prevent the widespread adoption of psychoanalysis and the subsequent work of those whose legacy has been the systems-psychodynamic approach to group and organisational life. In addition to considering how Melanie Klein's concepts of splitting and projection of emotions (1959), from one individual onto another, might be applicable in groups, the field considers the importance of anxiety as simultaneously a motivator for, and an impediment to, task performance (the task being undertaken to resolve an identified source of anxiety, but anxiety regarding the task triggering various unconscious defences that may interfere with the work). Unconscious responses to anxiety include the basic assumption behaviours of dependency, fight–flight, and pairing in small groups (Bion, 1961), the large group social defences (Jaques, 1955; Menzies-Lyth, 1960), and between the two (in the extent to which the response is concealed), Hirschhorn's "covert coalition" (1988). Adding elements of open systems theory and systems thinking, the model asserts the importance of leadership (a function that derives significant authority from the projections of followers) as a boundary function of group and organisation, defining the primary task for the group and taking numerous other responsibilities that both ensure operational functioning, but also "meaning-making", for those in the group.

When considering a global pandemic, we can look for evidence of all the phenomena outlined above, driving the behaviour of people in groups and countries. We can do this in different ways. If we take the position that the systems-psychodynamic perspective is a useful model for interpreting behaviour, we could be content to find examples that fit the model. But if we claim that the systems-psychodynamic model is not only useful, but is also true (despite the reservations of George Box above), and describes fundamentals of human nature, then we have an extended form of usefulness. We can both validate our model through the events we see, and also use it to consider what the future may hold … given that with the exceptions of asteroid impact and supervolcano eruption, so much of our future, even disasters like pandemics, will be the outcome of the collective activities of humans and their unconscious drivers.

The Covid-19 pandemic through the systems-psychodynamic lens

What are pandemics, these bushfires of the microbial world, unstoppably spreading fear, illness, and death around the planet? Perhaps understanding this will help us to think about them from a psychodynamic perspective.

Specialists in infectious diseases have suggested that eight criteria must be met to define a pandemic (McMillen, 2016):

1. Wide geographical extension
2. Disease movement
3. High attack rates and explosiveness
4. Minimal population immunity
5. Novelty
6. Infectiousness
7. Contagiousness
8. Severity.

Examined individually, these criteria give us clues about what psychodynamic processes might be evoked by *any* pandemic.

Wide geographical extension of the outbreak of infection means people will have an awareness of scale. Each person knows they are living through something extending far beyond their own span of action and control. This creates a feeling of powerlessness. It also creates opportunities to fantasise about the role of "others" (i.e. anyone, elsewhere) in spreading infection.

Disease movement is further linked to geographical extension—people know that the disease moves, carried in from other villages, towns, cities, or countries by returning travellers or outsiders. Suspicion and fear of others grows.

High attack rates and explosiveness—for example through super-spreader events—lead to a sense of mass casualty, rapidly evolving case numbers, and instability. We experience an enhanced perception of threat, not only to our health but also, in effect simultaneously, to that of close family, friends, and near neighbours. All we love, the very social fabric of our lives, is threatened, and quickly.

Minimal population immunity means that initially, no one is safe; anxiety can legitimately know no bounds when we, and all those we know, are simultaneously at risk.

Novelty means we cannot know what effects the disease will have on us, or anyone affected. We cannot know how things will end. Until there are plausible experts to advise us about the disease, fantasy and rumour are in charge.

Infectiousness evokes the dread of bodily invasion, contamination, corruption, and physical annihilation. Our bodies are no longer our own, our defences penetrated by unseen aliens that enter our being and make us sick.

Contagiousness brings the fear of contact, even (or especially) intimate contact, but also the necessity to avoid contact in order to avoid disease. With this come consequences; isolation, the loss of social pleasures, and perhaps also of our livelihood. Our choices are fearfully to isolate ourselves or fearlessly (even recklessly) to continue with our social and working lives as best we can.

Severity, finally, increases our personal likelihood of harm if we do develop the disease, with its attendant known and unknown risks of pain, death, disability, stigma. Greater personal threat brings greater anxiety.

I suggest that this combination of factors together acts to amplify anxiety, to mobilise individual defences against it, and to function as a focus for the deeper existential anxieties we all hold. Our habitual support structures for containment, in our personal or working lives, are either caught up in their own anxieties, or inaccessible to us through our fear or because of public health measures. Contact and work via phone or online platforms mitigate this isolation for some, but also introduce new anxieties. And contact with others exposes us to the anxieties of individuals and groups, and media reports of the evolution of the pandemic.

As individuals, we fall back on our own psychological resources, some stimulated by anxiety into selfish acts, others responding with altruism. In this and previous pandemics, there have been many remarkable examples of both. Selfish acts have included the panic buying of goods causing temporary shortages, and the flight of the privileged from infected cities to other parts of the country, even though this risks dispersing the disease. Altruistic acts included healthcare workers courageously treating patients even when they had major concerns (later sadly proved true) about the risks to themselves due to inadequate personal protective equipment; and the volunteering of many who helped vulnerable neighbours, returned to unpaid work in hospitals or vaccination centres, or supported public service workers with gifts, food, and home-made face coverings or surgical scrubs.

Unable to rely on our usual mechanisms to contain anxiety, we look to our leaders (political, medical, religious, and in the current age, social media) for containment of it. Sadly, in many nations, this containment has not been forthcoming, with leaders refusing to implement basic public health measures or to endorse face coverings (*BBC News*, October 20, 2021). In every pandemic some have preferred to trust those who deny the existence of the pandemic or the need to take measures against it. In the current pandemic, "Covid deniers" have influenced many to refuse treatment (even to leave hospital while unwell), eschew face coverings, and to protest against lockdown. Many have also joined with existing "anti-vaccine" movements of people who refute and refuse vaccination, and are highly connected via social media. Opinion and information, at variance with scientific orthodoxy and the public health strategies pursued by most governments, circulate; so great has the volume and impact of this been that the World Health Organization (2020) has labelled this an "infodemic" ... a "tsunami" of information, some true, some false and harmful, circulating at pandemic pace and breadth. This has not only taken the form of individuals creating and distributing false information about Covid-19 and vaccines within their own social networks, but also of more organised and widespread distribution of misinformation using automated social media accounts.

As groups, we respond collectively to each other's emotions and to the positions taken by leaders. In the current pandemic, prominent figures who broke the rules of public health measures, through forbidden travel or social contact, were rapidly and vigorously condemned and cast out of their roles, even though most individuals would privately admit to their own small breaches of regulations. New social defences emerged, for example in the United Kingdom in relation to its National Health Service (NHS). This cradle-to-grave healthcare service, provided free to all at the point of delivery, is often put forward as an exemplar of state-funded healthcare systems, offering value for money and high-quality care, training, and research. It enjoys enormous popular affection and respect. But it has many constraints, demographic and financial.

There is relentless growth in demand for healthcare and expectations of it, but governments have often not increased funding in line with these changes. The unspoken pact between government, media, and much of the population appears to be that the NHS must continue to meet unlimited demand within allocated resources, continually providing "more for less". Despite the reality that this is an impossible task, meaning that the service is *de facto* rationed (through waiting lists and other means), explicit discussions about this are confined to the fringes of any debate.

It is as if the NHS is acting not only as a healthcare organisation but also as a social defence against the anxieties of facing illness, death, and suffering in the context of finite resource. When the defence appears to function, the institution is loved. When the NHS appears not to function, the defence it provides crumbles, and popular anxiety is released, often as criticism of the service.

One notable trend in the course of the first wave of the pandemic was an emphasis on protecting the NHS, to prevent it becoming overwhelmed by large numbers of patients with Covid-19. As was seen in other countries, this can lead to very serious consequences for all patients in need, whether or not Covid-19 is their diagnosis. In the UK, there was a notable use of military metaphors in early talk about the pandemic and the NHS, as well as visible use of the military to develop surge facilities in case of mass casualties from infection. The effort was likened to a war against the virus, a common cause articulated in the phrase "we are all in it together". Staff were hailed as "heroes", an accolade many were uncomfortable with, not least because heroes in war are often sacrificed or sacrifice themselves. Was this an expectation, that staff who contracted Covid-19 might simply be seen as inevitable casualties of war? Perhaps government hoped that by casting the effort as a war, many normal processes of governance, oversight, and criticism, even of morality, might be suspended, a justification to be deployed in the aftermath if criticism arose. And while the NHS was protected, this did not mean people were protected from death; a high proportion of deaths in the first wave occurred in nursing and care homes.

A popular movement called "Clap for Carers" emerged in the UK. At an agreed time once a week, people gathered on their doorsteps, windows, or balconies to applaud for a few minutes. It was a brief moment of socially distanced, permitted, communal activity to honour hard-pressed healthcare workers (and over time, all essential workers). Prominent public figures, from royalty to politicians, joined the event, which quickly assumed the status of a ritual (Addley, 2020). Television coverage was reverential, featuring multiple shots of applauding people in diverse locations across the country, much like similar coverage of commemorative silences to honour the dead of war or disaster. This practice lasted for ten weeks during the first UK wave in 2020. As Covid-19 cases and deaths declined, and the pressure on the NHS eased, the ritual ceased.

Consciously, the Clap for Carers was a means for the nation to show its gratitude to healthcare workers. It also created connection with neighbours, a release of pent-up energy, and expressed a collective resolve against the coronavirus. It is not clear how health and social care staff felt about it (Manthorpe et al., 2021).

I suggest that it was also a transient social defence: against the anxiety of the NHS being overwhelmed and the other anxieties brought to the fore by the pandemic. For when the UK experienced a second wave of infection and death in 2021, there was no repetition of the public outpouring of gratitude. An attempt to revive the Clap for Carers in 2021 was abortive.

Why was this? The second wave was at least as severe as the first, and healthcare workers were under as much pressure as during the first wave, with the added challenge of trying to recover from their earlier experiences.

There could be several reasons: "compassion fatigue" on the part of the public (we know compassion is finite); the winter months being less appealing as a time to gather on doorsteps; the growing sense towards the end of the 2020 "Clap" that it had become politicised. But we should also note that by the time of the second wave, there had been major advances in treatment for severe illness, so that death from severe Covid-19 was less likely, and critically, the evidence was clear that effective vaccines had been developed; indeed, the mass vaccination programme had already been commenced in the UK. The public no longer needed the Clap for Carers as a social defence against pandemic anxiety … it had a new social defence, the mass vaccination programme.

Long-term changes

The most reliable way to predict the future is to create it.
—Abraham Lincoln

People ask me to predict the future, when all I want to do is prevent it. Better yet, build it. Predicting the future is much too easy, anyway. You look at the people around you, the street you stand on, the visible air you breathe, and predict more of the same.
—Ray Bradbury

Anyone can predict the future, but predicting it accurately is notoriously difficult. Traditionally, predictions are made by historians, economists, or other experts. The interested reader is referred to a comprehensive set of predictions considered by Ferguson (2021). Expert forecasting has many risks, dominated as it is by the thinking of a single person. Hence the alternative approach to future forecasting, of scenario planning, which involves the deliberate imagining—by an interested group, rather than an individual—of multiple possible futures, rather than a single set of events (Scoblic, 2020). Each imagined scenario is then subjected to detailed thinking to develop its features and implications. Effort can subsequently be put into planning not for one future but for several; the effect of planning in this way being to develop not just concrete plans for different eventualities, but the organisational agility to respond variably and to the unexpected. From a psychodynamic point of view, scenario planning strikes a compromise between an all-knowing (but highly likely to be "wrong") expert stance and an "all-unknowing" (but therefore always able to be "right") consultative stance of negative capability. If we were seriously wishing to predict futures from a psychodynamic perspective, this approach might bear fruit.

Will we learn lessons from this and previous pandemics? We know that governments often fail to prepare even when there is ample evidence that they should; that there are frequently good intentions to learn lessons for the future but that these are often not followed through; that pandemics expose and exacerbate existing social trends and especially inequities and injustices, disproportionately impacting on the poor and marginalised, while the advantaged are more able to protect themselves from economic and health impacts; that "others" (countries, or groups of people within them) are often scapegoated as being responsible for the development or transmission of the pandemic); and perhaps, too, that it is only when pandemics cause extraordinary levels of mortality and prolonged societal disruption that we can attribute changes in society to the pandemic, and not to other factors that preceded it (Ferguson, 2021). These themes link to psychodynamic principles including our capacity for denial, splitting, and projection, and our vulnerability to criticism (and hatred of experience) that affects our ability to learn.

Many changes took place during the acute phase of the pandemic, but it is questionable how many will survive the pandemic's end. Following a substantial switch to home and online working, consequent on the need to maintain office-based industries when offices were closed because of lockdown, it seemed likely that for many, the days of the office were numbered. Yet a very substantial return to the office is underway (though hybrid home-office work patterns may become established). Similarly, in countries such as the UK or the USA, where the adoption of face coverings was slow and contested, the removal of mandates for wearing face coverings has led to widespread discontinuation of the practice. A return to busy roads, and of a huge demand for overseas travel, suggests that the need or desire to travel, for work and recreation, has not been affected by the pandemic … even though the emissions associated with travel are significant parts of humanity's impact on the planet through climate change. Perhaps we should not be surprised. Although globalisation and its features seem critical in the genesis of the Covid-19 pandemic, it is hard to imagine this has caused enough disruption to trigger a substantial move away from this structuring of our world. Nor does it seem likely that the negative effects of the infodemic will lead to a flight from social media platforms or greater regulation of their content.

Different groups have fared differently. Social distancing and school closures had particularly difficult impacts for children. We may worry about the long-term developmental effects, on very small children, of prolonged periods of minimal interaction with others (except on virtual platforms), and of the extensive wearing of face coverings on their learning to recognise non-verbal cues. The teenage years should be filled with intense social development and educational activity, not lockdowns. What will the impact be? And children of all ages have had much more prolonged contact (in hours per day) with parents, sometimes in difficult domestic environments of deprivation and violence. The effects of this may be long term; child and adolescent mental health services have reported dramatic upsurges in child mental health problems.

Many young adults have seen their opportunities for beginning independent living, employment, and university education severely curtailed, while older adults have lost employment or income unless able to work virtually, impacting (sometimes delayed through state assistance) on housing and other essentials. The longer-term economic impacts are only just beginning to work through many economies. Wealthy older people have been relatively protected, but their risk of serious illness and death (but not, to the same extent, of long Covid) has been significantly greater than in the young, escalating dramatically with age.

And for women and people of colour, there is abundant evidence of them faring worse than white men both from the perspective of the economic and social impacts but also on their work prospects and chances of being made unemployed. Beyond this, the UK and the USA have seen disproportionate rates of death in black and minoritised groups, initially as a marker of social deprivation, more recently compounded by higher rates of vaccine hesitancy linked to mistrust of the authorities given the history of racially motivated abuses towards them.

What remain uncertain are the societal impacts of these very different effects of the pandemic on different age groups. Perhaps younger people will begin to resent the wealth, cost of care, and past careers of their elders, and be less willing in future to sacrifice their immediate opportunities and income for the benefit of much older people. Perhaps the way the pandemic has acted as a spotlight on the inequity we tolerate will trigger new political movements. At a global level, perhaps low-income countries, resentful of the unequal global distribution of vaccines and the inequities that underlie them, will find ways to act upon that resentment. But awareness of inequity and resentment, coupled with the economic aftershocks of the pandemic, might have destructive impacts rather than reforming ones, if they feed another important unconscious human emotion, envy. Finally, there may even be an environmental impact, if nations drive to "recover" economically as fast as possible using older technologies, including the polluting and climate-changing ones, the use of which, briefly, the world appeared pleased to pause.

Conclusions

> *The best lack all conviction, while the worst*
> *Are full of passionate intensity.*
> *Surely some revelation is at hand.*
> —"The Second Coming" (Yeats, 1920)

I alluded earlier to the shadows that humanity is already casting into the future. These include:

- The retreat of democracy with the advance of autocracies and populist leaders manifesting anti-democratic behaviours
- Increased polarisation of views about a range of issues linked to civil liberties
- Climate change and global warming
- Environmental degradation through deforestation, pollution, and plastic accumulation
- Continuing systemic discrimination over a range of visible differences, even in Western liberal democracies

- Worsening inequities in the global and national distribution of wealth and power
- Our long history, as a species, of violence and of the development of technology to further violence, which now encompasses nuclear, chemical, and—ironically at this time—biological warfare.

All of these furnish examples of:

- How our primitive anxieties, managed through splitting and projection, create "othering" and sow the seeds of conflict and envy
- How our need to organise into groups (to survive and thrive physically, mentally, and socially), and our anxiety at belonging to and surviving in them leads us not just to be "a group animal at war with his own groupishness" (Bion, 1961) but an in-group animal at war with other (out-)groups
- How our sense of "lack" drives us onwards to explore, consume, and deplete our world, the unconscious, but also wilful, denial of which creates a painful reckoning to come
- How our social institutions organise both as defences for those who belong and as offensive weapons against those who do not.

The pandemic has not removed these underlying threats, though in presenting all of us "in-the-mind", and some of us "in-the-body", with an immediate life-or-death problem, it has temporarily distracted us from them, and from the anxiety they engender. We have not, I believe, seen novel psychodynamic principles manifesting as a result of the pandemic. It is not so much a novel psychic force as a magnifier, in both senses of the word. It has made existing forces more powerful, and at the same time it has made them more visible.

These threats remain clear and present dangers to humanity that needed our attention before the pandemic began. Against them, only global collective action will be effective, action that may be hampered by the same psychodynamic responses to the anxiety of uncertainty as those we have seen in the Long Covid. Perhaps the biggest lesson of all that we could take from the Covid-19 pandemic would be a much more widespread recognition, within society at large, of the importance of the forces within our own unconscious, and their effect on us as individuals and in groups. Within those forces, if unchecked, lie the seeds of our destruction; but therein lies salvation, too, through the power of other unconscious forces: love, kindness, and altruism. Using our systems-psychodynamic insights, to help create more humane and engaging lives at work and at home, might be the most important change that could result from the pandemic if only this—the true lesson of history—were more widely understood and acted on.

References

Addley, E. (2020, May 28). Clap for our carers: the very unBritish ritual that united the nation. *The Guardian.* https://theguardian.com/society/2020/may/28/clap-for-our-carers-the-very-unbritish-ritual-that-united-the-nation (last accessed March 22, 2022).

BBC News (2021, October 20). Covid: Brazil's Bolsonaro "should be charged with crimes against humanity". *BBC News.* https://bbc.co.uk/news/world-latin-america-58976197 (last accessed March 22, 2022).

Bion, W. R. (1961). *Experiences in Groups and Other Papers.* London: Tavistock.

Brecht, B. (1950). *Mr. Puntila and His Man Matti.* J. Willett (Trans.). London: Eyre Methuen, 1977.

Callard, F., & Perego, E. (2020). How and why patients made long Covid. *Social Science and Medicine, 268*: 113426. https://doi.org/10.1016/j.socscimed.2020.113426 (last accessed March 22, 2022).

Charters, E., & Heitman, K. (2021). How epidemics end. *Centaurus, 63*: 210–224. https://doi.org/10.1111/1600-0498.12370 (last accessed March 22, 2022).

Davis, H. E., Assaf, G. S., McCorkell, L., Wei, H., Low, R. J., Re'em, Y., Redfield, S., Austin, J. P., & Akrami, A. (2021). Characterizing long COVID in an international cohort: 7 months of symptoms and their impact. *EClinicalMedicine, 38*:101019. https://doi.org/10.1016/j.eclinm.2021.101019 (last accessed March 22, 2022).

Ferguson, N. (2021). *Doom: The Politics of Catastrophe.* London: Penguin Random House.

Funtowicz, S. O., & Ravetz, J. R. (1993). Science for the post-normal age. *Futures, 25*(7): 739–755. https://doi.org/10.1016/0016-3287(93)90022-L (last accessed March 22, 2022).

Giubilini, A., & Charters, E. (2021). The end of the COVID-19 pandemic. *Practical Ethics* (blogsite, University of Oxford). http://blog.practicalethics.ox.ac.uk/2021/08/the-end-of-the-covid-19-pandemic/ (last accessed March 22, 2022).

Hirschhorn, L. (1988). *The Workplace Within: Psychodynamics of Organizational Life*. Cambridge, MA: Massachusetts Institute of Technology Press.

Hughes, T. (1960). November. In: *Lupercal*. London: Faber & Faber.

Jaques, E. (1955). Social systems as defence against persecutory and depressive anxiety. A contribution to the psycho-analytic study of social processes. In: M. Klein, P. Heimann, & R. Money-Kyrle (Eds.), *New Directions in Psycho-Analysis* (pp. 478–498). London: Tavistock.

Johns Hopkins University Coronavirus Resource Centre (2021). *COVID-19 Dashboard: Global Map*. https://coronavirus.jhu.edu/map.html (last accessed September 8, 2022).

Klein, M. (1959). Our adult world and its roots in infancy. *Human Relations*, *12*(4): 291–303.

Manthorpe, J., Iliffe, S., Gillen, P., Moriarty, J., Mallett, J., Schroder, H., Currie, D., Ravalier, J. M., & McFadden, P. (2021). Clapping for carers in the Covid-19 crisis: Carers' reflections in a UK survey. *Health and Social Care in the Community*, *00*: 1–8. https://doi.org/10.1111/hsc.13474 (last accessed March 22, 2022).

McMillen, C. W. (2016). *Pandemics: A Very Short Introduction*. New York: Oxford University Press.

Menzies-Lyth, I. E. P. (1960). A case study in the functioning of social systems as a defence against anxiety. A report on a study of the nursing service of a general hospital. *Human Relations*, *13*: 95–121.

NHS England (2021). Your Covid recovery. https://yourcovidrecovery.nhs.uk (last accessed March 22, 2022).

Nobel Prize nomination archive (2021). Sigmund Freud. https://nobelprize.org/nomination/archive/list.php?prize=3&year=1920 (last accessed March 22, 2022).

Our World in Data (2021). *Statistics and Research: Coronavirus (COVID-19) Vaccinations*. https://ourworldindata.org/covid-vaccinations (last accessed September 8, 2022).

Parasher, A. (2021). COVID-19: Current understanding of its pathophysiology, clinical presentation and treatment. *Postgraduate Medical Journal*, *97*: 312–320. doi:10.1136/postgradmedj-2020-138577.

Park, C., Chaturvedi, N., Sterne, J., Steves, C., Williams, D., & Ayoubkhani, D. (2021). Short report on long Covid. *UK Government: Office for National Statistics.* https://assets.publishing.service.gov.uk/government/uploads/system/uploads/attachment_data/file/1007511/S1327_Short_Long_COVID_report.pdf (last accessed March 22, 2022).

Rushforth, A., Ladds, E., Wieringa, S., Taylor, S., Husain, L., & Greenhalgh, T. (2021). Long Covid—the illness narratives. *Social Science & Medicine, 286*: 114326. https://doi.org/10.1016/j.socscimed.2021.114326 (last accessed March 22, 2022).

Scoblic, J. P. (2020). Learning from the future: How to make robust strategy in times of deep uncertainty. *Harvard Business Review.* https://hbr.org/2020/07/learning-from-the-future (last accessed March 22, 2022).

World Health Organization (2020, April 7–8). An ad hoc WHO technical consultation managing the COVID-19 infodemic: call for action. Geneva: World Health Organization. Licence: *CC BY-NC-SA 3.0 IGO.* https://who.int/publications/i/item/9789240010314 (last accessed March 22, 2022).

Yeats, W. B. (1920). The second coming. In: *Michael Robartes and the Dancer.* Churchtown, Dundrum, Ireland: Chuala.

CHAPTER 14

The future of organisations and leadership

by Leslie B. Brissett

This chapter seeks to explore the future of the constructs of organisation and leadership, by touching on some of the emerging forces that could shape how we hold these constructs in mind and, perhaps of equal importance, how we develop the individuals and the systems of today to be able to transform themselves to take up the fullness of the role challenges offered in the bright tomorrow of the post-pandemic world. The bright tomorrow has both detractors and advocates: some policy analysts and political theorists from both sides of the arguments hold a shared lens, however, indicating that humanity could be entering the fourth industrial revolution.

The future is an alluring prize into which many professionals and artisans have placed their ambitions, dreams, and hopes. No area seems as inclined to attract humans away from the creative and aesthetic as the hunger and lust for power and position over their fellow humans, and in some cases, all life in all contexts. The enduring lust for power is often enshrined, embedded, and reproduced as if in concrete. There is a concrete that is created without being manufactured and poured, but it acts as a substrate from which is hewn our most enduring human thought structures, namely, organisations. Some of these emergent-concretising properties can be captured as a set of dynamics that are best captured outwith academic or philosophical texts. Engaging in a new language to explore organisations and leadership for the future can be thought of as calling forth the creative arts such as poetry, painting, sculpture, and plays. One play that strikes me as an appropriate place to begin this exploration is Shakespeare's *Macbeth*. If we look at the herald-haunting three pronouncements taken from Lines 49 to 51 of Act 1 Scene 3 of Macbeth, we hear the future leadership of Macbeth called into being:

First Witch: All hail Macbeth! Hail to thee Thane of Glamis!
Second Witch: All hail Macbeth! Hail to thee Thane of Cawdor!
Third Witch: All hail Macbeth, that shalt be King hereafter!"

What we discover, evoked in the hearts and minds of battle-weary Macbeth and his companion Banquo on meeting the witches, is both curiosity and terror. Wanting the elevation to king on the one hand and envying the possible elevation of a companion on another, further complicated by the simultaneous seeking of prestige and fortune and with equal measure wishing to run from its acquisition. The revelation and unravelling of these complex juxtapositions are at the heart of the psychoanalytic endeavour in our organisational and leadership consulting work, whilst in the play, the stage is now set for what is to unfold on the stage. As spectators of the drama, we partake in the plot to slaughter and seize power at the expense of the current role holder, King Duncan. So, what does this scene have to do with our understanding of the notion of the future of leadership and organisation in the context of a post-pandemic world? As a starting point, it seems that the three witches are akin to our historic and contemporary sites of learning: the universities and professional training bodies, which have shared declaratory powers. These organisations have evolved, grown, and firmly established themselves as clarion heralds, proclaiming to eager, battle-weary executives (those who "execute"): "Come to us and we will see that you achieve your reward of king-hood of your department, discipline, or indeed the whole enterprise!"

The future

Civilisation is crumbling (Freud, 1930a) as the assumptions which have held us together begin to no longer hold. In the face of this discontent, the future has become a place of salvation and respite from the relentless anxiety of an uncertain today. First, let us have a look at the dynamics of the "future" as an idea, and what the conceptualisation of its dimensions opens up for us, since this act of opening up may allow us to find a new context into which organisation and leadership will have to fit in a post-pandemic world. Second, we can think about the nature of organisation itself and how it may alter and, interestingly, how its manifestations could change the very experience of being in or working for an organisation. Third, the chapter explores leadership and what it may come to mean in its new, broader societal context and the more immediate organisational contexts in which it is executed. Finally, the chapter ends with some musings, conjectures, and propositions that at first may seem tangential, but are themselves fundamental to the continuation or ending of the constructs of organisation and leadership as we know them.

Hirschhorn (2012), while reflecting on the financial crisis, talks about the impact of the capacity to imagine and how it is affected by the changing social context. I would suggest that the financial crisis of 2007–8 heralded the changes that were due to take place, so as to create the conditions for the further globalisation of the financial and corporate structures and methods for moving products and extracting value in more digital mediums. Schwab and Malleret (2020) describe a number of examples of environmental, sustainability, and governance (ESG) considerations that will be the hallmark of post-pandemic organisations and those that lead them. The requirement for employee activism and boardroom accountability for the actions of corporations will increase, and the self-serving actions of leaders and organisations will not be able to "hide" in the transparent omniscience of the digital age. The issue of visibility is currently shrouded in narratives about the loss of privacy, yet in the post-pandemic world, it seems that privacy will be seen or narrated as the act of hiding or wilful withholding.

This is a key contextual consideration: the shift in political and economic energy in global systems of production and value creation open an interesting line of investigation for our understanding of the world. The rate and pace of change, along with the depth and breadth of organisational and leadership revelations, require people to participate more fully in a process of thinking, conceptualising, and formulating a sensorial mosaic about those constructs that involve reimagining. This is a rather poetic way of describing the complex web of associations and emotions that need to be engaged with in order to bring into being a set of new possibilities, without fixing them as the "answer". In this way, the emergent "sense of the picture as a whole", the gestalt, shifts as the prevailing paradigms shift. These interdependent shifts can be experienced as a present discomfort by the person experiencing them. However, if we are in a process of giving birth to a new form, even a new species, then we are required to find a set of behaviours that are vortical in motion, beyond our current thinking and preoccupation with complexity. It has been argued by Emery and Trist (1997) that we are entering a vortical environment, which is more complex than a turbulent environment.

A turbulent environment was described as the fourth causal texture of an organisational context. The tools needed to engage beyond the fourth causal texture (Baburoglu, 1977) are of an entirely different order and perhaps require a new dimensionality rather than just a broadening of perspective. The co-occurrence of both rigid and dynamic forces are best captured in the paradoxical question: "What happens when an unstoppable force meets an immovable object?" The modern context of the fifth causal texture of organisation, the vortical environment, I suggest, is the impact of digitisation and what will emerge post-pandemic as the new social and organisational order. This new order has been described by some as a "great reset".

These adjustments have been articulated by Klaus Schwab (Schwab & Malleret, 2020) and the World Economic Forum in the text on the "great reset" in the form of a coordinated global response to Covid-19. The narrative put forward by Schwab is that the changes the world is going through are necessary in order to recalibrate systems and cultures so as to adapt to a more integrated and interdependent world economy. From the analysis propounded by Schwab, a concerted effort to "build back better" post-Covid-19 has many of the same themes and memes identified by Hirschhorn in his reflections on the post-financial crisis rhetoric. This indicates a blindness or inability to face what Freud (1911b) identified as the thanatic coagulation in our psychic structures; this is not simply the death wish, but the nature of the destructive drives across all systems, including those masquerading as creative and erotic.

At its widest stance, this could herald the total destructive drive latent in all social activity, from our foods laden with pesticides and chemicals to our education systems empty of meaning, producing automatons. I would like to turn to the work of Marshall McLuhan and invite us to think more radically about the way that we are using technology to add to the capacities that humans possess: in a sense we are extending the human being by "adding on" technology. When we consider the use of artificial intelligence and digital technology to extend or replace human functioning, the pace of such changes will only increase after the pandemic. Many of the governmental and industrial reactions to the coronavirus have involved harnessing technology in the service of rebuilding our economies and systems as part of an integrated, often international, Covid-19 response.

Language and technology

If the development of technology is changing how we think about the future, it can be argued that it is simultaneously also changing the perception of the past and the ability to be with the present as it is. Rather than imagination, it is the ability to see what is, as it is, in the here and now, rather than imagining what could be present through a formula of signification and meaning making, "as if" the present is a text to be read, decoded, and reconstituted. This idea that we live in and are constructed by language, that it opens the way for us to think about the capacity to use and engage fully with language in order to create the world around us, is well advocated by linguists and those who have studied social construction and social representations as tools to deconstruct our social order.

This use of language as both the prison and the gateway to freedom is at the heart of the "talking cure" in Freud and the profession he founded, psychoanalysis. This linguistic capacity to reveal meaning from contexts has its roots in the sophistry of the deconstructive rhetoric with its roots in antiquity; indeed, it is at the heart of the psychoanalytic canon and art of the "talking cure". However, in light of the critical thinking of McLuhan (1967), the communicative devices deployed to reveal meaning and purpose could be seen as a misappropriation of the tools of discursive practices, that lead us to a blind alley rather than offering a key to unlock the door to a particular crisis. We are considering here the methods of engaging people in thinking about the state of the world, and being free enough to see for themselves as an act of participation, rather than demonstrating their active citizenry in the act of compliance and conformity to the narratives as presented for digestion wholesale by those in authority. In essence, the dynamic between imagination and authority identified by Hirschhorn in relation to the financial crisis, is alive and thriving in relation to the Covid-19 crisis. How we listen to the intuitions and promptings of conscience will denote the extent to which actors are activists for an interdependent social and economic order. Perhaps the "talking cure" in our post-pandemic world might better be articulated as the "listening cure".

So, what do we mean by the future? A growing number of theorists from various disciplines have carved out a niche as futurologists, a role defined by the Oxford English Dictionary as a "person who studies the future and makes predictions about it based on current trends". Naisbitt (1984) and Gerber et al. (1991) offered a set of ideas about the ability to understand trends that emerged in the 1980s as a precursor to what may emerge in the decades due to arrive in the next thirty years. These texts were aimed at and desired by the wider non-specialist public audiences. Both Naisbitt and Gerber et al. focus primarily on the United States of America and the issues that will impact its economy and citizens. Globalisation had not yet taken root in the popular mind and the interdependencies across the social and political fabric were not deeply thought about (the World Trade Organization was not formed until 1995). Despite these geographic limitations, the analysis and themes identified are useful to highlight just how little grip we have on the future on the one hand, and how similar or constant some things remain over time on the other hand.

The key themes they identified in relation to the focus of this chapter include the following:

- A decline in the birth rate
- More women than men living longer
- Changing patterns of work and learning
- Larger institutions and more self-employment.

Yet we see an alternative viewpoint from Hamish McRae (1995) who suggests that his detailed, systematic analysis may be thrown off course by an unforeseen inevitability. Reflecting on what may negatively impact his thesis on the future, he says in the final chapter, "The Prize":

> The most worrying thought of all, though, is not that AIDS in its present form will continue to spread, but that the virus which causes it will mutate into something which is more easily transmitted. Nature's creation of a "new" disease, just at the moment when humankind thought it was well on the way to eliminating many of the "old" diseases, carries an awesome message: if AIDS, caused by a virus which is difficult to transmit, can suddenly burst on the world, are there other viruses out there which could follow it with even more devastating consequences? ... Now while it is reasonable to suppose that considerable progress will have been made against AIDS in its present forms, there is no guarantee that the virus will not change its form again and again, maybe to return in even more devastating guise. The reappearance in the West of diseases like tuberculosis which were thought to have been permanently eradicated should give pause for thought. We should not be so arrogant as to assume that throwing resource at a problem will solve it. (p. 273)

Role of trust and enquiry

In the above extract, McRae (1995) has identified the capacity to be blindsided by what has yet to emerge, but what interests me is that there is something else embedded in his narrative. Identifying this could offer us a clue that our organisational forms and our leadership practices hold the key to understanding how we will deal with the challenges of the future. I think the key rests in the call to a "grand narrative", typical of the Western academic and political discourses. Our current models of leadership and organisation are urging all citizens and policy makers alike to get on board and behind a dominant narrative in the face of Covid-19 and the need to recover that we:

1. Wear masks
2. Keep social distance
3. Wash hands
4. Above all: "Trust the science."

I am not suggesting that the future leadership and organisation ought not to trust the science, but perhaps the future is calling for a leadership and organisation that is more focused on enquiry rather than blind trust. In the face of the compliance narrative, it takes much social courage to enquire or question the direction of the dominant voice, its agenda, and how it is calling for compliance. This is our litmus test for the leaders of tomorrow—who can or will question the purposes of the context in which we find ourselves? Are leaders willing to forgo their place in the "inner ring" and find a place on the boundary of the systems they inhabit; could they function and think from that position? I think the question is equally applicable to apparently polar contexts such as China and Russia on the one hand as it is to Europe and America on the other. Both apparent polar contexts present their citizens with the same option, phenomenologically. Live according to the culture as dictated, or face rejection. It may be to capitalism or communism, but both "isms" require conformity to domination, and both have penalties for non-compliance.

What might that mean for us as we consider the nature of trust and enquiry? In order to approach that question, I think we need to go further back in our arsenal of texts and thinking, back to the founding father of Western philosophical traditions, as documented by Plato. Socrates, as captured in the dialogue with Alcibiades, is also a narrative of and for our time as we consider leadership for the future.

As ever, all the works of Socrates are collected in the form of an enquiry between Socrates and his object of the discourse. Using the translation by Professor D. S. Hutchinson of Toronto University, we discover that Alcibiades was the one young man that Socrates loved consistently. In so doing, he watched and took great care over the character development of this young man and when the time was right, as dictated by his "god", he could reveal himself and what he had to share with the object of his affections. The dialogue opens with Socrates telling Alcibiades about his arrogance and ambition and how he can help him to achieve his objectives.

In our modern world, management schools and leadership programmes "tap into" the aims of the potential students and offer them the chance to achieve their ambitions with the right training given by the right institution; if we continue with the metaphor, in this transaction, and the underlying lack that it is purported to remedy or to fill. The current institutional offerings to address learning for leadership effectively act like the seductive Socrates and the students are encouraged to take on the role of an ambition-hungry Alcibiades.

This current state of affairs in leadership education, with its underlying task of seducing the ambitious, is a corruption of an ideal, yet it is a corruption that was both necessary and (potentially) inevitable. The modern university was able to establish itself as the key producer of those trained individuals able to deliver the purposes of the Empire(s)—it was they after all that had funded the universities. These same university institutions have continued to receive funding and have also undertaken a gradual incremental reform ever since the Moors created the first universities in Spain and Portugal from 700AD. The Moors brought writing and text learning to Europe and spread throughout the Iberian Peninsula and as far north as Ireland and northern parts of Scotland. The processes of civilisation were rooted in the dynamics of education and artistic endeavour that also involved music and an appreciation and cultivation of the natural environment.

Let us now return to Socrates and Alcibiades, and have a look at a direct piece of their dialogue in order to understand what it is telling us about the nature of learning to lead. There are two excerpts that are worth considering. The first sets the scene and the tone for the second.

SOCRATES: Very well. What do you propose for yourself? Do you intend to remain in your present condition, or practise some self-cultivation?

ALCIBIADES: Let's discuss it together, Socrates. You know, I do see what you're saying and actually I agree – it seems to me that none of our city's politicians has been properly educated, except for a few.
SOCRATES: And what does that mean?
ALCIBIADES: Well, if they were educated, then anyone who wanted to compete with them would have to get some knowledge and go into training, like an athlete. But as it is, since they entered politics as amateurs, there's no need for me to train and go to the trouble of learning. I'm sure my natural abilities will be far superior to theirs. (section 119b, c page 576)

So Alcibiades makes his declaration that in order to study or to learn the art of political leadership he would need to invest, and such an investment he deemed unnecessary as his natural talents would suffice. This idea found resonance in the narratives of modern leadership discourses where management and leadership theorists wrestled with the ideas that leadership was an innate talent and could not be taught, on the one hand, or it was a developed sense of skills and capacities that could be taught, on the other.

If we now turn to the second of the discourses between Socrates and Alcibiades (which can sound like "I'll see bodies"), we discover that Socrates is asking Alcibiades to think about the nature of the soul and its relationship to the body, and the relationship of body and soul to the act of self-control or self-cultivation, and therefore its role in leadership. In essence the importance of looking at this dialogue in particular is to identify the importance of an education that addresses the soul. For the sake of brevity, I have omitted the responses of Alcibiades and only indicated the sayings of Socrates:

SOCRATES: Since a man is neither his body, nor his body and soul together, what remains, I think, is either that he's nothing, or else, if he *is* something, he's nothing other than his soul.
SOCRATES: What we mentioned just now, that we should first consider what "itself" is in itself. But in fact, we've been

	considering what an individual self is, instead of what "itself" is. Perhaps that was enough for us, for surely nothing about us has more authority than the soul, wouldn't you agree?
SOCRATES:	So the right way of looking at it is that, when you and I talk to each other, one soul uses words to address another soul
SOCRATES:	So the command that we should know ourselves means that we should know our souls.
SOCRATES:	And someone who knows certain things about his body knows about what belongs to him, not himself. (p. 589. Section 130c to 131)

When Socrates speaks of the self, it is derived from the Greek *auton*, from which we derive the English word autonomy. He is describing the impact of a leadership that is not well placed to lead, not knowing itself. This has resonance with my reading of Eric Miller. In his book *From Dependency to Autonomy: Studies in Organization and Change*, he discusses the delicate balance required of the awakened leader to manage the pressure to conform to dependency needs in a system. The leaders often begin to act as if superior and more knowledgeable than their subordinates, in order to facilitate the emergence of the feelings of inferiority in the minds of subordinates, thereby generating the removal of autonomy such that the subordinates "had in effect lost their boundaries as individuals and surrendered their ego functions" (1993, p. 227).

The Tavistock Institute of Human Relations developed its group relations learning programme to provide a method of learning about leadership that was antithetical to the top-down, command-and-control methods that preceded it. The learning for leadership methodology articulated by A. Kenneth Rice, building on the work of Wilfred Bion, was designed to draw out of the participant in the working conference, the skills, capacities, and thinking ability to function in the "work group" modality in the absence of a named, designated, leader. Through application of the anthropological frame to the psychoanalytic lens, a method of training leaders was developed that was radical and enduring.

McLuhan (1962) discussed the assumptions that underpinned the old paradigm of the textual base of Western learning and its shortcomings. Primary school education in England was structured about the necessities of Reading wRiting and aRithmetic, the 3Rs. Drawing on this as an idea, a new leadership curriculum rooted in the 3Rs of the future could be: Ro (Role), Re (Relatedness), and Rh (Rhizome). I will expand on those a little later, but first a brief look at the work of the army officer turned psychiatrist and psychoanalyst, Wilfred Bion. Bion took his insights into the treatment of army officers after World War 2 and offered them to the wider world. His insights into the working of groups and leaders was captured in his later published text, *Experiences in Groups* (1961).

Bion took a scientific approach to thinking about the psyche and like Freud, returned to the use of concepts from the physical sciences and mathematical formulae to articulate mental processes. Bion's typology consists of alpha function (the capacity to dream), beta elements (the concrete experiencing of sensation and emotion), and three links: ideas that connect psychic objects, namely, hate, knowledge, and love. Each is designated with a letter that can be thought about as having positive or negative polarities, for example: knowledge K or –K. It may be helpful to think about a leadership rooted in the capacity to relate to the system and the other actors along the lines articulated by Bion, but adapted to our new emerging context, functioning at the level of Role, Relatedness, and Rhizome.

Where Role is the idea in the mind, as articulated by Armstrong and Long, to name two authors from the group relations/systems psychodynamic orientation, Relatedness, which I think is the most exciting area of the 3Rs, is the capacity to hold the ideas about the other in relation to the self. This is a construct and as such it should not be collapsed into becoming a fixed or absolute reality. The capacity of an individual to hold an idea in the mind and recognise that this is simply an idea and not "reality" is a challenge both intellectually and emotionally. To hold an idea as reality requires the ability to tolerate that what appears to be external to the observer is actually or potentially a projection constructed from within the observer's mind that is then outwardly projected onto the screen of external objects and phenomena. The observer behaves in a subjective manner in relation to external objects. This process is further complicated or made more complex by the fact that it has to be assumed that the external world has some reality in and of itself and so can be able to do what the observer can do; in other words, it too has agency and can be a "subject" projecting meaning from within its mind onto external objects as it perceives them. The observer is therefore potentially rendered both subject (projecting its reality onto the external world) and object (receiving the projections of another subject in its role as an observer).

The reality co-construction process is thereby an intersubjective process. This intersubjective construction of reality runs counter to the Freudian (1927c) notion of the reality principle as a fixed external reality. The capacity to not collapse it into an absolute reality could be spoken of as the capacity to tolerate the unreality of the reality principle, namely that all apparent external phenomena are projected constructs from within the psyche of the thinker/beholder, while simultaneously having an independent existence to which an intersubjective meaning-making process could yield new formulations of both the entity observed and the observer (Baaquie et al., 2015).

Rhizome relates to the capacity to conceptualise the vast network of systemic relationships structured as both people and processes that formulate a given field at a given time. The Rhizome is taken from the observation in fungal networks that make up the soil substructure and provide nutrients and information flows within an ecosystem. Likewise, the leader of tomorrow will be able both to occupy the nodal position and possess the geospatial awareness to work with the interdependencies emerging within a context, moving smoothly between the worlds of creativity and growth on one hand and entropy, decay, and death on the other. The totality of growth and decay form a coherent whole as part of a cycle of emergent transformational properties within organisational trans-networked boundaries. This is the era of the artist, open, curious, exploring, and uncertain while working to hold the space for the yet unseen to emerge. In this way, Steve Jobs was able to work at levels of creative potential, effectively speaking from the realm of the dream (Bion's alpha function) and creating the conditions to manifest a network of collaborating scientists to deliver innovation for both consumers and governments.

Drawing from chemistry, the capacity for the leader to be both left- and right-brained in the way that they perceive and process information, the Rhizomatic leader will also be chiral. Chirality is a term taken from chemistry: it can be applied to an atomic structure as a totality and it can also be applied to the subatomic level. As such, there is a fractal component to atoms as there is a fractal component to systems. Molecules can be seen as having a degree of "handedness" that can also be identified at the subatomic level. As spin directions of electrons also demonstrate chirality, electrons exist within potential spaces, called orbits, which have a directional quality to them. It is possible to extend the idea of left- and right-handedness of molecules to the chirality of the human brain. Thoughts about the relationship and behaviour associated with the two hemispheres of the human brain have been argued by Tweedy (2013) and McGilchrist (2009). The unifying theme of their hypotheses sets out the evolution of the Western mind as a dance between the dominance of the left hemisphere with its commitment to rationality, logic, and reason and the suppression of the right hemisphere with its propensity towards creativity, holism, and embodied sense-making. The future leadership will be neither left- nor right-hemisphere-dominated, but will seek out and enhance the capacity to work across both in appropriate ways. This new way of engaging with the world of organisations and leadership will be a trans-modal way of being and as such will require a new curriculum. Boyle (1664) highlighted the ability to see and experience colours as requiring a new way to consider both parts of the brain and proposed a number of experiments to illustrate this. The future curriculum will also require experimentation to make it "alive".

The 3Rs curriculum will be one that is delivered in a range of settings across a range of media, from a network of institutional forms. As the differentiated marketplace emerges, the leader of the future will be able to be located in the metaverse which is a region of potential that is neither physical nor fluid. The leader of the future likewise will not fall into the hangovers of the hero narratives, and so their visibility and name recognition may be less of an issue than today, where much of our leadership discourse is located in the individual. In many ways, Jeff Bezos of Amazon and Jack Dorsey of Square are two who come to mind, while the tech giants of Twitter and Google have CEOs with low personality profiles while holding their enterprises in good shape and as nodal points in the networks to which they belong (Western, 2008).

Massachusetts Institute of Technology has been working to identify a new era of materials that can form superconductors with the capacity to be a liquid substrate, from and through which the information constructs, sub-particles of data will be able to replace the chips in the technology that we use today. These superconductive materials will form the framework of the new organisational forms.

Will there be a need for an office, or a place for people to take their bodies to work? If there is no need to take the body to work, what is it that the leader will use to conduct their tasks? This far-into-the-future question takes us far into the past to answer it. As Freud argued for us to consider the psychoanalytic process as an excavation, so too an archaic revival has been postulated by archaeologist Marija Gimbutas (1974) as a way to understand what may have been repressed or expunged from our collective memories. As a society moves to a point where old ways are redundant, there is a need expressed in the unconscious to go back to a point in time where things made sense. Often this return to the past is relatively close, as in the fall of feudalism and the emergence of the European Enlightenment when classicism was rediscovered. What we are about to face in the end of this era could generate a new rediscovery of our ancient selves, and a rediscovery of partnership and the collaborative mind as the current systems of hierarchy and stratification are no longer tolerable. The time frames for what our archaic revival may be could be in the thousands of years, rather than the hundreds. If we think about the vortical environment earlier elucidated, then we could be going as far back as the early community structures when we lived very close to the land and in small tribes.

As McLuhan (1967) has indicated, the advancement of technology may well render the use and presence of the human body unnecessary. As such, the leader of tomorrow will require a capacity for presence in absence—and this could almost be thought of as a textual negation, a rendering of the unthought known as coined by Bollas into the known unknown, speakable unthinkable (a sort of glossolalia—where what is heard is babbling to the listener, but to the speaker is coherent argumentation—otherwise known as speaking in tongues). In this realm of activity, the Tower of Babel could re-emerge as meaning is possible to be communicated across culture and linguistic ability as a near telepathic auditory ability emerges from the interface between man and machine—a true cyborgian state, where the mystery of the human capacity to dream meets the digital capability of the virtual realities underpinned by the intricate lattice work of computronium, a material able to turn organic matter into programmable computer material. This section could sound like science fiction, but the Google advisor, futurologist Ray Kurzweil (2005) has made such ideas open to investigation.

So, what will we be? Who and how will we lead?

We will observe a splitting of humanity into those who can cope and choose to transition into the new age, and those who choose to exit, forcefully or by design. Those who remain will be ready to download their consciousness into the metaverse and take up their role as a full-time generator of content and partaker in the games and functions of the meta. The machines will be equipped to learn and think and generate ever more efficient and effective processes for the production of goods that will be bought and sold using the digital currency and packaged and delivered by drones and self-driving vehicles. As in *The Matrix* movies, human beings will be the battery material that drives the system.

What I think we will need human beings for is our dreaming capacity: the ability to cross the dimensional divide between 3D and the other realms, wherein we can harvest new ideas and capture new thoughts and concepts and return them to 3D for investigation and development. The humans that will serve no function in terms of dreaming and inter-realm travel and therefore will not be needed, will be deleted.

The capacity to live and be in harmony will be a crucial one to understand. Will our togetherness be in 3D or in the realm of the virtual? If it is in the virtual, then our ability to think and feel and establish rapport and meaningful relationships will be the key skill for the future. When robots can be programmed to always be courteous and pleasant, it may well be the humans who argue for the deletion of the other humans in favour of the more agreeable and consistently behaved programmed intelligences.

As Rilke (1929) says in his letter to a young poet: "Be patient towards all that is unsolved in your heart and try to love the questions themselves. Live the questions now. Perhaps you will find them gradually, without noticing it, live along some distant day into the answer."

In summary

The world is undergoing a number of radical changes, many of which have been emerging since the 1980s, and our technological advances are moving us closer to a singularity or convergence of the human development and the technological capacity. The pandemic has been the global crisis narrative that has opened up a new way of seeing and thinking about the world post-pandemic.

The leadership narratives that we face will radically call into question the nature of our experience of hierarchies and the capacity of our species to work in collaboration and partnership where command and control once were. The ideas at the root of systems psychodynamic perspectives are helpful in framing the questions and the depths which we will have to plumb in order to reorient ourselves and face squarely our destructiveness and its ending, to usher in a new age of creativity and possibility, or to begin again another cycle of despair and destruction.

The thinkers of the 1960s had a vision of what is to come, and many were "on the money", such as the Tavistock Institute thinkers, Emery and Trist or the professor of media, Marshall McLuhan. Our organisational forms will move towards ever more complex networks and partnerships, and the leaders needed to work in such contexts will be more strategic and better able to work in and with not-knowing. The capacity to wonder, as Alastair Bain (2013) suggests, requires a mental capacity of "being able to hover at the edge". A wondering brain will be wide open and expectant, in a poetic sense, behaving like the female womb/matrix preparing to release a child into the world. The leadership of tomorrow is an embodied ability to remain open and expectant, and as such will represent the dynamics of birthing. As an expectant mother knows only too well—something will emerge, but what?

I will end the chapter with this comment from Bion:

> I would warn against the phrase "empirically verifiable data" which I employ in 100 [he means a section of the book]. I do not mean that experience "verifies" or "validates" anything. This belief as I have come across it in the literature of the philosophy of science relates to an experience which enables the scientist to achieve a feeling of security to offset and neutralize the sense of

insecurity following on the discovery that discovery has exposed further vistas of unsolved problems—"thoughts in search of a thinker". (1990, p. 166)

References

Baaquie, B. E., Carminati, F., Demongeot, J., Galli-Carminati, G., Martin, F., & Teodorani, M. (2015). *Quantum Psyche*. Switzerland: GuigiEditions.

Baburoglu, O. (1997). The vortical environment: The fifth in the Emery-Trist Levels of Organizational Environments. In: E. Trist, F. Emery, & H. Murray (Eds.), *The Social Engagement of Social Science, A Tavistock Anthology: Volume 3. The Socio-Ecological Perspective* (pp. 203–229). Philadelphia, PA: University of Pennsylvania Press.

Bain, A. (2013). Wonder and socioanalysis. In: S. Long (Ed.), *Socioanalytic Methods: Discovering the Hidden in Organisations and Social Systems*. London: Karnac.

Bion, W. R. (1961). *Experiences in Groups*. London: Tavistock.

Bion, W. R. (1990). Differentiation of the psychotic from the non-psychotic personalities. In: *Second Thoughts* (pp. 43–64). London: Karnac.

Boyle, R. (1664). *Experiments and Considerations Touching Colours*. London, December 28, 2004 [eBook #14504, most recently updated: April 8, 2021] (last accessed September 20, 2021).

Emery, F., & Trist, E. (1997). The causal texture of organizations. In: E. Trist, F. Emery, & H. Murray (Eds.), *The Social Engagement of Social Science, A Tavistock Anthology: Volume 3. The Socio-Ecological Perspective* (pp. 53–65). Philadelphia, PA: University of Pennsylvania Press.

Freud, S. (1911b). Formulations on the two principles of mental functioning. *S. E., 12*. London: Hogarth.

Freud, S. (1927c). *The Future of an Illusion*. *S. E., 21*. London: Hogarth.

Freud, S. (1930a). *Civilization and Its Discontents*. *S. E., 21*. London: Hogarth.

Gerber, J., Wolff, J., & Klores, W. (1991). *Lifetrends: Your Future for the Next 30 Years*. New York: Avon.

Gimbutas, M. (1974). *The Goddesses and Gods of Old Europe, 7000 to 3500 BC: Myths, Legends and Cult Images*. London: Thames & Hudson.

Hirschhorn, L. (2012). The financial crisis: Exploring the dynamics of imagination and authority in a post-industrial world. In: S. Long & B. Sievers (Eds.), *Towards a Socioanalysis of Money, Finance and Capitalism: Beneath the Surface of the Financial Industry*. London: Routledge.

Hutchinson, D. S. (1997). Alcibiades. In: J. M. Cooper (Ed.), *Plato Complete Works*. Indianapolis, IN: Hackett.

Kurzweil, R. (2005). *The Singularity Is Near: When Humans Transcend Biology*. New York: Viking Penguin.

McGilchrist, I. (2009). *The Master and His Emissary: The Divided Brain and the Making of the Western World*. New Haven, CT: Yale University Press.

McLuhan, M. (1962). *The Gutenberg Galaxy: The Making of Typographic Man*. Toronto, Canada: University of Toronto Press.

McLuhan, M. (1967). *Understanding Media: The Extensions of Man*. London: Sphere.

McRae, H. (1995). *The World in 2020: Power, Culture and Prosperity: A Vision of the Future*. London: Harper Collins.

Miller, E. (1993). *From Dependency to Autonomy: Studies in Organization and Change*. London: Free Association.

Naisbitt, J. (1984). *Megatrends: Ten New Directions Transforming Our Lives*. London: McDonald.

Rilke, R. M. (1929). *Letters to a Young Poet*. C. Louth (Trans.). London: Penguin, 2011.

Schwab, K., & Malleret, T. (2020). *Covid-19: The Great Reset*. Geneva: World Economic Forum.

Shakespeare, W. (1606). *Macbeth*, 2nd edition. Glasgow, UK: William Collins, Sons, 1983.

Tweedy, R. (2013). *The God of the Left Hemisphere: Blake, Bolte Taylor and the Myth of Creation*. London: Routledge.

Western, S. (2008). *Leadership: A Critical Text*. London: SAGE.

CHAPTER 15

Dark beam of light: what Covid is telling us about race relations

by Leslie B. Brissett

Introduction

To see clearly one has to close one's eyes and see with the inner eye. The capacity to see from within is what makes women aware of danger on dark streets and black people aware of danger wherever white people are in authority. To make sense of Covid-19 and race we need to enter a murky world of disinformation and conspiracy, where conjecture and unpicking the seams of the not-written can open us up to new ways of seeing, understanding, and being.

Carl Jung (1929) says,

> The gods have become diseases; Zeus no longer rules Olympus but rather the solar plexus, and produces curious specimens for the doctor's consulting room, or disorders the brains of politicians and journalists who unwittingly let loose psychic epidemics on the world. (Collected Works, Vol 13, section 54)

Gordon Lawrence (1998) identifies a distinction between invention and discovery in his narration of the emergence of social dreaming as a discipline. He says that:

Bion (1975) in the second of his Brazilian lectures, says that Freud, in correspondence with Lou Andreas-Salome, wrote "that when he was investigating a very dark subject he sometimes found it illuminating to investigate it by artificially blinding himself". Bion goes on to say that perhaps Milton's blindness was induced by the unconscious need to be so, in order that he could investigate "those things invisible to man", which he reveals in Book III of *Paradise Lost*. This idea of artificially blinding oneself, which is a creative posture, is a key element of the capacity to be available for discovery (Bion, 1975, pp. 62–63). Such a posture is one that yields the kind of original and intense insights that are "won from the void and formless infinite". (p. 11)

I invite the reader to join with me in the creative act of self-blinding to all that we know or think we know about race as we explore this chapter. Why should we perform that violent act of self-blinding? Because to do so may, as Lawrence describes, open us up to the realm of discovery. So much of our scholarly practice and training has taught us to defend what we have to say, leading to the conditions of us not really listening fully to the other, but rather seeking an opportunity to attack and counter what we hear. The same attitude is applicable to the complex and contested matters of race and disease; much of what we have been told about race and disease is still richly contested and, more significantly, sometimes runs counter to our lived experience. Perhaps, like the thinking of Freud in Bion's quote, what we are about to investigate is something so very troubling that it lurks beyond our conscious reach and resides in the dark matter of the ever present "void and formless infinite". Perhaps the quantum scientists, with their narratives of dark matter as the background to all living matter, indicate that the void that is already there and with the aid of our systems psychodynamic lenses we will be able to perceive the as yet unseen.

The mental exertion it takes to hold our critical, intelligent, well-read, wild-horse-like intellects at bay long enough to listen to any full story, like the one in this chapter, is not to be underestimated. So, let it simmer and see what emerges. I make no assertions of truth or universal validity in what I am about to share, rather I offer a set of observations, associations, and reflections on associations that may well illuminate something about the current state we find ourselves in, in relation to race relations and the Covid-19 experience since February 2020.

My story

I was born in North London in Tottenham (what is now called Stoke Newington), in the Bearsted Memorial Hospital for Jewish Mothers. My parents came to England from Jamaica to assist in the call to "build back better" the National Health Service and industry as Britain faced labour shortages, and called on the colonies. My parents came filled with stories of welcome and potential prosperity but found hostility and ghetto-isation. They passed down well-told tales of signs on prospective homes saying "No Blacks, no Irish, no dogs"—and landlords unwilling to house anyone deemed impure or dirty. They eventually found homes, careers, and each other, and had me. I was told very early on the "truths" of the system into which I was born. They told me that no matter what, I will always be judged by the colour of my skin, and that for some reason that they were unable to explain, white people did not like black people, and they will try to hold you down at best, and destroy you at worst. I would say repeatedly, "I can only be me, I cannot be what someone else says I am or must be." Regardless, my parents insisted that the world was dangerous, and I had to take care, and the key part of that care was understanding what it means to live in a black body. It turns out, in retrospect, that my reaction to their narrative, one that I resisted with my whole being, came to be my inoculation against the race war that I denied. So, what I am about to share is able to exist due to my inoculation against the mimetic infection of systemic racism, as I knew who I was and where I came from.

Along comes 2020 and the coronavirus pandemic. I begin by sharing the reality that I have lost members of both my blood and chosen family to Covid-19. At one time my mother and older sister were both in hospital due to Covid-19 complications, the latter in an induced coma for three and a half weeks. At other time periods there were two cousins similarly in induced comas. I have seen these infected people emerge well and recover on the one hand, and on the other, I had to attend funerals, online and in person, for those that did not recover. The infections, the pain, and the loss are real. What is also real and much harder to accept, tolerate, and explore is the onslaught of the confusion and anger at the apparent disproportionate impact on black people (who I refer to as beings in black bodies). The black body is one that is rich in melanin. Melanin is the carbon protein that produces dark pigment in the skin and other parts of the body. What is it about those beings in melanin-rich bodies that makes them susceptible to death from Covid-19? Is there anything in the chemistry of the SARS-CoV virus that attracts it to melanin, or, more worryingly and difficult to articulate, are there professional, social, and cultural factors that lead to the deaths of beings in black bodies?

The reaction to the emergence of the Covid-19 virus is a very interesting phenomenon on its own, and yet its convergence with the police murder of a black man, George Floyd, in Minneapolis, USA, created a complex nexus when considered through the lens of race. Race itself is a contested term and therefore thinking about race relations is also a contested conceptual and operational space. This chapter sets out to think about these matters from the gaze of the group and the framework of a history that is long and equally complex, and therefore unlikely to be adequately covered in any attempt. The ambitions are partial and so I only hope to connect some historical matters with our contemporary situation. Are we simply in the midst of a "little bit of history repeating"?

I would like to start this exploration not in Wuhan or Minneapolis, but in 1870s Ghent, and its relationship with the Congo via the International Africa Association under the leadership of King Leopold of Belgium (Ascherson, 1963). From there we will travel across the Atlantic to think about the manifestations of the relations of power and privilege, and brutality and exclusion, and ideas of race. Having set a historical framework, we can then explore what the psychoanalytic voice has to say about race, drawing on inferences made from the writings of Freud, in particular "Moses and Monotheism", and what it can tell us about the historical foundations of psychoanalytic thought that might yet open up new ways of seeing and thinking about race.

We then turn to the contemporary philanthropical and scientific discourses of the Bill and Melinda Gates Foundation and CEPI (the Coalition for Epidemic Preparedness Innovations) and think about the parallels that they reveal with the King Leopold International Africa Association. The chapter then goes on to connect with the "beam of intense darkness" that James Grotstein identifies when thinking about the impact of the work of Wilfred Bion on our appreciation of thinking and experiencing our interconnectedness as human beings on earth. So, let us begin to enter the darkness of our subject matter. I call upon two authors: Dr Wade Nobles (1997), who said that "One has to understand history in order to remove the white man's mystery," and Joseph Conrad, following his invitation to take a journey into the "Heart of Darkness" and see what we can discover.

European philanthropy meets the Dark Continent

There is a long legacy of war and battle in Europe that has left millions dead and seen kings and queens deposed in favour of political secular regimes. Simultaneously, various swings between religious sensibilities as the driving force for, or the halting dynamic behind, the cessation of said wars, have been a significant factor in the development of the European mind. The Dutch Kingdom of the Netherlands relinquished control of the Belgian territory after the Belgian Revolution of 1830. The people chose to adopt a hereditary monarchy as their governing model. Their second king is the monarch of primary interest in our journey into the darkness.

King Leopold II of Belgium began a programme of broad philanthropic activity. He called together a council that met as "The Brussels Geographic Conference" that took place in September of 1876. The conference voted to create a vehicle for their joint philanthropic efforts, "The International African Association", more fully described in its deeds as "The International Association for the Exploration and Civilisation of Africa". The association was represented by all the European royal houses and their associated political machinery performed the facilitating execution. Each nation set up its own committee that reported in via the international association that had elected King Leopold as chair. The original idea was that chairmanship of the international committee would rotate such that each nation would be represented in turn at the helm, and thus the enterprise would be a shared endeavour. Things fell apart as the European nations began to organise and execute their own expeditions and each claimed land and resources for themselves, rather than the shared endeavour articulated in the setting up of the International Association.

The scramble for Africa, as this phase of European history has been termed, had to be curtailed somehow, and the idea to call another conference was agreed, this time to be held in Berlin. The Berlin Conference took place between November 5, 1884 and February 26, 1885. Before and after the conference there were many bilateral meetings leading to agreements, deals, and negotiations that secured agreement over who would get what in terms of land and resources in Africa. Fourteen nations took part in the conference and all secured areas of Africa except Denmark, The Netherlands, Austria-Hungary, Sweden-Norway, and the USA. The map of Africa that we work with today was a product of the work of the European powers in Berlin in 1885.

So why is this set of historical events significant to a 2021 pandemic and the way we think of race relations? I suggest that the relevance lies in what Fred Emery (Emery & Trist, 1973) refers to when he comments on Levi-Strauss's inaugural address as Chair of Social Anthropology at the College de France, where his talk

> presents an analysis and a vision, conceives the viable future as an achievement of societal self-regulation made possible by the culture of the second industrial revolution. This would bring to an end the epoch we have known as history and have called civilisation. Yet there can be no simple return to a Type 2 world in which large numbers of small societies existed independently; rather will there come into being a matrix in the inter-dependent networks of which values will be such that pluralism can be tolerated. (pp. 210–211)

This move to an interdependent network requires the capacity to work as equals in a number of arenas. The European powers' collaborative efforts for the invasion of Africa and the systematic dehumanisation and brutality employed to achieve the domination, have left a significant challenge in the minds of both dominator and dominated.

The statisticians and historians have an assemblage of the enormity of the brutality that the Europeans used when they ravaged across Africa in the colonial period. The methods of systematised control and the dehumanisation that accompanied the brutality allowed people to unleash the same sorts of inhumane conditions to which we subject our "animal" earthlings that we "farm" for food. For the organisers of the African colonies, and other colonies structured along race/pigmentation, the justification of the regimes' attitudes created a context that called forth the narratives of race and the associated distribution of privileges along racial grounds. But these forces of oppression and brutality were not just unleashed on the black populations: melanin-recessive people were also subjected to brutality in order to achieve their compliance and subjugation to the systems.

Brian Davey (2016) illustrates this rapacious abuse well, in regard to the treatment of the Irish at the hands of the English colonial forces and their collaborators. He says, "Having thus degraded fellow human beings as low as they could go through applying 'economic principles', the sociopathic gentlemen then witnessed the resulting wretches and failed to recognise their own handiwork."

Accompanying Queen Victoria in Ireland, historian Charles Kingsley commented:

> I am daunted by the human chimpanzees I saw along that 100 miles of horrible country. I don't believe they are our fault. I believe that there are not only many more of them than of old, but that they are happier, better and more comfortably fed and lodged under our rule than they ever were. But to see white chimpanzees is dreadful; if they were black, one would not feel it so much. (Gallagher, 1995)
>
> What is called "political economy" then was a set of doctrines that suited a gentleman elite of genocidal sociopaths. The statement is not written to be read as indignant rhetoric, but as strictly factual. I seek to describe the world as it was then, not as I would have liked it to have been. There is plenty of evidence. The art and journalism of the time shows how these men regarded themselves. (Davey, 2016)

The capacity to dehumanise in order to justify further abuses is a hallmark of the colonial mindset. What does all this tell us when considered in the contemporary context of Covid-19? It indicates that there are grounds for the mistrust of the Big Pharma and the politicians at two levels, first when they say that black people and the poor are disproportionately affected, and second, when they encourage the poor and black people to trust them and take the medicine in the form of the vaccine. There is a historical precedent to the nature of systematic abuse, and the memory of the people and their descendants lingers on in the minds, memories, and the unconscious of peoples and of nations. In the same way that the descendants of the Nazi Holocaust survivors say, "We will never forget," it seems that there is an unspoken but enacted sentiment. The descendants of the colonised have behavioural demonstrations of the same sentiment, this time voiced as "We will not take the vaccine." How we collectively make the space to face the reality of the rational paranoia of those who will not take the vaccine or trust the medical professions or politicians, I suggest is the task of the next one hundred years, in this, our postmodern ecology.

The skills and sophistication required to deal with these tensions and dilemmas lie in the hands of the psychoanalytically informed practitioners, theoreticians, and scholars. A collaborative engagement, working alongside the anthropologists and artists who are still able to engage critically and reflexively with the public discourse on the racialised experience of the vaccine and Covid infections, may yet reveal new resources for our understanding to progress.

Freud and the unthought known

In "Analysis Terminable and Interminable" Freud (1937c) says something of such significance that I am going to quote it in its entirety.

> Moreover, we know that we must not exaggerate the difference between inherited and acquired characters into an antithesis; what was acquired by our forefathers certainly forms an important part of what we inherit. When we speak of an archaic heritage we are usually thinking only of the Id and we seem to assume that at the beginning of the individual's life no ego is as yet in existence. But we shall not overlook the fact that Id and ego are originally one; nor does it imply any mystical over evaluation of heredity if we think it credible that, even before the ego has come into existence, the lines of development, trends, and reactions which it will later exhibit are already laid down for it. The psychological peculiarities of families, races, and nations, even in their attitude to analysis, allow of no other explanation.

> Indeed, more than this: analytic experience has forced on us a conviction that even particular psychical contents, such as symbolism, have no other sources than hereditary transmission, and researchers in various fields of social anthropology, make it plausible to suppose that other, equally specialised precipitates left by early human development are also present in the archaic heritage. (pp. 240–241)

I take this quote to mean that he recognises that what we instinctively carry from generation to generation is embedded within the cultural fabric into which all human beings are born. This cultural fabric is not separate and located in the individual ego, which is only formed as a result of the life experiences that each individual faces. Rather, the archaic transmission is located in the id itself, which from the perspective of group relations could be argued to be the location of the group unconscious identity. Wilfred Bion (1990) describes the process that an individual psyche has to undertake in order to metabolise societal and socially located fragments of the ego. He says,

> the particles which have to be employed share, as we have seen, the qualities of things. The patient seems to feel this as an additional obstacle to their re-entry. As these objects which are felt to have been expelled by projective identification become infinitely worse after expulsion than they were when originally expelled, the patient feels intruded upon, assaulted, and tortured by this re-entry even if willed by himself. (pp. 62–63)

These two perspectives invite us to consider that perhaps the trauma that remains unspoken and unexplored is the trauma of the European in general and the European in a melanin-recessive body in particular. The exoticisation of the black and African inherited trauma of slavery could also be a projection of the split-off trauma of the European—in the same way that the notion of the "black brute" was a projection onto the black body by the enslaver to legitimate their brutality to tame the wild beasts.

The delicate balance of resource and feared object can be elucidated by ideas of race and role by later group relations thinkers.

Purity, race, and role

Allan Shafer (2020) draws on the writing of earlier and more recent writings of Gouranga Chattopadhyay (2018) to introduce the ideas of the colonial domination and its implications for both the dominated and the dominator. Chattopadhyay (2018) identifies a comprehensive narrative of the impact of the European coloniser in particular, and what he proposes as the replication and internalisation of the coloniser mindset into the colonised. The argument draws skilfully on the Indian subcontinent's experience of colonial rule and the existing caste system to offer a further refinement of the idea of the basic assumption group behaviour expressed by Bion (1962).

> The idea of a basic assumption stipulates that a work group can be engaged in "as if" behaviour that is anti-task and can be assumed to be seeking dependency, pairing, or fight/flight. There were two further basic assumption groups identified by later proponents in the group relations tradition. Pierre Turquet (1974) articulated basic assumption oneness, followed later by Lawrence, Bain and Gould (1996) who used their experiences to illustrate how certain work groups suddenly ceased to behave as a group and became a congregation of individuals *as if* each member has to look after only her/his interest for survival. They called this the "fifth basic assumption baMeness. (Shafer, 2019, p. 2)

The stage is set for what he articulates as the sixth basic assumption, baPu (basic assumption purity/pollution). Essentially, a hierarchy is created in which some are invested with superior skills, attributes, or power and ultimately it is enshrined in systems and procedures that authorise the minority group to have and maintain positions of privilege over the impure majority. The creation of the idea of "blue bloods", families who manage the purity of their bloodline and thereby their inheritance of wealth and privilege, Chattopadhyay locates in the constructed family networks that we now call royalty and their wider support group that he refers to as the aristocracy.

The idea of the aristocracy endures beyond the existence of the royalties who created them, as is pointed out by the continued use of the term in Germany and France, for example. What Chattopadhyay interestingly points out, is the nature of the location of the authority for the behaviour and span of control that these historic families hold and their created systems legitimate. The citing of the role of the Vatican and the use of papal decrees to permit such action is striking.

> Religion has also played its role in upholding the idea of baPu. An example comes from the Papal Bulls known as the Bulls of Discovery. Way back around 15th Century the Pope had decreed that any geographical territory not occupied by Christians, which by definition was also white persons in that era, such as explorers or people seeking new lands to expand trade, were to be known as unoccupied and discovered by those white Christians when they first arrived there. At one stroke this created a pure group of white Christians as opposed to non-whites of various "impure" shades. Since then Whiteman arrogated to themselves [sic] the right to settle, conquer and plunder land belonging to non-whites. Holding on to the idea of purity of blood, they have rationalised rapaciousness as White Man's Burden. From the dehumanising caste system of India to various other institutions that rationalise establishing privilege for minority groups under the umbrella of preserving purity of bloodline and such other phenomena as skin colour have been described as the sixth basic assumption of Purity/Pollution. (pp. 2–3)

Introjected elements

In this section we will look at what both authors have to say from their perspectives. I will then add to that narrative by linking it to the matters of indigeneity of the European. What I seek to do is to suggest that the cause of the desire to dominate could be located in envy. My suggestion is that what is envied is the imagined sense of connection that the black body has to the soil from which it sprang, and that the soil is one that is fertile and generous. In contrast, the European has rejected its soil because it has been barren, hard to farm, and has offered a hostile context for growth due to the impact of the ice and cold of northern Europe. The lack of fertility of the soil has meant that the European has had to struggle against "nature", to dominate it and render it fertile while fighting against the cold and wind that has been experienced as trying to kill the inhabitants. This reaction to the hostile cold could be connected to the superior innovation of the Scandinavian countries and those who migrated to the lowlands of Western Europe.

Perhaps this primary envy towards the forces of nature themselves are at the root of the European brutality towards those who are surrounded by sun, fertile soil, and abundance. The relationship to a nurturing "mother earth", who provides abundantly with little effort, could underpin projections of lazy and idle Africans. It is countered by the containing drives of the industrious, diligent European who has had to hold on to a "Protestant work ethic" for survival. This idea of the good enough mother was advocated by David Winnicott as a way of thinking about human development and its roots in childhood rearing.

Winnicottian perspectives on ego-relatedness and id-relationships

So, what is the impact on the psyche of the progeny who have not experienced "good enough" mothering from their context (sky and soil)? Winnicott offers some ideas that might be worth thinking about. In approaching Winnicott, let us do what Shafer (1999, 2019, 2020) did in applying the thinking of Turquet (1974) in the large group in a group relations conference to wider society and what Khaleelee and Miller's (1985) application did in shifting our understanding from large group to analysis of societal forces. If we think about the experience of the mother in the world as a projected relationship onto the mother in the home, I think that this is the work that Freud was advocating in his later work. What might we discover if we thought more psychoanalytically about the mother as context or culture, which shapes our experience of the mother as parent? This was the work that Freud was undertaking, I believe, and the relationship to the mother that he intended to address was not the mother that gave birth but was the mother as the context in which the mother gives birth, namely the socially constructed notion of civilisation or culture—where culture represents the repository of what Freud called the archaic. We can study race relations as dynamic between people in relation to their environment and as an integral element of their embodiment of the culture, as a microcosm.

Vandana Shiva (2020) has written forcefully about the ecological understandings of the current social dilemmas in regard to race and Covid-19, where she draws parallels between the origins of the pharmaceutical industry and the thanatic, destructive forces of the chemicals that they produce, to kill pathogens, insects, plants, and indeed humans. There are resonances with her stance on the 1% in terms of global wealth and how they map directly onto the old aristocracies and oligarchs who have seen their wealth increasingly concentrated into fewer and fewer hands. She speaks starkly about the military industrial complex and the enormous amounts of money spent on the machinery of war and destruction and how the death tolls in these exercises disproportionately affect those in lower social and economic classes and those from black and other minority groups.

Africa has been a significant resource for Europe not just in terms of gold, uranium, diamonds, teak, coffee, and cocoa, but also intellectual and spiritual resources to fuel Europe's devised and concretised positions of authority. Part of that intellectual tradition that has been used by the European mind to dominate its enemies has been the field of psychology in general and psychoanalysis in particular. A striking coincidence occurs in the 1930s. Freud constructs his final book prior to his death, while he was living as a refugee, driven from his Vienna home and newly settled in London: "Moses and Monotheism", in which he elucidates the Ethiopian/Egyptian origins of Moses. He raises the question of legitimacy of inheritance and the necessary destruction of his identity from the minds of his European ancestors, at the same time as the National Socialist German Workers Party was beginning its cleansing of Europe of Germany's supposed/perceived enemy, namely, the Jews who had cleansed the African roots of their religion. The desire for eradication seemed to transcend time and space and culture.

CEPI—the re-emergence of a new philanthropic paradigm/return of the repressed?

So now we return once again to the Covid-19 pandemic and what it tells us about contemporary race relations. The World Economic Forum 2017 in Davos, Switzerland was the site of the launch of the Coalition for Epidemic Preparedness Innovations. The governments of Norway, Germany, and Japan, and the Wellcome Trust and the Gates Foundation were the founding partners. This was an initiative to tackle the enduring nature of pandemics and how to ensure their eradication. This coalition agreed billions of dollars to prepare for vaccines to cleanse the world of the impurity of pandemics. But that same narrative of world war has been used for poverty, famine, and terror, and with each declaration of war we see more death and displacement. For some scholars, such as Shiva (2020) and Chattopadhyay (2018), the risk of destruction is posed to those people deemed poor and those deemed impure.

The very darkest of thoughts emerge when we shine what Bion called the "beam of intense darkness" into our self-blinded state. We bring into sharper relief the idea that the Nazi "final solution" agreed at the Wansee Conference was the descendant of the solution agreed at the Berlin Conference, which was itself in turn the descendant of the Brussels Conference. Might perhaps the birth of the CEPI also be a descendant of the forefathers of Berlin, Brussels, and the Wannsee? Might the vaccination programme also be a targeted "plandemic" to eradicate those people deemed to be "human chimpanzees" who have no part in the New World Order? Many people, who have been joining the dots for aeons, saw on the horizon things that the rest of the population did not want to see. They were often labelled heretics and madmen, and found their fate in death or imprisonment. So rather than risk such a fate, the wise keep quiet, and turn a blind eye. Our task in the coming one hundred years is to blind our eyes not to avoid, but to confront things that are not yet visible, and to pay attention to the patterns as they seek to emerge.

Beam of intense darkness

Illumination is a process that unfolds due to a range of matters and assumptions that are no longer allowed to remain untested and unexplored. The idea of race and in particular the abuse and misuse of those with dark skins and African appearance has been used as a vehicle to form the social hierarchies that have dominated the human story in the last 500 years. If we are to turn our eyes to look closely at what may be as yet discussed or even thought about, as a portal for transcendence, a new age of human relations may emerge. The tools of oppression of beings in black bodies have now been experienced by all people, thanks to Covid-19. First, everyone is a possible vector for disease; second, mistrust and surveillance are the order of the control mechanism by the systems of power; and third, social distancing and the control of movement are responsible for creating ghettos out of our homes.

This assault on the freedom and liberty of those in white (non-melanin-rich) bodies have opened them up to the subtleties of suppression and forces of divide and rule that have shaped the Covid-19 trail. The calls that "all lives matter" is not simply a rejection of black lives, it is genuine recognition that the system has devalued all life, and it is now acknowledged as intolerable on the level of human flourishing and unacceptable as a method of social development. The intensity of the experience of the Covid-19 era has indelibly printed on the psyche of the people what it must be like to be denied one's humanity in the midst of the narratives of infection and pollution. This could be seen as a collective awakening to what it means to be human, and the injustice and cruelty that has operated just below the level of our experience. The Covid-19 journey of race and ethnicity has opened us up to a new layer of experience.

Conclusion

In conclusion, I wish to suggest that part of the key work that Covid-19 has surfaced is that the ideas embedded in our social systems are the product of historical factors. These historical factors are rooted in the organised, systematic, and systemic nature of the planning driven by the royal houses of Europe and their associated political and administrative systems across time and geography. The institutional transformations of oppressive regimes are embodied and transferred epigenetically across time and races, such that the elites of all societies contain the same thought structures and values regardless of biological phenotypes. For example, in the Black Lives Matters marches that sprang up all over the world amid the pandemic, we saw images of police in all cultures battering their citizens. Thus we can see that the brutality of authority and misuse of power is embedded in the fabric of our social system, regardless of the race and ethnicity of the role holders. It was not just white police officers in Minneapolis who battered their citizens; black officers in Trinidad did the same thing. The infections of Covid-19 and racism are transmitted intergenerationally and we have been systemically slow to respond to the debates of how this transmission occurs. I believe that we have been misled to focus on the content of melanin in the skin of the perpetrator rather than interrogating the thought structures that role-holders possess. It is not about white oppression, per se, it is about first of all understanding what it is that black bodies possess that makes them a target for dehumanisation. Second, it is about questioning the replication of systems of oppression, domination, and corruption across races that may reveal how people become consumed from within by ideas that eventually destroy them—much like the infection from Covid-19.

Covid-19 has brought into sharper focus a range of processes that have been hidden but known for centuries so that we can see together (etymological roots of *co* and *vid*). Our seeing is paradoxically at its best when we deliberately blind ourselves, so that we may discover anew what we have been as yet unable to behold. Perhaps the "gas chambers" of 2021 were the Nightingale hospitals and the ventilators of the world where many died. Ivan Illich (1973) described a set of processes that are created to keep people subdued and bound in an unquestioning manner to the dominant narratives of their society. He describes schooling that does not educate and medicalisation that does not heal. He argues that the biggest threats to health are in the hands of modern medicine and the tool to ensure compliance with its domination is an educational system that teaches people how to conform. What he offers us is a window from which to see our collective blindness to the harm done by the systems that are created to heal us.

Race relations are not the issue—we are one race of humans, and some of us, as a result of envy and brutality, are no longer human. And how do we help them to recover what they have lost? Through the healing of the descendants, we can clean up the whole; a win from the formless infinite void, no less.

References

Ascherson, N. (1963). *The King Incorporated: Leopold the Second in the Age of Trusts.* London: Granta.

Bion, W. R. (1962). *Experiences in Groups and Other Papers.* London: Tavistock.

Bion, W. R. (1990). Differentiation of the psychotic from the non-psychotic personalities. In: *Second Thoughts* (pp. 43–64). London: Karnac.

Chattopadhyay, G. P. (2018). The sixth basic assumption baPu (basic assumption purity/pollution). *Organisational & Social Dynamics*, 18(1): 105–121.

Davey, B. (2016). Economics in Darwinist mode—the competitive struggle for existence. https://credoeconomics.com/economics-in-darwinist-mode-the-competitive-struggle-for-existence/ (last accessed July 18, 2021).

Emery, F. E., & Trist, E. L. (1973). *Towards a Social Ecology: Contextual Appreciations of the Future in the Present.* London: Plenum.

Freud, S. (1937c). Analysis terminable and interminable. *S. E.*, 23: 211–254. London: Hogarth.

Gallagher, S. (1995). Body schema and intentionality. In: J. Bermúdez, N. Eilan, & A. J. Marcel (Eds.), *The Body and the Self* (pp. 225–244). Oxford: Oxford University Press.

Illich, I. (1973). *Celebration of Awareness: A Call for Institutional Revolution.* Aylesbury: Penguin Education.

Jung, C. G. (1929). *Alchemical Studies. Volume 13, Collected Works.* 2nd Edition. H. Read, M. Fordham, G. Adler, & W. McGuire (Eds.). Princeton, NJ: Princeton University Press, 1967.

Khaleelee, O., & Miller, E. (1985). Beyond the small group: society as an intelligible field of study. In: M. Pines (Ed.), *Bion and Group Psychotherapy.* London: Routledge & Kegan Paul.

Lawrence, W. G. (1998). *Social Dreaming @ Work.* London: Karnac.

Nobles, W. W. (1997). To be African or not to be: The question of identity or authenticity—some preliminary thoughts. In: R. L. Jones (Ed.), *African American Identity Development: Theory, Research and Intervention.* Hampton, VA: Cobb & Henry.

Shafer, A. (1999). Colonial domination and the struggle for identity: Socio-analytic perspective. *SOCIO-ANALYSIS: The Journal of the Australian Institute of Socio-Analysis*, 1(1): 34–47.

Shafer, A. (2019). Colonial domination and the struggle for identity: a 2019 exploratory perspective. *Socioanalysis, Journal of Group Relations Australia*, 21: 1–16.

Shafer, A. (2020). Racism and Covid-19. Blog. https://grouprelations.org.au/racism-and-covid-19/ (last accessed September 30, 2021).

Shiva, V., with Shiva, K. (2020). *Oneness versus the 1%: Shattering Illusions, Seeding Freedom*. White River Junction, VT: Chelsea Green Publishing.

Turquet, P. M. (1974). Leadership—the individual in the group. In: G. S. Gibbard, J. J. Hartman, & R. D. Mann (Eds.), *Analysis of Groups*. San Francisco, CA: Jossey-Bass.

Resources (all last accessed November 8, 2021 to March 23, 2022):
https://en.wikipedia.org/wiki/Berlin_Conference
https://en.wikipedia.org/wiki/Leopold_II_of_Belgium
https://en.wikipedia.org/wiki/International_Association_of_the_Congo
https://en.wikipedia.org/wiki/International_African_Association#Further_reading
https://gutenberg.org/cache/epub/14504/pg14504-images.html#Page_50
https://en.wikipedia.org/wiki/Treaties_of_the_Holy_See
https://en.wikipedia.org/wiki/Heart_of_Darkness
https://en.wikipedia.org/wiki/Chikungunya#Virology
https://en.wikipedia.org/wiki/Coalition_for_Epidemic_Preparedness_Innovations
https://en.wikipedia.org/wiki/Robert_Boyle
https://en.wikipedia.org/wiki/Antoinette_Bourignon

CHAPTER 16

The traumata of Covid: learning from the pandemic

by M. Gerard Fromm

In a 1972 conversation with US Secretary of State Henry Kissinger, Chinese Premier Zhou Enlai was asked about the significance of the French Revolution, and famously responded, "It's too soon to tell." Actually, he was addressing a question about the ongoing effects of the 1968 student revolt in Paris, but the story has had staying power because it wittily underlines the wisdom of taking a long view of history. With regard to the significance of the pandemic, as I write this chapter in the autumn of 2021, we are only in its second year, and the disaster of Covid-19 is by no means over. We as individuals, the organisations through which we work, and indeed society as a whole hoped that we were seeing light at the end of the tunnel just a few months ago. Now that light seems to have been a short and rather blinding brightness before the next tunnel, and many worry that it will eventually be the oncoming train of a new, vaccine-resistant variant. In this context, what can we actually say about learning from the pandemic?

Of course, one thing we can say with sad confidence is that the pandemic has been enormously traumatic for so many people in so many ways—through illness and death, complex grief reactions, lost livelihoods, lost homes, and so on. Indeed, we are seeing collective trauma on a massive scale, compounded by the physical and psychological effects of cumulative and cyclical traumatic stress. While there must be enormous learning accruing at an everyday individual level—most basically in terms of how to get through—at the societal level, it tends to be the fate of trauma that its lessons slip below the surface when bad times are finally past. "Men learn from history only that men learn nothing from history," said WWII General Francis Braceland (1946, p. 587), paraphrasing Hegel—a sentiment echoed in the work of the trauma theorist, Judith Herman (1992).

There are, of course, good reasons for this: the relief people feel when the horror is over, the wish to protect other family members from their suffering, the desperate need to forget, the desperate need to rebuild, and so on. There are less ethical, though still understandable, reasons to forget as well. The history of plagues is also a history of societal fracture—those who can afford to leave and those who can't; those whose status is threatened, and those scapegoated for causing the suffering—and so post-trauma denial spares people the shame and guilt associated with how they behaved during the trouble. These all too human societal dynamics are costly. They erase the lessons trauma can so painfully teach, and they deny the truth of what happened, thereby alienating further the traumatised person from the human resources that make trauma more bearable. Indeed, as I have written elsewhere (Fromm, 2022), this denial is one of the things that makes trauma traumatic.

So, in the midst of the pandemic and the widespread trauma it has brought, and in the face of eventual post-trauma repressive forces, the question of learning from the Covid experience becomes a highly speculative one, to be approached with caution and open-mindedness. From my perspective—here in the United States, working with mental health professionals and organisations, and leading an international dialogue group—I will focus, in this chapter, on my own learning, with the hope that some of it has broader significance.

Stress tests

One bit of my and others' learning during the pandemic, of course, is that *pre-existing conditions* tended to make the effects of the virus much worse. This was most obviously true at the physiological level; many of those who died from the virus were severely compromised by diabetes, chronic lung disease, and a host of other, often lifestyle-related, illness conditions. Pre-existing psychological conditions—depressive tendencies or substance abuse, for example—also created greater vulnerability to Covid's physical and social effects. And pre-existing family conditions—everything from the number of people sharing a small space to the nature of people's livelihoods and the ability to manage home–work boundaries—became hugely important factors in determining how families would survive pandemic stress.

In organisations too, pre-existing conditions were enormously consequential for how these groups adapted to the stresses and the operational disruptions inflicted by the pandemic. In many organisations, tensions erupted between those who could—and should, for everyone's safety—work from home and those whose jobs required their physical presence in the workplace. A latent envy and class rivalry surfaced. There were also feelings of loss and resentment about having to adapt to new ways of working—a "we want it back" mentality—and a mistrust of the "wishful thinking" of leadership. Team functioning suffered in so many organisations, both because essential but heretofore informal in-person communications now needed to be organised intentionally and because containment of tensions was left unattended and task definition in the face of change left unarticulated.

Wishful thinking, on the one hand, versus a more clear-eyed recognition of the challenges did indeed distinguish many leaders within organisations. Organisations operating on what Bion (1961) would call basic assumption dependency habitually turned to their leaders for "answers", and their leaders were in the habit of giving them. But during the pandemic, no one had answers, leading to a kind of identity crisis for these leaders and their employees. This identity dynamic was exacerbated in some organisations when their "brand" was insufficiently integrated into their functioning. For example, a company known for its progressive attitudes towards female leadership panicked in the face of the pandemic and regressed to reliance on its male operations staff and a command-control mentality.

This company and others seemed caught up in what the psychoanalyst Jacques Lacan (1977) would call a "supposed to know" way of leading, which could not take in vital information from below nor attend to the relationship and containment tasks that were far more important to managing both the organisation's mission and the workers who were to accomplish it. What emerged was a powerful distinction between these organisations and those whose leaders led with presence, transparency, a willingness to listen and adapt, and an attitude of "I don't know the answer to that question but let's see if we can figure it out together." This is not simply a distinction between leaders but between the organisations themselves—their structure and dynamics—which pre-existed the pandemic but were exposed and exacerbated by it. Perhaps, one lesson of Covid is that something like the "stress tests" that banks were subject to during the financial crisis of 2009 would be valuable for organisations more broadly, as we learn more about the new stresses of the twenty-first century.

Failure at the task of containment, through an articulation of mission that workers can feel and join, led to disillusionment and passive resentment in many organisations. Whereas the CEO of one well-functioning but profoundly stressed organisation could say, "We love the work, *and* we pull our hair out," the staff of other organisations seemed to be saying in action, "We are doing a job, and we won't let it get to us." Indeed, an extreme form of this reaction can be seen in the phenomenon of "lying flat", or *tangping*, which began in China in April of 2021, just a little more than a year into the pandemic. "Lying flat" describes something of a movement, primarily among millennials, that rejects career ambitions and opts for a slower, more self-determining lifestyle, a lifestyle outside what are seen as—and indeed often are—the oppressions and exploitations of organisations. As Rosenblum (2021) put it, in this era of demands on workers to meet the challenges of the pandemic: "Work has become intolerable. Rest is resistance."

Unemployment figures in the US are being interpreted through this lens, as though the forced joblessness of the pandemic has opened the eyes of employees to the job conditions they had been suffering all along, the possibility of now having a choice, and the rejection of returning to a cog-in-the-machine status quo ante. There is much to celebrate about this twenty-first-century emancipation, but to the degree that it reflects leadership's failure to link work to mission and workers to leaders, there is also a sadness in it, a disconnection between Freud's "love and work" values that, in his view, gave meaning to life. It's as though, during

Covid, many employees have come to feel, "No one is taking care of me, so I'd better take care of myself." This disillusioned bit of learning may be freeing and even empowering, but it also brings cynicism and interferes with the development of a "potential space" (Fromm, 2022; Winnicott, 1971), in which leaders and workers can come to believe that "We can do something good together."

To vax or not to vax

Of course, another pre-existing condition was exposed and exacerbated during the pandemic, this one at the societal level. To give only one statistic: as of July, 2021, 86% of self-identified Democrats in the US had had at least one vaccine shot and only 54% of Republicans had. How might we understand this massive disparity? One answer to this question—supported, for example, by the fact that the 2020 Republican convention dispensed with having a platform—is that the distinction between political parties in the US is no longer about visions of the nation or about policies or strategies; it is about *large-group identity*.

As most clearly developed by Volkan (2020), large-group identity has to do with common, often highly charged identity elements held by thousands, even millions, of people who will never meet each other. Rooted in generational history, they provide a secure and continuing answer to the question "Who are we?" Those answers may have to do with race ("I am black"), religion ("I am Muslim"), nationality ("I am a German"), some combination of these ("I am an Irish Catholic") or some other large-scale group designation ("I am a Communist"). Large-group identity is not a conscious process and does not begin in the late adolescent phase of identity formation (Erikson, 1959)—crucial as that phase is to the individual's further identifying with, or differentiating, from the large group.

Rather, large-group identity is an emotional phenomenon beginning in early life, with a child's earliest identifications, and continuing during the phase when a toddler is, both excitedly and fearfully, experimenting with leaving the home base of mother to explore a brand new world. In the course of this, the child quickly takes in messages of "Here, with me, is safe. There is dangerous." And "here" generalises from mother to family to home to village to religion to nationality.

It also generalises from safety to pride and morality. Things that belong "here" are good. Things that belong "there" are dirty or bad. Erikson (1959) noted "the subtler methods by which children are induced to accept ... prototypes of good and evil" (p. 27); the way that "minute displays of emotion ... transmit to the human child the outlines of what really counts" (p. 28).

Large-group identity involves deeply internalised meanings related to one's own group—of sameness, safety, goodness, pride, and belonging—and meanings related to those outside the group as well—of otherness, shamefulness, and potential danger. If a group's anxiety is low, those meanings about the other may include less problematic emotions, like curiosity and generosity. But if a group's anxiety is high, latent meanings of the other group as alien, threatening, or dirty may become prominent, and at critical moments, a process of societal regression can be set in motion. Erikson, writing in a totalitarian era, described a process of "othering", now enacted on the left as the "cancel culture" and on the right in more blunt-force fashion: "Where the human being despairs of an essential wholeness, he restructures himself and the world by taking refuge in totalism ... an absolute boundary is emphasized ... nothing that belongs inside must be left outside, nothing that must be outside should be tolerated inside" (1959, p. 133). In societal regression, Erikson's "absolute boundary" is demarcated, the other becomes only an object of projection, and one's own ranks are ruthlessly purged.

One sobering lesson of the pandemic may well be that large-group identity is far more powerful than a person's fear of death or illness and more powerful than sentiments based on transcendent values, like working together to protect everyone or respecting the outcome of an election. Certainly, Donald Trump's winning the presidency in 2016 indicated that large-group identity within a major segment of American society was already mobilised. It may have taken the differential reactions to the virus and to the vaccine to show us just *how* powerful the feelings and identity elements embedded in what has come to be called the MAGA world are (Make America Great Again). One of those feelings involves the effort to purge its ranks of RINO's—so-called Republicans-in-name-only. Another involves a profound craving for narcissistic triumph: the desire to "own the libs".

Nashville is undefeated

Owning other people—the right and the power to do so—was what led to the American Civil War, the death toll from which roughly equals the number of military deaths in all other American wars combined and has just been surpassed by the death toll from Covid. Might that phrase—"owning the libs"—have a deeper resonance? In March of 2020, in the midst of the first surge of the virus, a young shirtless and maskless male partier paraded down one of Nashville's main streets with his mates, yelling "Nashville is undefeated!" He was referring to the fact that local politicians had rejected the Center for Disease Control's advice about no large gatherings, social distancing, and wearing masks. So spring break revelry rolled along, untroubled by the dangers of Covid.

But why "undefeated"? Margaret Mitchell, the author of *Gone with the Wind* and a journalist in Atlanta during the first half of the twentieth century, once commented that she had been taught all there was to know, every single detail, about the "War of Northern Aggression", except for one thing: that the South lost! Learning that at the age of ten was a "violent shock": "I didn't believe it when I first heard it, and I was indignant. I still find it hard to believe, so strong are childhood impressions" (Perkeson, 2012). And so strong were childhood loyalties to the Confederate soldiers and plantation owners in her family's history. Beyond the reality of trauma—the horrors and losses of the Civil War, for example—Mitchell's comments could be heard as describing what Volkan (2020) calls *chosen trauma*.

Chosen traumas are traumatic experiences that over time have come to represent and to organise the collective identities of the large groups who suffered the historical trauma. They are passed down through emotionally charged narratives from one generation to the next—a form of transmission of trauma (Fromm, 2012)—and become a nexus of stories, feelings, and symbols that shape large-group identity. They characterise and distinguish each group of people as who they are, and sometimes anchor those identities in a stereotyped definition of the "Other". Both sides of a societal conflict come to know themselves, both sides feel their membership in something larger, and both sides do so through projections onto the "Other".

The concept of "chosen trauma" refers to a powerful psychological process shared by members of a large societal group and taking place over many years. Devastating events at the hands of an "Other" in the history of any group must be mentally and emotionally processed over time. When members of the victimised group are unable to bear the humiliation, reverse their helplessness, or mourn their losses, they pass on to their children powerful, emotionally charged images of their injured selves, which bind the next generation to them and pass along psychologically restorative tasks the younger group is implicitly charged with taking up. Chosen trauma emerges virulently in times of crisis. In a sense, it reflects the infection—a loaded word in the context of Covid—of a group's mourning process (Volkan & Fromm, 2016): an interference with efforts to come to terms with, and move beyond, the actual trauma. Its reactivation links group members to a shared, endangered sense of identity, which can be used by political leadership to promote large group movements, some of which may turn deadly, as we saw on Capitol Hill in January, 2021.

Has the pandemic shown us that, in the United States, large-group identity associated with the Civil War—including nostalgic romanticising about the "lost cause" and gut-level fears and guilt associated with having had a black president—remains a powerful force, available for exploitation by demagogic leaders? Is vaccine refusal, which is now killing three times the number of Trump voters than Biden voters, driven by both current and ancient anti-government rage, much of which has its unconscious source in chosen trauma? Does that young man's proclamation of being "undefeated"—and the implicit entitlement to go maskless that he and so many others claim—carry, without his knowing it, the humiliation of a long ago defeat his people suffered but have yet to truly accept?

I can't breathe

On May 25, 2020, two months into the pandemic, George Floyd was murdered by a police officer in the course of an arrest for allegedly using counterfeit money. His final words, as the officer's knee pressed on his neck, were "I can't breathe." These words—heartbreaking and enraging as they are in their original context—have developed an uncanny resonance and, in a sense, become ubiquitous. Residents of the American West have said these words as they choked from the smoke of forest fires. Residents of the American East felt their meaning as they tried, and sometimes failed, to keep from drowning in sudden hurricane-driven floods. A different police officer, trying to protect the US Capitol on January 6, screamed these words as the mob pinned him against the wall. Some in that mob scream them when, back home, they were required to wear a mask upon entering a public building. And, of course, Covid kills by depriving its victims of oxygen. "I can't breathe" was the last-gasp horror for so many people.

The pandemic has become a context for a dire form of intersectionality. Covid anxiety, like Covid itself, begins invisibly, but its contagious, boundary-dissolving nature merges with climate anxiety and anxieties driving social unrest, and gathers into what Strozier (2021) calls *apocalyptic dread*. The breath of life in Genesis—that first inspiration—threatens to become a can't-breathe expiration at so many levels. The plague has brought its other horsemen with it.

This kind and degree of collective anxiety, what the psychoanalyst Donald Winnicott (1974) called a *"primitive agony"*, makes it extremely difficult for people and their leadership to think clearly and contain panic. Leadership may reflexively respond by mobilising some aspect of a society's chosen trauma—like pride in defeating the so-called authorities—which reassures the group about their large-group identity while also unleashing regressive processes. Something in the direction of Erikson's absolute boundaries—in the US, border walls or draconian immigration prohibitions—are attempted as fantasy solutions to the threat to identity. The invisible boundary dissolutions of the pandemic, not to mention helplessness in the face of catastrophic climate events, expose the irrationality of this solution as it also escalates the anxiety. An incredible irony, bordering on psychotic thinking, is that, in some southern US states, the large-group identity boundary established by leadership is *against* a boundary—masks—that would actually contain the contagion.

In psychological terms, this is an extreme splitting defence, in which all good is here, all bad is there, and no mixing of these absolutes can occur. Within this mindset, which the psychoanalyst Melanie Klein (1946) called the paranoid–schizoid position, any questioning of one's own virtue and the other's vices—a questioning that would actually reflect a mature capacity to own one's shortcomings and to see the actions of both sides as making sense somehow—is unacceptable. Erikson linked the splitting/purification dynamic to a group's "despair of an essential wholeness" (1959, p. 133), and indeed what have come to be called "deaths of despair" have plagued a segment of the mostly Republican electorate for years now. Historical trauma and its aftermath may well have led to profound despair in this group about its "essential wholeness", now regressively clung to in a fantasy of whiteness, while the larger society seems to be moving on without them. In the face of current trauma from the pandemic, a huge number of American citizens seem deeply damaged, stubborn, potentially humiliated, and secretly hopeless about ever being made whole again.

Only I

In this context, it is no surprise that a society would want, and be vulnerable to, a leader who promises to restore collective self-esteem and, in a sense, "treat" profound narcissistic injury. Donald Trump's projection of power and pride—his claim to lack nothing and be entitled to everything—must have sparked an instinctive quickening in his followers that all might not be lost. Regressed societies look to the leader as a saviour, and Trump's message that "Only I can save you" must have had visceral appeal. The basic trust ordinarily given to leadership in a benefit-of-the-doubt way became blind trust (Volkan, 2004) in the MAGA world.

Narcissistic leadership involves a mirroring dynamic between leader and follower, each thriving on the image the other offers them. While rooted in a fundamentally important developmental process, mirroring between narcissistic leaders and their followers is profoundly risky. The large group, damaged over time by losses and humiliation (Alderdice, 2012), regressively attempts to bypass loss in favour of reversing the humiliation. An entitlement ideology (Volkan, 2020)—which Weintrobe (2021) links to the climate crisis—emerges, and collective illusions about both sides assume a life apart from reality. Processes of idealisation and denigration escalate, intense emotions are enacted towards the group seen as threatening one's entitlement, and the kind of polarisation we saw in the US under President Trump and still see in the nation's reactions to the pandemic becomes the new normal.

For Lacan (1977), the mirror and the gaze of the other are a seduction, a partial truth that vulnerable people want to believe is the whole truth. The mirroring dynamic defines what he called the Imaginary Order, in which narcissistic needs are gratified, but simultaneously an inevitable paranoia develops. Deep down, people know that the image in the mirror—or in the adulatory gaze of followers—is not the whole truth; indeed they know that that truth, whatever it might be, cannot be seen in the mirror. For the wishful-thinking narcissist, seeing is believing. For the paranoid, what is *not seen* is believed. And for Lacan, these are two sides of the same person. Witness the vulnerability to conspiracy theories in Trump's followers.

Narcissistic leaders, and the mirroring dynamic they mobilise, present a major risk to the societal self-esteem they are meant to restore. Mirroring is an imaginary process, involving people's emotionally driven, wishful fantasies about themselves and their leaders. It denies truths it doesn't want to see and increasingly separates itself from reality. Illusions become more like delusions. The futile effort to restore a traumatised society through mirroring takes a paranoid turn, as what is not seen threatens to invade what is seen. In this context, Covid is not only a dire threat from what Lacan calls the Real, but also the perfect metaphor for this form of large group anxiety.

Covid, like climate change, is nature: it's biology, chemistry, and physics. It can come to be known, and to a degree managed, through science. What it can't be is permanently denied, seduced, or conquered. In an interesting op-ed article, Thomas Friedman (2020) plays with the idea that Trump, so identified with the all-powerful father, thought he could treat Mother Nature as just another woman, who would eventually submit and not expose the sense of profound inadequacy narcissistic people feel to be the core truth about themselves. Covid's threat to the magical 30,000 Dow Jones mark seems to have triggered an escalating narcissistic crisis within Trump's bubble. Potential economic collapse and electoral loss threatened to break the mirror and expose shameful weakness. Hence, the initial denial and subsequent antics about the virus.

When there are so many

In its first line, W. H. Auden's magnificent elegy "In Memory of Sigmund Freud" (1940) frames another aspect of the challenge and the potential learning from the pandemic:

When there are so many we shall have to mourn

How does loss on such an immense and ongoing scale affect the task of mourning? Human beings do not have a choice about whether the mourning process occurs, only a degree of choice about how it is taken up. Though it has its biological and social dimensions, mourning is, first of all, a psychological process, a process of allowing images and memories of the lost loved one to come to mind, with feeling, in order to integrate them into the internal relationship with that person and to say goodbye to the external relationship. It is a conscious and unconscious process that has its own trajectory, its own pain, and to be sure, its own complications. For example, unfinished emotional business with the lost other, especially to the degree that it involves negative feelings, may well lead to depression. But mourning is made bearable through the help of others and the "holding" sociocultural rituals of bereavement.

The Covid context has profoundly affected this process. It has heightened two fundamental kinds of anxiety: a paranoid–schizoid anxiety associated with harm coming from the other person and a depressive anxiety associated with harm I myself might do. To the degree that these forms of harm are linked to less conscious feelings and fantasies about oneself and others, anxiety is amplified. Moreover, the social distancing, necessary to protect oneself and others, affects the mourning process in at least two ways. Certainly, it has interfered with the social and religious rituals of mourning. Wesley Carr, former Dean of Westminster and a leader within the field of group relations, designed and conducted the funeral of Princess Diana in 1997. He describes how the flow of a funeral liturgy is meant to carry mourners into, hold them through, and bring them out of a regressive emotional experience, a collective relaxing of defences in the service of healing (Carr, 2010). In the context of Covid, when people cannot gather in this way, how does this happen? Have mourners adapted and found creative ways of doing this? What happens if they haven't?

The second way social distancing has affected mourning occurs in the dying process itself: loved ones and the person they are losing cannot physically be with one another. In many cases, they can't see and certainly can't touch each other. To the trauma of loss and of helplessness is added the trauma of aloneness for both parties. As Coates and her colleagues (2003) note—first of all in the title to their volume about post-9/11 clinical work, *September 11: Trauma and Human Bonds*— exposure to trauma is mitigated by the emotional presence of others, and intensified by their absence. But dying from Covid has a terribly sad Winnicottian element to it (1974): Covid has introduced a profound *emptiness* into the dying process, a traumatic moment of "nothing happening" when something extremely important might have happened.

We have all learned to live with social distancing and to do without the ordinary physicality of human relationships. Largely, people have adapted, from elbow bumps to kisses blown through a mask to closing emails with "Hugs". But for mourners-to-be and for the loved ones they are losing, these adaptations don't work. Even if loved ones view each other through a windowpane or a small screen, it is still "through a glass darkly", and often an excruciating experience of being so near but prevented from the longed-for touch that nearness yearns for. Among the many wrenching challenges faced by healthcare workers (Awdish, 2020), one involved a dying man's daughter who "couldn't bring herself to come in alone, so she asked me to take a picture of her dad's body for her. I didn't know if it was OK … I said a prayer and I took it. I'd never done that before." The task of a doctor resigns itself to the task of a minister, and a daughter can't bear a last chance. At this point in the Covid trajectory, we don't know what the effects of this emptiness will be on mourners, how they will recognise it within themselves, and how they may find meaningful ways of filling it.

The frailty of our conscience

The next few lines of Auden's poem frame another aspect of mourning in the aftermath of Covid, at least in the context of the United States:

> when grief has been made so public, and exposed
> to the critique of a whole epoch
> the frailty of our conscience and anguish

Rituals of bereavement are affected not only by protective restrictions, like social distancing, but also by society's attitude towards its institutions. For example, in post-WWI Britain (Newcombe & Lerner, 1982), immense loss did not lead to increased churchgoing, as one might expect; in fact, just the opposite. Why? One answer has to do with that society's profound change in attitude towards authority: the governmental authority that had, seemingly so blithely, sent young men to their deaths and the clerical authority that supported it. In their anger and grief, people left divine authority alone on Sunday. Within the field of group psychology, authority became a new area of study.

Trauma—whether traumatising horror or acute loss—occurs in a context, even if awareness of that context is obliterated in the traumatic moment. Part of healing is the restoration of context, both as a "holding environment" (Winnicott, 1960) but also for the task of understanding its contribution to the traumatic experience. Sometimes, as more recent theorists of war trauma have noted, context is a critical contributor to the trauma, particularly as it inflicts on the traumatised person what has come to be called *moral injury*. That term, coined by Jonathan Shay (2014), refers to a kind of identity crisis, particularly to the way in which a person may experience a deep sense of having witnessed or participated in actions that profoundly violate his or her core sense of "what's right". This very personal experience may refer to one's own action or to that of someone in authority, in which case feelings of betrayal intermix with feelings of violation. Moral injury tends to occur in a high-stakes situation, when physical and psychic survival is on the line.

Moral injury—sometimes in the form of traumatic disillusionment—is now understood to be a major factor in trauma; indeed, in some instances, it *is* the trauma. Is moral injury part of the trauma of Covid? That maskless partier on spring break in Tennessee was representative of a set of attitudes—lived out in super-spreader events—that undoubtedly have contributed to the number of Covid casualties. The politicisation of science, of governmental authority, and of what it means to be strong or weak, among other things, reshaped a medical crisis into a social and moral one. In Auden's words, it exposed "the frailty of our conscience", such that people have acted recklessly, indifferently, and cruelly towards others, and thereby brought a new level and kind of "anguish" into American life.

How do members of a society mourn when a significant part of that society is implicated in the loss? How do we deal with the "frailty of conscience" that has brought this about? How is a mourner's grief affected by a powerful grievance against one's community, sometimes one's own family? There may well be, for many mourners, a feeling of moral injury for continuing to participate in such a system. In their pain and anger, mourners may feel that the community they have been a part of did not deserve their lost loved one nor do they as mourners want to return to it. Covid may leave so many people with a terribly disillusioned truth: that some of the people you thought cared about you didn't. This anguished sense of betrayal by both leadership and fellow citizens—a failure of its and our responsibility to protect each other—is a key element in the moral injury inflicted by the pandemic.

Their souls speak to us

On February 22, 2021—the day the United States reached the "grim heartbreaking milestone" of 500,000 Covid deaths—President Biden addressed the nation's loss and the way that trauma-related defences work against acknowledging it (Miller, 2021). With 500 candles in the background, he said that "We have to resist becoming numb to the sorrow. We have to resist viewing each life as a statistic … We must do so to honour the dead. But, equally important, to care for the living." The process of mourning means that those left behind *need* to feel this sorrow in order to go on as whole persons, and they need to feel it in the company of people who can feel it with them. The black bunting, lowered flags, and moment of silence that followed were meant to lead this process on a collective level. In large and small, traditional and innovative ways, others across the US and the rest of the world are doing that too.

Recovery from Covid-related trauma requires this kind of leadership into collective mourning. Beyond acknowledging, remembering, and feeling loss at an individual level, something more encompassing is needed by a nation. And, to the degree that the US as a society has not been "in it together", the healing process requires a larger set of rituals or acts of communal remembering that can be joined over time, even by those who failed to appreciate the level of suffering when it was happening. Memorial moments—eventually anniversary ceremonies and monuments—established by national and local leadership, assert that those lives mattered. In providing places and times to remember and to honour, to empathise and even forgive, leadership helps people recognise that, in the act of speaking about those we have lost, their lives speak back to us, and that that process will be healing.

In 2016, Barack Obama, the first sitting US president to visit the Hiroshima Peace Memorial asked: "Why do we come to this place? … To force ourselves to imagine the moment when the bomb fell … to feel the dread of children … [to] listen to a silent cry … [to] remember all the innocents killed … to mourn the dead … Their souls speak to us." This is the work of mourning that depressive-position leaders (Klein, 1946) can help societies achieve. Crucially, it includes the leader's being willing to bear guilt and shame, associated with aggression, on behalf of his own group. President Biden was elected as a depressive-position leader, and, in his remarks, he recognises that healing from traumatic experience needs a kind of witnessing (Laub, 2018), a truthfulness, and a being with, at the family, community, and societal levels. How we and others across the world do this will be one of the essential learnings from the pandemic.

References

Alderdice, J. (2012). Speech to the United Nations General Assembly, New York, September 13.

Auden, W. H. (1940). In memory of Sigmund Freud. In: *Another Time*. New York: Random House.

Awdish, R. (2020). The shape of the shore. *Intima: A Journal of Narrative Medicine*, ISSN 2766-628X.

Bion, W. R. (1961). *Experiences in Groups*. New York: Basic Books.

Braceland, F. (1946). Psychiatric lessons from World War II. *American Journal of Psychiatry, 103*: 587–593.

Carr, W. (2010). A dynamic reading of The Funeral of Diana, Princess of Wales. In: H. Brunning & M. Perini (Eds.), *Psychoanalytic Perspectives on a Turbulent World* (pp. 141–158). London: Karnac.

Coates, S., Rosenthal, J., & Schecter, D. (Eds.) (2003). *September 11: Trauma and Human Bonds*. Hillsdale, NJ: The Analytic Press.

Erikson, E. H. (1959). *Identity and the Life Cycle.* In: G. S. Klein (Ed.), *Psychological Issues* (pp. 1–171). New York: International Universities Press.

Friedman, T. (2020, May 19). Is Trump challenging Mother Nature to a duel? *The New York Times.* .

Fromm, M. G. (Ed.) (2012). *Lost in Transmission: Studies of Trauma across Generations.* London: Karnac.

Fromm, M. G. (2022). *Traveling through Time: How Trauma Plays Itself Out in Families, Organizations and Society.* Bicester, UK: Phoenix.

Herman, J. (1992). *Trauma and Recovery: The Aftermath of Violence—From Domestic Abuse to Political Terror.* New York: Basic Books.

Klein, M. (1946). Notes on some schizoid mechanisms. *International Journal of Psycho-Analysis, 27*: 99–110.

Lacan, J. (1977). *Écrits.* New York: W. W. Norton.

Laub, D. (2018). Testimony as part of the therapeutic process in psychoanalysis. In: E. J. Schreiber (Ed.), *Healing Trauma: The Power of Listening* (pp. 97–108). New York: International Psychoanalytic Books.

Miller, Z. (2021, February 22). Biden mourns 500,000 dead from COVID-19 in White House ceremony. *PBS News Hour.*

Newcombe, N., & Lerner, J. (1982). Britain between the wars: The historical context of Bowlby's theory of attachment. *Psychiatry, 45*: 1–12.

Obama, B. (2016, May 28). Excerpts from "The memory of the morning of August 6, 1945, must never fade". *The New York Times.*

Perkeson, M. (2012, March 12). Interview with Margaret Mitchell from 1936. *PBS American Masters.*

Rosenblum, C. (2021, August 22). Work is a false idol. *The New York Times.*

Shay, J. (2014). Moral injury. *Psychoanalytic Psychology, 31*(2): 182–191.

Strozier, C. (2021). Covid and the psychology of the pandemic panic. *Psychoanalysis, Self and Context, 16*(3): 205–211.

Volkan, V. D. (2004). *Blind Trust: Large Groups and Their Leaders in Times of Crisis and Terror.* Charlottesville, VA: Pitchstone.

Volkan, V. D. (2020). *Large-Group Psychology: Racism, Societal Division, Narcissistic Leaders and Who We Are Now.* Bicester, UK: Phoenix.

Volkan, V. D., & Fromm, M. G. (2016, January 28). We don't speak of fear. *Georgetown Journal of International Affairs.* https://georgetownjournalofinternationalaffairs.org/online-edition/we-dont-speak-of-fear. Washington, DC: Edmund A. Walsh School of Foreign Service of Georgetown University.

Weintrobe, S. (2021). *Psychological Roots of the Climate Crisis*. London: Bloomsbury.

Winnicott, D. W. (1960). The theory of the parent-infant relationship. In: *The Maturational Processes and the Facilitating Environment* (pp. 37–55). New York: International Universities Press, 1965.

Winnicott, D. W. (1971). Playing: Creative activity and the search for the self. In: *Playing and Reality* (pp. 53–64). New York: Basic Books.

Winnicott, D. W. (1974). Fear of breakdown. *International Review of Psycho-Analysis*, *1*: 103–107.

Follow the Covid Trail

by Halina Brunning and Olya Khaleelee

When the earth shakes in its foundations, when the lightness has been replaced by darkness and forms its pole opposite the "new normal" so you no longer know where you are located, when the human race has run out of power to control its destiny, how can you spark the last vestige of faith when all hope is gone?
Chapter I

> The pandemic is a real threat, and not to fear the spread of the virus can only be seen as denial. The pandemic, the invisibility and dangerousness of the virus, the distancing, the hygiene procedures, and the knowledge that we may be a (potentially deadly) threat to someone else also activates neurotic anxiety: what might I suddenly feel the urge to do? Kiss a stranger (and thus kill him)? Our attempts at controlling the pandemic and the risk of catching the infection from someone close to us underscore how pervasive our loss of control is.
> Chapter II

Dreamers reported living in times where all has changed and became unrecognisable:

The town was my own town, yet it was different, there were no people around, nobody I could trust to take care of my children. Life cannot go on without breathing. What kind of future will our children have without towns and without breathing?

Chapter III

> Besides being a haunting ghost, a terrible memory of the past, epidemics have recently also become a present nightmare, a source of individual and collective fears, so much harder to bear in that they symbolically represent all the unseen or disavowed insecurity, complexity, and vulnerability belonging to our current life, as well as the archaic anxieties and "nameless terrors" belonging to every human being's early childhood experience.
>
> Chapter IV

> *A new lexicon exploded into our lives: quarantine, lockdown, Zoom, exponential, ratio, flatten the curve, unprecedented … on and on it went, the emergence of the vocabulary we would need to begin to navigate this reality. Not new words of course but an alien language to most, with a futuristic feel, but also echoes of the past. Paradox and contradiction were all core to this experience as time would continue to prove.*
>
> Chapter V

In the event, it was people's fear of the unknown threats of this infectious disease that made people stay at home. This created a double intimidation, partly from the virus, partly from the oscillation in government policy between lax and stringent policies that earned them a reputation for unreliability. Such vacillation was born of anxiety in leadership when dependability was urgent. This double intimidation resulted in inner confusion for citizens.

Chapter VI

> *The symptoms of coronavirus, a lung infection that makes breathing difficult, are similar to breathing hard when people are afraid. There's a denial of life, an unconscious fear that you're "not good enough", that saps life's power all the time. In Confucianism, the ultimate goal is to become a flawless sage, which unconsciously forms a very common tendency to pursue perfection. Therefore, a kind of caution comes into being…*
> Chapter VII

In this time of an extraordinary if involuntary social experiment, we need to be philosophers as well as epidemiologists. We all have an underlying condition, called life, and it is universally fatal, but the trouble is, we still do not altogether believe that. According to Freud, death is not inevitable in our unconscious reasoning.
Chapter VIII

> *A little virus, a small part of nature, has taken over and now governs the rulers of the world's largest countries. Hence, we can see the virus as an elusive rupture that might entail a new notion of our relationship with nature and the earth. The virus and its effects demonstrate the frailty and fragility of humankind which, we are only now beginning to understand, can be easily completely disrupted.*
> Chapter IX

Covid pandemic is a warning, it is an amplifier of what already exists. It warns us to lose our attachment and devotion to human omnipotence, and to traverse the fantasy that the ethos of modernity can save us. There is an urgent demand to start developing new narratives that recover our lost sense of belonging to this planet, and to learn to live with precarity, fragility, connectedness, and interdependence in new ways.
Chapter X

> *The Western mind does not want to confront the sense of the images it perceives. It is ready to develop a string of self-deceptive rationales, permitting to stay asleep, or maybe rather—sleepwalking. Hence, multiple fetishistic narratives (...) find their place in the symbolic sphere, forging the new imaginary.*
> Chapter XI

Finally, an equally grave possibility lies in changes in society, whereby distrust of government and a failure of containment will tend to mobilise more authoritarian leaders, leading to a greater dismantling of democratic structures. The question remains as to whether citizens, now more in touch with the power of their citizen roles, are able to use their authority proactively to rebuild their communities democratically from the bottom up so as to enable greater integration of wider society; or whether governmental failure is so profound and the fractures so deep that this proves impossible to achieve.
Chapter XII

> *We have not (...) seen novel psychodynamic principles manifesting as a result of the pandemic. It is not so much a novel psychic force as a magnifier in both senses of the word. It has made existing forces more powerful and at the same time it has made them more visible.*
>
> *... Using our systems-psychodynamic insights, to help create more humane and engaging lives at work and at home, might be the most important change that could result from the pandemic if only this—the true lesson of history—were more widely understood and acted on.*
> Chapter XIII

The world is undergoing radical changes, many of which have been emerging since the 1980s, and our technological advances are moving us closer to a singularity or convergence of human development and technological capacity. The pandemic has been the global crisis narrative that has opened up a new way of seeing and thinking about the world post-pandemic.

The leadership narratives that we face will radically call into question the nature of our experience of hierarchies and the capacity of our species to work in collaboration and partnership rather than in a system of command and control.

Chapter XIV

> The ideas at the root of systems psychodynamic perspectives are helpful in framing the questions and the depths which we will have to plumb in order to reorient ourselves and face squarely our destructiveness and its ending to usher in a new age of creativity and possibility, or to begin again another cycle of despair and destruction.
>
> Covid-19 has brought into sharper focus a range of processes that have been hidden but known for centuries so that we can see together (etymological roots of *co* and *vid*). Our seeing is paradoxically at its best when we deliberately blind ourselves, so that we may discover anew what we have been as yet unable to behold.
>
> Chapter XV

How do members of a society mourn when a significant part of that society is implicated in the loss? How do we deal with the "frailty of conscience" that has brought this about? How is a mourner's grief affected by a powerful grievance against one's community, sometimes one's own family? There may well be, for many mourners, a feeling of moral injury for continuing to participate in such a system. In their pain and anger, mourners may feel that the community they have been a part of did not deserve their lost loved one nor do they as mourners want to return to it.

Covid may leave so many people with a terribly disillusioned truth: that some of the people you thought cared about you did not. This anguished sense of betrayal by both leadership and fellow citizens—a failure of its and our responsibility to protect each other—is a key element in the moral injury inflicted by the pandemic.

Chapter XVI

Conclusions

This book was started a year into the global pandemic in April 2021 and finished after nine months of gestation in December 2021.

At the beginning of that period the world was taken by surprise and dominated by a novel virus and then a series of new variants of the same virus, causing widespread damage to the populations and economies of the developed, developing, and Third World countries around the globe.

The world was "wrapped around" and unexpectedly connected by this dangerous virus as well as by the climate crisis that has become more severe with each passing season. Despite differences in the impact of both calamities—the virus and rising global temperatures—these were the major problems which the world had to deal with during 2021, culminating in COP26, an international conference held in Glasgow, UK, devoted to agreeing urgent action on climate change. The other global event of that period was the discovery of effective vaccines against Covid-19 and the unrolling of an international vaccination programme.

Both catastrophes, the viral pandemic and the changes in global climate, affected some countries more than others, just as the benefits of the fightback against these phenomena were greater and more effective in the global North than the global South.

Despite superficial similarities across the globe, the underlying differences and inequalities will only get worse with time. In the face of enduring deprivation of sustainable life environments in poorer countries, already affected by conflicts, deforestation, and rising sea levels as well as rising air temperatures, these factors will cumulatively result in Third World citizens wishing to look for an alternative place to live. The migration to the rich North will continue. Currently 54 million people are on the move in a desperate search for a new home (Brunning & Khaleelee, 2021).

We also observe the speed with which some authoritarian rulers are already weaponising the migrants' desire for a better, safer life in Europe, as dramatic scenes, reminiscent of past historical traumas, are being re-enacted, for example, on the border between Belarus and Poland. "These migrants are victims of a high stakes game of geopolitics played to expose the West's weaknesses, heighten international tensions, stoke divisions and shred credibility. (…) For now the Kremlin holds the initiative. It can turn the migration crisis off. It can turn to another target … " says Edward Lucas (2021).

The political scene worldwide demonstrates a steady growth of authoritarianism, a hybrid phenomenon of "illiberal democracy", populism, and deep societal splits within each society, fuelled by social media. Recently, we saw an attempt to realign the international powers, one example being the formation of AUKUS, a new trilateral security pact between Australia, the United Kingdom, and the United States of America focused on the Indo-Pacific region. This pact was announced in September 2021, its main purpose: to enhance the collective security of the three member states. China immediately criticised this initiative, thus revealing itself as the main reason for this pact having being formed. China is seen by many countries, especially by the West, as the chief source of danger, due to expansionism in the South China Sea and aggression towards Taiwan (Wintour, 2021).

While Russia is also seeking new alignments, especially in Africa, it continues to demonstrate its disruptive hybrid powers primarily against the European Union. This includes the UK as a post-Brexit standalone country, and of course, shows a provocative attitude towards NATO

(Harding, 2020). There are also signs of a growing co-operation between China and Russia which might destabilise the West.[1]

China, in the meantime, is spreading its industrial might by creating dependency on its markets in major developed countries around the globe. Sooner or later this dependency will come home to roost. There are already visible effects of our dependency on China such as lack of vital equipment and supplies ordered and purchased by the West.

After four years of a chaotic, dangerous, risky presidency by Donald Trump, which ended in the storming of the Capitol by his supporters, enraged at Trump losing the election, the USA is now in the hands of an old, weak, Democrat president. Despite the hopes of many citizens, Biden is demonstrating to the world that the United States is gradually weakening and losing its position of international leadership. This change in the way the US is enacting its role on the world stage was demonstrated by the disorganised and sudden withdrawal of troops from Afghanistan in August 2021, leaving it in the hands of the Taliban.[2] High inflation, unrest at the borders (Sullivan & Jordan, 2021), and the polarisation of the population, mirrored by even deeper internal splits between Republicans and Democrats, is leading some commentators to a conclusion that a civil war might break out in the USA.

Power is being exercised not only by country states as such, but also by newly emerging groupings and subgroupings within each political system. Western countries are being tested by the growing power of, initially, a small group of citizens mobilised against Covid vaccination, who subsequently joined forces with white supremacists, thus forming an anti-establishment irritation and provocation. This new movement

---

[1] Since completing this manuscript world events have moved very quickly and therefore the book would be incomplete without mentioning that Russia began a "special operation" by invading Ukraine on February 24, 2022. Its stated aim was to rid Ukraine of "Nazism", despite Ukraine's leader, Volodymyr Zelensky, not only being Jewish but from a Holocaust-surviving family. The war is ongoing at this point in April 2022 with Russia's forces massing to take over the eastern part of Ukraine, including the Donbas region.

[2] However, perhaps in the light of Biden's leadership in mobilising NATO countries against Russia for its 2022 invasion of Ukraine and noticing the generosity of the US in supplying the Ukrainians with sophisticated armoury, maybe the view of Biden as a tired "sleepy Joe" should thus be reassessed?

is becoming aggressive as it appeals to identity politics, generating splitting and anger within Western societies.

Russia as a state is winning its battle against the local opposition movement. Alexey Navalny remains imprisoned and seriously ill after the Novichok poisoning, as he and his supporters have been oppressed and suppressed by Putin's authoritarian regime.[3]

The freedom movement in Hong Kong has been squashed; nobody dares to protest on mainland China, whilst Xi Jinping is positioning himself as China's most authoritarian leader since Mao (Sheridan, 2021).

This growth of authoritarianism is not only confined to the present regimes of China and Russia, which pre-existed Covid, but is a more widespread response to heightened present day uncertainty and fear of annihilation (Covid + climate change), and the wish for visibly "strong leadership" to counteract what is going on beneath the surface. In Hungary Viktor Orbán, a right-wing authoritarian leader and key ally of Putin, has recently been re-elected as prime minister, and in France, Marine Le Pen, another right-wing ally of the Russian leader, threatened to upset Emmanuel Macron's plans to win the forthcoming second vote in the French election, but narrowly failed. Thus we see the continuing rise of nationalism and the growth in popularity of authoritarian leadership to counteract splitting, fragmentation, and the high levels of uncertainty prevailing in contemporary society.

If we stop to consider what is really going on beneath, for many it will be a combination of heightened existential anxiety, together with an underlying melancholy, and for others, active grieving at the losses sustained. Mourning is the natural conscious response to the many deaths worldwide, amounting to nearly 5.5 million at the time of writing in December 2021. Related feelings of anxiety and melancholia, on the other hand, will often be unconscious, resulting from losses that may relate to death, the loss of love, and of family structure. Therefore, we can expect the yearning for "strong leadership" to continue, to provide the containing structures that are now lost from many lives.

---

[3] As the war in Ukraine continues, repression in Russia has increased dramatically, with the arrest of thousands of Russians protesting against the war, and the threat of fifteen years' imprisonment for those citizens perceived to be spreading disinformation, such as using the word "war" instead of "special operation".

The intriguing new phenomena of three billionaires—Bezos, Branson, and Musk—having taken their own rockets into space during 2021 can also be seen as a symbolic manic defence against this fear of annihilation of life on earth.

These terrible Covid and climate change events of flood, fire, and plague, together with our defensive responses to them (primarily denial and reaction formation), raise the question of whether societies can change, or whether we are condemned to repetition compulsion as a defence. Will we continue to smile in the face of adversity, keep calm and carry on, while generating hundreds of thousands of new cases of Covid each day worldwide, or can we change in response to these threats? The lessons learned from the Spanish flu of 1918, in which at least 50 million people died, mostly through medical ignorance, can be summed up as: vaccination, isolation, and social distancing.

As we know, history tends to repeat itself, only never in quite the same way. We as a global population are capable of massive developments, whether in response to climate change, through the development of solar and other forms of power as replacements for fossil fuels, or in the rapid development of vaccines in response to this latest threat. Yet at present, we are still dominated by this mighty powerful little virus and its polarising effects on our populations' reactions in democratic countries. Most importantly, the loss of trust in our leaders' judgements only makes things worse.

Let us end on a quote from our earlier book, *Danse Macabre* (2021):

> Taking all these issues into account, the combined picture indicates a world in which simultaneously there exists a closer geographical proximity between cultures and religions, yet a greater emotional distance between the faithful, where the ease of communication and human exchange is available at a touch of a button, yet where conflicts increase and reach a boiling point much faster; where the leaders whom we are still able to choose no longer represent us; where the poorest in society will remain poor while being exposed to vicariously observing the festival of wealth and fortunes of those who are and will continue to be rich; a world where we "live life to the max", but are also fast destroying the planet in the process. (Brunning & Khaleelee, 2021)

Our Covid book is finished.
But Covid has not yet finished with us!
Just as we write the last sentence, the Omicron variant is leading this *danse macabre* ... where to, only time will tell.

Halina Brunning and Olya Khaleelee
December 31, 2021

References

Brunning, H., & Khaleelee, O. (2021). *Danse Macabre and Other Stories: A Psychoanalytic Perspective on Global Dynamics*. Bicester, UK: Phoenix.

Harding, L. (2020). *Shadow State: Murder, Mayhem, and Russia's Remaking of the West*. London: Guardian Faber.

Lucas, E. (2021, November 13). Vladimir Putin weaponises human misery in this new proxy battle in Belarus. *The Times*.

Sheridan, M. (2021, November 20). The mysterious rise of Xi Jinping. *The Sunday Times Magazine*, pp. 23–38.

Sullivan, E., & Jordan, M. (2021, October 22). Illegal border crossing driven by pandemic and natural disasters soars to record high. *The New York Times*.

Wintour, P. (2021, September 16). What is the AUKUS alliance and what are its implications? *The Guardian*.

Index

Abel-Hirsch, N., 20
Abram, J., 24
actor-network theory, 145 *see also* network(s)
Addley, E., 204
AfD *see* Alternative für Deutschland
Agamben, G., 130
AIDS, 38, 40, 51, 52, 91, 219
Aidt, N. M., 27
Alderdice, J., 260
alpha function, 224, 225
Alternative für Deutschland (AfD), 113
Ambrosiano, L., 54
Anderson, G., 141
anger, 26, 166, 181–182
anxiety, 12, 45, 182, 198, 199, 201–203, 209, 259, 270, 278
    Covid and, 12–13, 71, 72, 259, 262
    group, 256
    primitive, 50
    survival, 177
Anzenbacher, A., 127, 128
Arendt, H., 167
aristocracy, 242–243, 245

Armstrong, D., 17
Ascherson, N., 236
Auden, W. H., 262
authoritarianism, 276, 278
Awdish, R., 263

Baaquie, B. E., 225
Baburoglu, O., 217
Badiou, A., 130, 140
Bain, A., 229
baPu *see* basic assumption purity/pollution
BART *see* boundaries, authority, role, and task
basic assumption purity/pollution (baPu), 242, 243
Bateson, G., 151
Bauman, Z., 53, 152
Benjamin, W., 83
beta elements, 178, 224
Bion, W. R., 48, 51, 55, 114, 134, 176, 199, 209, 229–230, 234, 241, 253
    alpha function, 224, 225
    beta elements, 224

containing, 23
group behaviour, 114–115, 242
selected fact, 20
typology, 224
black
bodies, 233, 235–236, 241, 243, 246, 248
identity, 112, 255
and minoritised groups, 207, 239, 245
Black Lives Matter, 90, 146
blame, 181–183
Bollas, C., 30, 44, 84, 90–91
Bonnerup, B., 22
Book of Job, 100
borderline psychotic state of mind, 84
boundaries, authority, role, and task (BART), 152
Boyle, R., 226
Braceland, F., 252
Brague, R., 168–169
Brecht, B., 193
Brunning, H., 119, 276, 279
Buechler, S., 22
Burdeau, C., 175
Butler, J., 127, 131

Cabinet Office Briefing Rooms (COBR), 174
Callard, F., 197
capitalism
extractive, 142
modernity and, 153
and science, 140, 143, 149
caring
justice and, 128–129
moral concept of, 128
Carr, W., 262
Castells, M., 145
CEPI *see* Coalition for Epidemic Preparedness Innovations
Charters, E., 194
Chattopadhyay, G. P., 242–243, 246
Cheltenham Races, 62
Chinese
culture and Jung, 99

mythology, 98–99
"Oil Peddler, The", 102–103
chirality, 225–226
citizenship, 111–112
Clap for Carers, 45, 71, 204–205
Coalition for Epidemic Preparedness Innovations (CEPI), 236, 245–246
Coates, S., 263
COBR *see* "Cabinet Office Briefing Rooms"
Coffey, H., 172
collective *see also* fear
anxieties, 45
fears, 54
healing process, 265–266
mental space, 47
trauma, 110, 251–253
unconscious, 99, 176
Conference of Parties (COP26), 186
Confucianism, 99–100, 271
confusion, 178–180
connectedness, 132–134, 136
connectivity and interdependence, 147–148
contagion, 42–43 *see also* epidemics
containment, 93, 130, 134–135, 136, 184, 186, 253, 254
COP26 *see* Conference of Parties
Cowper, A., 87

Davey, B., 239
Davis, H. E., 196
defences, 46
paranoid, 43
and protection, 45
psychological, 44
social, 44–45, 46
defensive dynamics, 49–50
of managing fear, 88–91
dehumanisation, 238–239, 243, 248
Deleuze, G., 152
denial, 157–159 *see also* repression
fetishistic narrative, 159–160, 162–163, 167
perspective on past and present, 168–169

transference neuroses, 161, 163–164
and trauma, 252
Verleugnung, 158, 160, 162
Western mind, 165–166
despair, 181–183, 260
Di Nicola, V., 130
disorientation, 9–10, 10–11, 19–20, 22–23
divided self, 142
Douglas, M., 91, 92
dreamers, 30, 33–34 *see also* social dreaming
Dunn, K., 178
Dying: A Memoir, 75

ecocide, 89
Eco-Leadership, 146
    connectivity and interdependence, 147–148
    eco-mindsets, 149–150
    ecosystems, 146–147, 148
    four discourses of, 147–148
    leadership spirit, 148
    organisational belonging, 148–149
    principles of practice, 149–150
    systemic ethics, 148
ego-relatedness, 244–245
Eisold, K., 49
Eliot, T. S., 141
Ellery, B., 175
Emery, F., 216
Emery, F. E., 238
environmental stewardship, 152–153
environmental, sustainability, and governance (ESG), 215
epidemics, 37, 40, 194, 270
    centuries of fear, 38–40
    and contagion, 42
    and crises, 97
    effectiveness of psychoanalysis, 54–57
    fear, 41, 54
    flu, 40
    HIV, 40
    learning from experience, 56–57
    pandemics and social order, 52–53
    psychic, 97
    as psychosocial processes, 42–52
    unveiling hidden social issues, 52–54
Erikson, E. H., 255–256, 260
ESG *see* environmental, sustainability, and governance
ethics, 127
    based on justice, 131
    and morals, 128
    systemic, 148
eudaimonia, 112
eugenics, 141

fear, 41, 176–178. See also epidemics
    of abandonment, 43
    "bodyguard" against, 46
    centuries of, 38–40
    of death, illness, and need for dependency, 82–84
    defensive dynamics of managing fear, 88–91
    epidemic of fear, 48
    exported fear, 88
    fantasy in fear of epidemics, 43
    fear of contagion, 43
    healing collective fears, 54
    managing, 88–91
    of mortality, 177
    normal and pathological, 44
    "politics of fear", 41
    social defences, 41
    spaces and symbols of, 42–52
    splitting and projection into demonised Other, 41
    stranger, 113
    of unknown threats, 270
Ferguson, N., 195, 205, 206
fetish(ism), 159–160, 161, 162–163, 165, 167
Foucault, M., 50–51
fragility, 100–101
Freedland, J., 85–86
French, R., 55, 134
Freud, S., 12, 198
    blows to human narcissism, 122
    concepts of defence mechanisms, 158
    controversy over theories, 198–199

death, 105, 271
fear, 41, 43
forms of anxiety, 12
future, 215
Group Psychology and Analysis of the Ego, 41
morality, 128
Moses and Monotheism, 245
mourning, 25–26
mourning and melancholia, 83–84, 161
object relations theory, 114
reality principle, 225
thanatic coagulation, 217
and unthought known, 240–241
Friedman, T., 261
Fromm, M. G., 252, 255, 257, 258
Funtowicz, S. O., 197

Gaburri, E., 54
Gallagher, S., 239
Gerber, J., 218
Gilbert, S., 85
Gilligan, C., 128, 131
Gimbutas, M., 227
Giubilini, A., 194
glossolalia, 227
Goethe, 126
Gosling, R. H., 176
Gray, J., 153
Green, C., 85
grief, 26–27, 180–181
group
  anxiety, 256
  behaviour, 114–115, 242
  large, 91, 92, 176, 199, 244, 261
  small, 117, 176, 199
group relations, 91, 152, 176, 223, 241, 242, 244, 262
Guerrera, F., 57
Gwynne, G. V., 113

Hancock, M., 85, 87, 173, 174, 182
Haraway, D. J., 143, 144
  sympoiesis, 154
  thinking, 151–152

Harding, L., 277
Harvey, C., 55
Hasselager, A., 22
Heidegger, M., 140
Heitman, K., 194
Helferich, C., 126
Helland, M. R., 135
Herman, J., 252
Hinshelwood, R. D., 24
Hirschhorn, L., 199, 215
Höffe, O., 127, 131
Hoggett, P., 89
Hopper, E., 92
Horgan, J., 122
Hørslev, L., 16
Hughes, T., 193
human
  emotions, 44
  and non-human actants, 145
  vs. nonhuman animals, 126–130
humanity, 130–131, 208–209
  of care and connectedness/communion, 132–136
  splitting of, 228
humiliation, 124–125, 132, 260
Hutchinson, D. S., 220
hypoimmunity, 98
  Chinese mythology, 98–99
  collective unconscious, 99
  Covid-19, 99–100
  fragility, 100–101
  immune system, 98
  recovery, 102–104
  Taoism, 102–103
  weakness, 101

Ibarra, H., 135
id-relationships, 244–245
Illich, I., 248
Imaginary Order, 261
individuals and society, 42–43, 176
International Listening Posts, 106, 117, 175–176, 185–186
  experiences of, 106–113, 115, 117
  breakdown of society, 183–185
  collective unconscious, 176

confusion, 178–180
fear, 176–178
grief, 180–181
shame, blame, anger, and despair, 181–183
International Social Dreaming Matrices, 30–35 *see also* social dreaming
International Society for the Psychoanalytic Study of Organizations (ISPSO), 33, 35
ISPSO *see* International Society for the Psychoanalytic Study of Organizations

Jaques, E., 199
Jordan, M., 277
Jung, C. G., 97, 128, 233
    Chinese Buddhism and Taoism culture, 99
    collective unconscious, 99
    ethics and morals, 128

Kaës, R., 46
Kahn, J., 178
Khaleelee, O., 88, 176, 244, 276, 279
Klein, M., 25, 199, 259, 266
Klores, W., 218
Kohlberg, L., 128
Krantz, J., 41
Krebs, A., 126
Kurzweil, R., 228

Lacan, J., 151, 253
    desire of the Other, 163
    Imaginary Order, 261
    the Real, 140, 143, 153, 155, 261
Laing, R. D., 142
language, 217–219
Laplanche, J., 158
large-group identity, 255–256, 257, 258, 259, 260
Lasch, C., 164–165
Latour, B., 143, 144, 145
Laub, D., 266
Lawrence, W. G., 29, 109, 150, 233–234

leadership *see also* Eco-Leadership
    authentic, 135
    narcissistic, 260–261
    spirit, 148
    women in, 32
Leadership: A Critical Text, 145
Leder, A., 165
Lerner, J., 264
Life after Loss, 24
Lillie, P. J., 173
Listening Post *see* International Listening Posts
loneliness, 21–22
long Covid, 84
    Covid-19 and, 195–197
    metaphor of, 79, 197–198
    societal, 84
loss, 13
    of data, 15–16
    as a gift, 24
    and grief, 24–25, 26–27
    and meaning, 23–24
    of micro moments, 16–17
    overlooked, 18–19
    of relationships, 21
    of routines, 17–18
    of time, 13–14
Lucas, E., 276
lying flat, 254

Macbeth, 214
MAGA *see* Make America Great Again
Make America Great Again (MAGA), 256, 260
Malleret, T., 215
Manthorpe, J., 204
matrix, the, 29. See also social dreaming
Matrix, The, 228
McDonnell, B., 152
McGilchrist, I., 226
McLuhan, M., 218, 224, 227
McMillen, C. W., 194, 200
McRae, H., 219
Menand, L., 165
Menzies, I. E. P., 41, 176
Menzies-Lyth, I. E. P., 200

micro moments, 16
Miller, E., 223, 244
Miller, E. J., 113, 176
Miller, J. A., 140, 143, 151
Miller, Z., 265
Milner, M., 51
mirroring, 260–261
Morgan-Jones, R. J., 81, 82, 92
mourning, 25–26, 27, 273, 278
    anxiety, 262
    loss and development through, 24–25
    and melancholia, 83–84
    "Mourning and Melancholia", 25
    and narrative fetishism, 160
    process, 262–263
    story of inevitable experiences of, 10–11, 22–23
    transformation of, 43–44, 49
    and transgenerational traumas, 26–27

Nagel, C., 122, 134, 136
Naisbitt, J., 218
narcissism,
    decay, 47, 53
    and Freud, 122
    leaders, 260–261
    moral, 131
    personality, 164–165
National Health Service (NHS), 61, 63, 64–65, 76, 84, 95, 107–108, 203–204
    funding, 87, 185
nature, 126, 129, 152–153
    and Covid, 261, 271
    and humankind, 121–122, 123–124, 125, 130–131, 132–133, 151, 154, 243–244
    and modernity, 140–141, 142, 143, 152–153
Neilson, S., 172
Nestor, R., 89
network(s), 148, 150, 225, 226, 229, 238
    family, 242
    identity, power, and influence (NIPI), 152
    social, 203
    society, 145, 147
    travel, 195
Newcombe, N., 264
NHS *see* National Health Service
NHS England, 197
NIPI *see* network(s)
Nobles, W. W., 237
novel coronavirus, 9, 12, 171, 173–174

Obama, B., 90, 266
object(s)
    containing, 23–24
    external, 50, 225
    fetishistic, 162–163
    internal, 25, 47, 49
    relations theory, 114–115, 241
"Oil Peddler, The", 102
Organisation for Promoting Understanding of Society (OPUS), 106, 174, 175, 176, 185
othering, 256
Other, the, 43, 127, 258
    demonised, 41
    desire of, 163
    paranoid transformation of mourning, 43–44, 49

pandemic, 195, 209, 269
    behaviour during, 202–203
    coronavirus, 80, 84–85, 91, 142, 144, 145, 146, 172
    fear, 48
    flu, 40
    and health workers, 93
    HIV, 197
    lessons from, 206, 251–266
    long Covid as metaphor, 197–198
    psychologist's work, 65–67
    restrictions, 12
    role of psychology in, 75–76
    and social groups, 91–93
    social media, 196
    societal impact, 208, 209
    systems psychodynamic lens, 200–201

as threat, 13
and unregulated economy, 90–91
paranoid defences, 43
paranoid–schizoid
    anxiety, 262
    mindset, 181
    position, 259–260
Parasher, A., 196
Park, C., 197
Pasini, W., 37
Perego, E., 197
Perini, M., 40
Perkeson, M., 257
personal protective equipment *see* PPE
PHE *see* Public Health England
PHEIC *see* "Public Health Emergency of International Concern"
P.I., 140
    age, 154–155
Piketty, T., 166
Pilgrim, D., 141
plague-spreader, 48, 50
Plato, 131
Pontalis, J.-B., 158
PPE (personal protective equipment), 73, 76, 87, 90
precarious-interdependence (P.I.) *see* P.I.
proning, 72
"Public Health Emergency of International Concern" (PHEIC), 172
Public Health England (PHE), 173
purity, 242–243

Raab, D., 116, 173
race relations, 236, 244, 245, 248
Rankine, C., 79, 90
Ravetz, J. R., 197
repetition compulsion, 56, 83
repression, 160–161, 163 *see also* denial
Republicans-in-name-only (RINO), 256
resilience, 109, 115–116
Rilke, R. M., 228
RINO *see* Republicans-in-name-only
Rosa, H., 14
Rosenblum, C., 254

Rosenthal, J., 263
Rowlands, M., 126
rupture, 130
Rushforth, A., 197

Santner, E., 159–160
    fetishistic narratives, 162, 163, 167
SARS, 171
SARS-CoV-2 infection, 195–196, 197
Schaverien, J., 88
Schecter, D., 263
Schelling, 126
Schnirring, L., 172
Schut, H., 27
Schwab, K., 215, 216
Scoblic, J. P., 205
Sebald, W. G., 160–161
self
    -blinding, 234
    -containment, 135
    divided, 142
    the, 223
Sensi, J., 185
"severe acute respiratory syndrome" *see* SARS
Shafer, A., 242, 244
Shakespeare, W., 214
shame, 181–183
Shay, J., 264
Sheridan, A., 151
Sheridan, M., 278
Shiva, K., 245, 246
Shiva, V., 245, 246
Sick Child, The, xxi
Simpson, P., 55, 134
social
    death, 113
    defences, 41, 44–45
    disruption, 145–146
    distancing, 263
    epidemics as defences, 49
    group, 91–93
    imaginary, 164
    isolation, 115
    issues, hidden, 52–54
    skins, 92

social dreaming, 29, 233–234 *see also* International Social Dreaming Matrices
    dreamers, 30, 33–34
    matrix, 110–111
society, breakdown of, 183–185
splitting
    defence, 259
    of humanity, 228
    and projection of emotions, 199
SSI *see* Statens Serum Institut
Statens Serum Institut (SSI), 18
Steiner, P., 142
strangers, 50, 113–114
stress tests, 252–255
Stroebe, M., 27
Strong, P., 40, 43, 48, 49, 51, 52–53
Strozier, C., 259
Sullivan, E., 277
superego, 128, 163
    brutal, 22
Sykes–Picot Agreement, 141
sympoiesis, 154
systematic abuse, 239–240
systemic ethics, 148

talking cure, 217–218
tangping see lying flat
Taoism, 98, 99, 102–103
Tavistock Institute of Human Relations, 223
Taylor, C., 75, 153, 163–164
Taylorism, 142
technology, 217–219
    advancement of, 227
    communication methods, 180
    cyborgian state, 227–228
thinking, insights into, 151–152
Thomsen, S. U., 11, 14, 23
3Rs, 224
    Relatedness, 224–225
    Rhizome, 225–226
    Role, 224
transference neuroses, 161, 163–164
    see also denial

trauma, 72–73, 83–84, 130, 143, 241, 263, 264
    chosen, 257–258, 259
    collective, 110, 117, 252
    Covid-related, 265–266
    historical, 159–161, 163, 164, 260, 276
    transgenerational, 26–27
    transmission, 257
    unresolved, 90
triple disruption, 145
    environment emergency, 146
    Leadership: A Critical Text, 145
    social disruption, 145–146
    technological revolution, 145
Trist, E., 216
Trist, E. L., 238
trust
    and enquiry, 219–228
    loss of, 186
Tsing, A. L., 143
Turner, T. S., 92
Turquet, P., 91, 92
Turquet, P. M., 176, 242
Tweedy, R., 226

unconscious
    collective, 99, 176
    and death, 105
    forces, 210
    responses to anxiety, 199
    undifferentiated, 29
unthought known, 227, 240–241

vaccine(s), 5, 20, 83, 84, 85, 95, 97, 106, 123, 139, 144, 162–163, 168, 184, 194, 205, 207–208, 239–240, 275
    anti, 202–203
    and identity, 256–257, 258
Verleugnung, 158, 160, 162 *see also* denial
Volkan, V., 24, 26
Volkan, V. D., 255, 257, 258, 260
Vossenkuhl, W., 126
vulnerability, 111

Wandle Trail, xix
weakness, 101
Weintrobe, S., 89, 260
Western, S., 140, 143, 145, 146, 152, 226
    four discourses of Eco-Leadership, 147
    three principles of practice for organisations, 149
WHO *see* World Health Organization
Winnicott, D. W., 22, 255, 263
    "holding environment", 264
    primitive agony, 259
    Winnicottian perspectives, 244–245
Winston, B. E., 135

Wintour, P., 276
Wolff, J., 218
Woodward, A., 172
Woolhouse, M., 171
World Health Organization (WHO), 171, 202, 218
Wren, B. A., 66

Yeats, W. B., 208

Zhuangzi, 98, 102
    "Paoding dissecting the ox", 102–103
Zintl, E., 24